Loma 7

DATE DUE
at Home Office Library
N/W National Life Insurance Co.

5-30-73	Falstad	
5-30-75	Porisch	
5-30-76	Carney	
5-30-77	Ackland	
8206a 9-63		

Home Office and Field Agency Organization—Life

Home Office and Field Agency Organization— Life

By **R. WERNER LEDERER**, M.A., FLMI, CLU

Manager of Educational Services

Life Office Management Association

Third Edition

Published for **LIFE OFFICE MANAGEMENT ASSOCIATION**

100 Park Avenue, New York

By **RICHARD D. IRWIN, INC.**, Homewood, Illinois

To Alice and Eric

Preface to the Third Edition

Like its two predecessors, this edition has been prepared primarily to present students in the LOMA Insurance Education Program with an overall picture of the agency organization of a life insurance company, both in the home office and in the field.

Agency developments in the life insurance business have generally been evolutionary. For the majority of companies, they probably still are. Hence, this revision includes updating of subject matter together with substantial rewriting and some rearrangement.

For an increasing number of companies, however, changes have been extensive and more rapid, especially since the second edition was published. Accordingly, a new chapter has been added to consider such recent developments as mutual funds, variable annuities, variable life insurance, mass marketing, changes in corporate structure and consumerism —chiefly with reference to their potential effect upon companies' agency operations.

Once again the author is indebted to the many persons upon whose experience and advice he drew and to the Life Insurance Agency Management Association, which granted him access to its many current reports and studies. Among his

LOMA associates the author wishes to recognize Helen H. Wachsman, FLMI, whose thorough review of the entire manuscript and numerous suggestions were extremely helpful.

He also gratefully acknowledges the assistance of his review committee: John A. Miller, CLU, vice president, company relations, LIAMA; W. J. Reid, FLMI, superintendent of field training, North American Life Assurance Company; Lothar A. Vasholz, FLMI, CLU, vice president—marketing, North American Life Insurance Company; and E. J. Moorhead, FSA, vice president, Integon Life Insurance Corporation. The author gladly expresses his particular appreciation to Mr. Moorhead, who served outstandingly as a member of the review committee for all three editions.

R.W.L.
October, 1971

Contents

1 | *Who Buys Life Insurance*

Miller calls on Bennett. Miller discusses with Bennett personal financial problems of a type common to most people. Miller takes some papers out of his briefcase, asks Bennett a number of questions about himself, opens a book containing various life or health insurance figures,[1] asks Bennett some additional questions and records the answers on a printed form that Bennett reads and signs. When Miller calls on Bennett again, usually a few days later, he brings with him a printed document known as a policy or contract and gives it to Bennett, who in turn gives Miller a check.

Who is Miller? Where does he come from? What does he do? And who is Bennett? Why does he listen to Miller? Why does he buy from Miller?

Miller is a life insurance agent. He works out of an agency or sales office for a life insurance company whose home office may be several hundred miles or more away from Miller and Bennett. Miller sells the right kind of life insurance to those who need it and can afford to pay for it. Bennett is such a person; Miller would call him a "prospect." Bennett listens to

---

[1] The procedure would be similar in the case of a health insurance policy.

Miller because the latter has recognized and explained a financial need of Bennett's. Bennett buys from Miller because he believes that this need can best be met by insurance.

The foregoing describes, in oversimplified form, the sale of a policy by an agent to a prospect. But a lot of agency or sales organization is necessary before this seemingly simple transaction comes about. In this book we will try to explain the development and operation of this agency organization as found in the United States and Canada.

THE MARKET FOR LIFE INSURANCE

The financial situations of a few adults may be such that they do not need life or health insurance, but their number is extremely small. Many persons may maintain that they do not need this protection, or at least not right now; analysis of the facts by a qualified soliciting agent usually will show them to be in error.

Our relationships with other persons, especially our families, usually involve one or more human needs. For those of moderate means—and that includes most of us—life insurance is the only way of discharging adequately our responsibilities to our families and such others as may be dependent on us. At times the systematic accumulation of funds, as in a savings account, is advocated as an alternative method of meeting these responsibilities. Even granting that we may be the exceptional persons who have the perseverance to save regularly, there still is no assurance that we shall achieve our objectives. Premature death, i.e., death before our objectives are attained, unemployment or disability can prevent us from "following through" on our resolves. Those who plan to save via savings accounts to meet future needs should recognize that a great deal depends on "if I live"—and no one can be sure how long he will live. Life insurance, on the other hand, "creates an immediate estate." Payment of the first premium on a policy creates a liability on the part of the company to pay the face amount at the insured's death to a beneficiary, provided the policy is kept in force. (Similarly, payment of the first premium on a health insurance policy creates a liability on the part of the company to pay the insured a specified income if he becomes totally disabled as defined in his policy. Health insurance will be treated in more detail in chapter 15.)

Assume that each of two men of the same age plans to save $400 yearly to accumulate $10,000 at the end of 20 years, one by bank savings and the other by life insurance. Assume further that each dies shortly after two payments. The man who deposited his money in a savings bank would leave his beneficiary $800 plus interest. The other would leave $10,000.[2]

In any discussion of needs, it is easier to think of persons who have them than of those who haven't. The wealthy are no exception. Death taxes must be paid before the proceeds or assets of an estate can be distributed. There have been many instances where various taxes and the necessity to pay them promptly—with resultant conversion into cash of the best assets of an estate at an inopportune time—have drastically reduced a sizable fortune.

A Typical Life Insurance Situation

A basic purpose of life insurance is to help maintain as long as possible the living standards to which a family became accustomed during the lifetime of the breadwinner. Consider the common family situation of a husband, his wife and young children owning a home with a mortgage. Among their immediate basic needs are food, clothing, shelter. Long-range needs or objectives include education for the children and retirement income to supplement such governmental or employer-sponsored benefits as the parents may receive.

Even this brief description of a fairly common family situation illustrates how life insurance provides a practical solution to financial problems. While the husband and father is alive, the presumption is that he will be able to earn and provide.

---

[2] Generally, people do not die so soon after buying life insurance, but such cases can and do occur.

But if he dies before he can meet his several needs or objectives, money will be needed to provide:

1. A cleanup (or last-expense) fund to pay outstanding funeral, medical, hospital, household and similar expenses. A policy payable in cash should be used to meet these outlays.

2. A fund to pay off the remainder of the mortgage. An obligation of this kind can be insured either through a regular policy on a permanent plan, or through a decreasing term contract.

3. A guaranteed monthly income for the family until the children are grown, and a life income to the widow thereafter.

4. A readjustment and emergency fund to help the family adjust to a smaller income and take care of unexpected expenses.

With respect to Nos. 3 and 4, often the widow eventually can establish or reestablish herself as a wage earner. But meanwhile her expenses and the need for income continue. With the continuing extension of Social Security coverage in the United States, and with the establishment of similar legislation in Canada, more and more survivors will be eligible for some income. Such amounts, however, are not intended to be adequate to maintain the family's former scale of living. Life insurance can satisfy the needs of Nos. 3 and 4 in the form of a policy for the specific primary purpose of providing adequate income while the family is adjusting to a more modest way of life after the death of the breadwinner. Thus the widow-mother, free from immediate financial pressures, can train herself for suitable employment and decide whether to sell the house and move to smaller quarters, etc.

5. An educational fund so that the children will be financially able to go to college.

Most parents desire the best for their children and want to enable them to compete on equal terms in the economic world. Today, more and more jobs require higher education. For many positions only college graduates will be considered; a high school diploma is no longer enough. As this trend continues, the economic prospects of those without a bachelor's degree are likely to decline.

Concurrently, college education is becoming increasingly expensive. Formerly many students were able to work their entire way through college. Today college costs are such that it is almost impossible for a young man or woman to defray all expenses without outside resources. A policy can be purchased for the primary purpose of making funds available at the time a son or daughter is ready to enter college.[3]

· · · ·

The foregoing discussion shows how life insurance meets needs if the father's death prevents him from meeting them himself. Needs may also arise during his lifetime. Injury or disease may render him totally unable to earn a livelihood. Health insurance or a disability income benefit in a life insurance policy will guarantee money for himself and his family if he becomes totally disabled because of injury or disease.

Another lifetime need is an income when the father reaches retirement age. Compulsory retirement at age 65 or 70 is becoming increasingly common. Virtually all wage earners in the United States are now paying taxes in return for some federal government-administered benefits at retirement, usually under the Social Security system. Legislation similar to that of the United States is also in effect in Canada. The Canada Pension Plan is operative in all provinces except Quebec, which established its own provincial plan. Also, pension plans paid for wholly or partly by the employer are increasing in number. Nevertheless, the breadwinner may need to supplement income obtained from these sources by means of a life insurance policy or an annuity or a combination of the two, so that he will receive a more substantial life income starting at his retirement.

---

[3] There has been a great increase in the amount and number of scholarships and grants. However, availability and eligibility are uncertain factors.

Other Common Situations Involving Life Insurance Needs

We have dealt with the situation of a man with a wife and young children. Examples of other situations for which needs can be met by life insurance include:

1. Provision by a son (or daughter) for his parents—Parents may be dependent on an adult child for support. An adequate amount of life insurance payable to the parents will protect them if their child predeceases them.

2. Provision for a disabled brother, sister or other close relative—As with a parent, life insurance will guarantee a disabled beneficiary continued income if the insured dies first.

3. Wife insurance—The death of the wife and mother usually is a severe economic loss to a family, especially if the children are young. Insurance on the life of the wife will help to compensate for the loss of her services in the home.

4. Savings plan—Many young, unmarried persons have no one dependent on them. Purchase of an endowment contract will help them develop systematic savings habits and accumulate a fund for emergencies, or for retirement if they do not marry.

5. Provision for philanthropy—Many would-be benefactors of charitable, religious and educational institutions are unable to give substantially during their lifetimes. Life insurance enables persons of moderate means to leave a bequest to their favorite philanthropy.

6. Business uses of life insurance—Business enterprises as well as individuals have needs that can best be met by life insurance. Both the material and the human assets of a business are important to its success. Insurance of the material assets—buildings, equipment, inventories—will indemnify the owners against loss from fire and other hazards. It is just as important to protect a business against the loss by death of its human assets—those men

who are primarily responsible for its success. The subject of business insurance in relation to "keymen," sole proprietorships, partnerships and corporations is a specialized study. It is mentioned here only because life insurance can be used to replace the money value of the human assets of a business.

· · · ·

The savings element in life insurance is also important. Permanent plans accumulate cash values that may be a financial backlog or emergency fund during a man's lifetime or until he retires. Because of the flexibility of life insurance contracts, these cash values can be used advantageously in many situations.

WHY LIFE INSURANCE HAS TO BE SOLD

We have now seen, briefly, how life insurance meets various human needs. In the specific example of the husband-father, life insurance enables him to provide for his family as he wants to do and expects to do if he lives. On the assumption that human beings are a fairly reasonable lot, they might be expected voluntarily to apply for and buy the protection they need for themselves and their dependents.

The fact is that most people do not.[4] Thousands of persons variously known as agents, soliciting agents, special agents, salesmen, field underwriters or life underwriters are engaged in the occupation of persuading other people, known in insurance parlance as prospects, to do something for their own good or the good of their families.

Why don't people buy life insurance of their own accord? As far back as the 18th century, farsighted individuals pondered this question. Benjamin Franklin (1706–1790) stated: "It is a strange anomaly that people will insure their houses, their

---

[4] Actually, some people *would* apply of their own accord. A considerable proportion would be either uninsurable or insurable only at substandard rates. Without active solicitation by agents, relatively few persons insurable at standard rates would apply for adequate amounts.

ships, their merchandise, and yet neglect to insure their lives, surely the most important of all to their families, and more subject to loss."

In Franklin's time there were very few organizations that sold life insurance even if people wanted to buy it. Today, however, that excuse hardly applies; there are more than 1,900 legal reserve life insurance companies, as well as numerous other organizations, selling life insurance in the United States and Canada. Otherwise the general picture has not changed greatly in the past 200 years. Men voluntarily insure their homes and furnishings against fire and other loss, their automobiles against liability, fire, theft and otherwise, their wives' furs and jewelry against theft, and so on. If Franklin were alive today, he might still wonder why men readily insure their tangible (but usually replaceable) assets against loss but neglect to purchase life insurance to protect their dependents against the loss of irreplaceable assets—their lives.

There are a number of reasons why life insurance has to be sold. Among them are:

1. The idea of the intangible. The enjoyment and benefits of a new car, a new house, a new color television set or an expensive vacation are clear and immediate. These are "assets" a man can impress his friends with. The purchaser of life insurance receives a printed piece of good quality paper as the only tangible evidence of his purchase of future benefits. The contrast is obvious.

2. The idea of procrastination or "putting it off." A painful tooth abscess soon sends us to the dentist whether we want to go or not. And a burst water pipe sends us after the plumber in a hurry. For most of us the *need* for life insurance is just as great, but the urgency is less apparent. Human beings consider death as remote. If we don't buy the protection we need today, we can do so tomorrow or next week or year. Unfortunately, the *urgency* of the need may not be apparent until too late. The prospect

who is going to buy life insurance "when I get around to it" may die leaving loved ones unprotected, or he may be alive but no longer insurable.

3. The idea of sacrifice, particularly for others. A man seeking life insurance protection provides for the future. The premiums he pays for such protection, however, take money he could otherwise use to satisfy the present wants and desires of himself and his family. Instead of enjoying something now, the person buying life insurance foregoes, or at least limits, that pleasure for the greater good of the future. Such sacrifice is not easy, especially when others, however dear, stand to benefit financially from one's own death.

4. A kind of simple optimism that "the Lord will provide." There has always been some of this attitude. It has not disappeared with the development of Social Security, unemployment insurance, group insurance and employer-funded retirement plans. These benefits, however, desirable as they are, are not designed to eliminate the individual's responsibility to provide for himself and his dependents. They are supplements to, rather than substitutes for, such responsibility.

5. Unfamiliarity with what life insurance can accomplish. Approximately 140 million[5] of the United States and more than 11 million[6] of the Canadian population—men, women and children—are insured under one or more policies issued by life companies. But even the majority of adult policyowners have only a limited concept of how life insurance will help them and their dependents. To the average person, an insurance policy is something he pays premiums on until he dies, when the face amount is paid in a single sum to his beneficiary. He has little understanding of the flexibility of a life insurance con-

---

[5] *1971 Life Insurance Fact Book*
[6] *1970 Canadian Life Insurance Facts*

tract and of the many favorable provisions it includes for his benefit.

Even today many believe that life insurance is a proposition where "you have to die to win." Actually, for a number of years living benefits—matured endowments, annuity payments, disability payments, surrender values and policy dividends—have exceeded annual death benefits paid by companies. Nevertheless, inadequate understanding of the benefits of life insurance makes people reluctant to buy of their own accord.

The trained, qualified agent knows what life insurance can do and what policy plans are best suited for certain needs. Here, as in many other situations, he renders a valuable service to his prospects by explaining what life insurance can do for them, by tailoring his recommendations to their best interests, and by urging them to buy.

SUMMARY

Whether or not people recognize the fact, most of them need life insurance. The wealthy are no exception.

In the typical family situation—husband, wife and young children—one result of the breadwinner's death is that money will be needed for a number of purposes. Most people can meet their needs best by means of life insurance, if in fact they can meet them any other way.

Nevertheless, few persons will voluntarily apply for and purchase the protection they need for themselves and their dependents. Salesmen, commonly known as agents, are engaged in the task of persuading the public to obtain the life insurance protection they need.

QUESTIONS FOR REVIEW

1. Discuss the feasibility of achieving one's financial objectives solely by means of systematic savings.

2. For what specific purposes will money usually be needed in the

event the head of the family dies before attaining his financial objectives? Explain briefly how these needs can be met by life insurance.

3. To what extend do people buy life insurance entirely of their own accord? Explain why.

2 | *Who Sells It*

In legal terminology, life insurance is an agreement between an individual and a company whereby the latter, in return for a consideration called the premiums, promises to pay the insured or his beneficiary a designated amount of money upon the happening of death or some other specified event. Less formally, it is a plan that enables an individual to buy money, or an income, for future use, paying for it on the installment plan, much as he would pay for a home or an automobile or for household equipment, such as a washer, refrigerator or freezer.

TYPES OF ORGANIZATIONS

Since life insurance is something that people need and will buy if salesmen stimulate their wants and imagination until the need is recognized, we will now consider the organizations that offer this commodity. These include:

Individual Underwriters

Today these are only of historical interest. However, life insurance did not come into its present state full blown. Before the corporate form of insurance organization was developed, insurance, life and other, was available only through individual underwriters. These were persons operating singly or banded together informally. For a given premium or charge, they would assume a certain risk, originally ship cargoes. This type of coverage was followed by temporary or term insurance on the lives of the captain and crew. Still later, the idea was extended to other persons. This arrangement was not satisfactory for the insurance of lives, for a number of reasons. To name only one, life insurance is a long-term commitment and an individual underwriter lacked the necessary permanence. Suppose the underwriter predeceased the insured, as could and did happen? Insurance by individual underwriters can be satisfactory for short-term risks, but experience soon indicated its unsuitability for life insurance.

The well-known Lloyd's of London is an organization of individual underwriters. Until fairly recently Lloyd's did not insure lives except to cover some unusual case. This status may soon change. Statements in the insurance press indicate that Lloyd's, for the first time in its 300-year history, will shortly enter the long-term life insurance field, probably through a subsidiary corporation.

Under the present laws of the various states and provinces, individual underwriters would be precluded from selling life insurance today.

Companies or Corporations

The overwhelming proportion of life insurance in force in the United States and Canada, well over 90 percent, is sold by organizations; i.e., companies operating under the corporate form. In fact, most people think of policies written by the legal reserve companies when various aspects of life insurance are discussed. As of Dec. 31, 1970, there were more than 1,900 such legal reserve companies *domiciled* in the United States and about 75 in Canada. Some small companies operate only in their home state or province of registry. Some of the larger United

States companies operate in all or most of the 50 states and in one or more of the Canadian provinces. A number of the larger Canadian companies are almost as active in the United States as in Canada. Several of them operate outside North America as well, as do also a very small but growing number of United States companies.

Fraternal Orders

A fraternal benefit society has been defined as "any corporation, society, order or voluntary association, without capital stock, organized and carried on solely for the mutual benefit of its members and their beneficiaries, but not for profit, and having a lodge system with ritualistic form of work and representative form of government and which shall make provision for the payment of benefits. . . ."[1]

At one time fraternals were quite prominent in the sale of life insurance. Today they are less so, for a variety of reasons. Many were organized on an unsound financial basis and disappeared by liquidation or merger. Several of the larger organizations have become legal reserve companies and thus are no longer classified as fraternals. The great development of group insurance has cut sharply into what was formerly a major market for fraternals.

An additional reason for the declining importance of fraternal insurance in proportion to all life insurance in force is that interest in fraternalism is generally waning. Hence those orders that limit their sales to members only are likely to have a shrinking market.

Most of the more than 150 fraternals providing life insurance benefits today operate on sound insurance principles. As of Dec. 31, 1970, fraternal insurance societies in the United States and Canada had more than $24 billion of life insurance in force.[2] About half this amount was with the three largest orders; the five largest accounted for two-thirds.

---

[1] New York State definition
[2] *1971 Life Insurance Fact Book*

Assessment Associations

These are commercial organizations formed for profit, but the term has been extended to include mutual aid associations and burial societies. They have been compared to fraternal societies but are neither fraternal in character nor organized on the lodge system. Assessment associations had their period of greatest growth about the same time as the fraternals. They experienced the same difficulties resulting from unsound operation but without the cohesive or unifying force of the fraternals. There has been no growth for a number of years. Although there are several hundred assessment associations, the amount of life insurance in force as of Dec. 31, 1967, the last year for which figures are available, was only $830 million.[3]

Formation of such organizations is now illegal in Canada and in some of the states.

Savings Banks

Legal reserve life insurance may be sold by savings banks "over the counter," i.e., without an agency force, in a few states. Massachusetts was the first state (1907) to empower *mutual* savings banks to establish an "insurance department" and to engage in the life insurance business with persons residing in or working in that state. Subsequently New York and Connecticut also enacted legislation to permit mutual savings banks to sell life insurance policies and annuities. It may be noted that 13 of the largest United States life insurance companies are domiciled in these three states. No savings bank life insurance is sold in Canada.

This form of insurance had a relatively slow but steady growth for many years. In the past decade, however, the growth has been more rapid, and the amount of business in force has more than doubled in the past five years. As of Dec. 31, 1965, the amount in force in all three states totaled about

---

[3] *1970 Life Insurance Fact Book*

$2.1 billion. By Dec. 31, 1970, this figure had risen to more than $4 billion.[4]

None of the foregoing organizations are government-sponsored. Two government sources or means of providing insurance should be mentioned.

Government

The United States government made life insurance available to members of the armed forces serving in World Wars I and II and in Korea. At the end of 1970 United States Government Life Insurance (World War I), participating National Service Life Insurance (World War II), and nonparticipating National Service Life Insurance (Insurance Act of 1951) totaled about $38 billion.

In addition to the foregoing programs, federal legislation enacted in 1965 established Servicemen's Group Life Insurance for men and women on active duty in the uniformed services. Under this program $5,000 or $10,000 of group life insurance is available to each individual on a voluntary basis. Practically all of those eligible have taken this protection.

SGLI is supervised by the Veterans Administration and is in part underwritten by more than 500 legal reserve life insurance companies.[5]

(Federal Employees' Group Life Insurance (FEGLI) is described in chapter 15.)

The Canadian government made life insurance available to World War II veterans after completion of their military service. Such insurance is sold without medical examination. It is intended primarily for veterans whose impaired health would preclude their qualifying for insurance with private companies. Pensions paid for out of general taxation provide income for dependents of service personnel who died while active mem-

---

[4] *1971 Life Insurance Fact Book*
[5] *1971 Life Insurance Fact Book*

bers of the armed forces. A $5,000 death benefit is also paid.

The Canadian government has not offered life insurance to the general public, although federal civil servants have been permitted to purchase insurance since 1896.

Old Age and Survivors Insurance[6]

The United States government has enacted Social Security legislation whereby those in so-called covered employment may become eligible for monthly retirement income or income disability benefits, and their survivors may become eligible for monthly survivors' benefits and a small death benefit.

In July 1965 Congress enacted legislation familiarly known as "Medicare." Briefly, it provides compulsory hospital and voluntary medical insurance through social security taxes for persons 65 or over. Medicare and related "Medicaid" will be treated in more detail in chapter 15.

Laws of the types outlined above are subject to frequent amendment. Thus it is virtually impossible to be specific and current at the same time.

·   ·   ·   ·

To a considerable extent, Canada's Old Age Security Act resembles the U.S. Social Security legislation described above. It provides for a (uniform) income to eligible workers upon retiring at age 65. The present monthly amount (1971) is $80. Unlike the United States system of contributions by employer and employee, these payments are financed out of general taxation in Canada. Under the Canada Quebec Pension Plan the maximum monthly retirement income at this time (1971) is $44.17; the maximum cash death benefit is $530. There may also be income payment to widows and dependent children. The Quebec Plan, which also provides for disability income up to retirement at age 65, will not be in full operation until 1976.

---

[6] While this coverage is entitled "insurance," this designation is not entirely accurate. These benefits are not set up on an insurance basis as life insurance company representatives and many others would understand the term.

THE CORPORATE FORM

The long-term nature of life insurance obligations requires permanency and solidarity on the part of the organization undertaking to furnish such protection. These requirements are best satisfied by the corporate form.

Under an economic system of private enterprise, the bulk of life and health insurance will be sold by corporations, or, as they are generally known, life insurance (assurance is common in Canada) companies. Of the other nongovernmental forms, the individual underwriter arrangement lacks the necessary permanency and safety; further, it would be illegal in most states and provinces. Fraternal orders are less influential insurance-wise than formerly; assessment associations are insignificant. Savings bank life insurance is sold in only three states and not at all in Canada. Also, experience suggests that relatively few will buy protection entirely of their own volition. Hence, our further discussion will concern life insurance as issued by corporations in the United States and Canada, unless otherwise specified.

Stock and Mutual Companies

Life insurance corporations are of two types, stock and mutual. In a stock company, ownership is represented by shares of stock held or owned by stockholders (usually known as shareholders in Canada). The stockholders own the company. They share the profits or losses—by dividends on the stock or by changes in its market value—and elect the board of directors. In Canada the law requires that one-third of the directors of a domestic stock life company be elected by its participating policyholders. These are known as policyholders directors.

A mutual corporation has no stockholders and no capital stock. It is owned by the policyowners,[7] each of whom has the

---

[7] This term has become quite common and will be used as a synonym for "policyholder" in the remainder of this text, although there are situations when the person whose life is insured is not the *owner* of the policy.

right to vote in the election of directors. Any profits from the company's operations belong to the policyowners. Such profits are either distributed to them as policy "dividends" or held for their benefit as "surplus."

COMPANY ORGANIZATION. The board of directors determines general policy of the corporation. As a rule, its members are not expected to participate actively in company management. Whether the company is stock or mutual, directors elect or appoint the officers. Frequently certain senior company officers are elected to the board, such as the president, who is usually the chief executive officer, and one or more vice presidents.

Most corporations have some kind of organization chart, formal or informal, that shows who does what, who reports to whom, etc. Figure 1 shows an organization chart for a representative life insurance company selling ordinary business only. In appraising it, we must remember that there are more than 1,900 legal reserve companies of various sizes and lines of business in the United States and Canada. Obviously, no one chart can more than suggest general divisions of activities.

Basic Company Activities

Irrespective of the number of officers, the specific titles used or the size of the organization, each company must discharge certain basic activities. At the top or policy-making level will be the board of directors to whom the president, as chief executive officer, and sometimes other executives report. Somebody has to sell policies; hence the sales or agency activity. Somebody has to decide whether applicants are acceptable risks and, if so, on what basis; hence the home office underwriting (or selection of risks) activity. Life insurance companies are prepared to offer protection to all those who can qualify. They are in business to accept rather than to reject applicants. Consequently, they exert every effort to find some basis on which coverage can be granted to all who apply. More than 95 percent of the applicants for ordinary or whole life insurance are accepted for some form of coverage.

Somebody has to determine such matters as adequate and

FIGURE 1

Specimen Organization Chart of a Life Insurance Company
(doing "ordinary" business only)

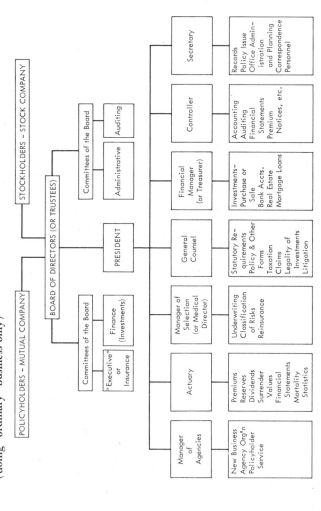

Note: This chart shows only the principal duties of each department. Other duties and functions are described in the text.

The above is not a standard or uniformly followed organization by departments. Organization and duties of departments (or officers) vary considerably in different companies. For example, claims are, in many companies, under the secretary; office administration and planning are sometimes under the controller; policyowner service may be under the secretary. The particular organization shown is, therefore, to be considered as a "sample" or "specimen" organization.

competitive premium rates and valuation of reserves; hence the actuarial activity. Somebody has to invest prudently the money received from premiums and other sources; hence the investment or finance activity. Somebody has to record the various bookkeeping and related transactions; hence the accounting or controller activity. Somebody has to safeguard the legal interests of the company and of its general body of policyowners; hence the law activity. A company's many insurance and investment operations necessitate strict conformity to statutes and regulations to guard against unintentional failure to comply with some particular requirement. In the event of litigation the law department arranges to protect in court the interests of the company and those of the policyowners generally.

The larger the organization, the greater the division of activities is likely to be. In the case of a life insurance company, there is a kind of cycle. As a starting point we may trace the general route of an application for insurance from the time the agent receives the signed application form from the applicant. The field office sends the application to the home office underwriting department. If the case is approved, the policy is issued and sent to the agent or the agency for delivery of the applicant. At the same time various records are set up for the home office and the field office. Premium payments are remitted to the home office and provide funds for investment. Eventually the policy goes off the books by expiry, lapse, surrender, or maturity as death claim or endowment.

Numerous departments of the insurer are involved in the cycle just described:

1. Actuarial, which determines sound premium rates for the company's policy contracts
2. Law, which determines the wording of policy contracts and the validity of claims under these policies
3. Agency, which as the sales department organizes the field and appoints managers and agents
4. Home office underwriting, which sets standards of selection and passes on applications for life insurance

5. Issue, which prepares and issues policies
6. Accounting, which sets up records and enters income (premium and other) and disbursements on the company's books
7. Financial or investment, which invests the funds the company receives from various sources, such as premium income
8. Claim or benefit, which pays out policy proceeds at death, maturity or surrender
9. Administrative, which is responsible for personnel and office services and integrates operations of the various home office departments

Each of the foregoing departments performs numerous duties in addition to those mentioned above. The distribution of work among departments depends considerably on the size of the company.

The Sales Department

The sales department is important in any business organization that offers something for sale. It is particularly so in the case of a life insurance company, whose "product" is a service, a promise to perform at some future date. The agency department is the sales department of a life insurance company. A brief analogy to sales organizations generally may be in order at this point.

Most large corporations do not sell their products directly to the general public. An automobile manufacturer does not sell us a car direct; neither do we buy a stereo phonograph direct from the maker. Both enterprises have contracts with dealers or representatives who stock automobiles and stereo phonographs and from whom the general public can buy these products.

The objectives[8] of such sales organizations are:

---

[8] Terms such as objectives, duties, functions, responsibilities, etc., often are difficult to distinguish. One individual may consider as an "objective" what another views as a "responsibility." At the risk of repeating terms frequently, we will try to be consistent. Once we refer to something as an "objective" or a "responsibility," we will always try to call that particular something an "objective" or a "responsibility."

1. To sell their products in sufficient volume to people who can afford them to yield adequate profit for the corporations (stockholders) and for the dealers
2. To develop and expand the company's territory intensively or extensively or both
3. To make certain that the dealers run their business affairs so as to win satisfied customers who will buy again and tell others about their satisfaction with what they have bought (and where they have bought it)

The objectives of the sales, i.e., agency, department of a life insurance company are somewhat similar, although there are important points of difference. Its objectives are also threefold:

1. To sell good business in adequate volume and at reasonable cost so as to show a profit to the company whether stock or mutual[9]
2. To develop and expand the company's territory intensively or extensively or both
3. To furnish field service to policyowners (and their beneficiaries)

Later we will enlarge on the objectives of the agency department and what it does to attain these objectives. The next chapter, however, will deal with systems of selling life insurance and health insurance and with the agency system. In fact the discussion in the following chapters will apply generally to health insurance as well as to life insurance. The bulk of health insurance is sold by life companies today; thus, the same agent usually sells both. Some points of difference will be considered in chapter 15.

SUMMARY

Life insurance is, or has been, sold by individual underwriters, fraternal orders, assessment associations, savings banks, the federal government and corporate organizations known as

---

[9] In a mutual company, the profits are paid to the policyowners in the form of policy dividends.

legal reserve life insurance companies. The last named are of two types, stock and mutual. Since the bulk of life insurance in the United States and Canada is in force with companies, this text will deal with life insurance as sold by companies.

Like corporations generally, life insurance companies have some kind of organization chart, formal or informal. Among the most important departments is the sales or agency department. Its main objectives are: (1) to sell good business in adequate volume at reasonable cost so as to show a profit to the company; (2) to develop and expand the company's territory intensively or extensively or both; (3) to furnish field service to policyowners (and their beneficiaries).

QUESTIONS FOR REVIEW

1. List the various nongovernmental organizations that sell life insurance. Discuss the relative importance of each.
2. Compare the life insurance evolution and relative prominence today of fraternal orders and assessment associations.
3. Describe briefly the government-sponsored life insurance available in the United States and Canada.
4. Explain why the corporate form is best suited for the marketing of life insurance.
5. Outline the basic activities that must be discharged in a life insurance company.
6. Compare briefly the objectives of the agency department of a life insurance company with those of the sales department of a manufacturing corporation.

3 | *Sales Organization*

If people voluntarily applied for all the life insurance they need, there would be no necessity for a sales force. Actually, very few do apply of their own accord. Salesmanship and fairly vigorous solicitation are necessary. Up to the 1850s those who sold life insurance rarely devoted their full time to that activity. As might be expected, relatively little business was sold in this manner, and companies soon recognized that some form of sales organization would be necessary.

It is estimated that today life insurance sales personnel number about 450,000. Approximately half that number derive 50 percent to 100 percent of their income from the sale of life insurance; the other half derive less than 50 percent.

THE AGENCY SYSTEM

An expression that is likely to arise in any discussion of the distribution of life insurance is "the agency system." Life insurance people refer freely to the agency system, although the expression is rarely defined or explained.

As applied to *life insurance*,[1] the agency system is that

---

[1] The term "agency system" has a somewhat different connotation in nonlife insurance.

25

means which most companies use to sell their products—life insurance policies and annuities. The term embraces the concept of a body of agents who are under contract to an insurer through a general agent or a branch manager to sell life insurance to those who need it, can pay for it and can qualify for it, i.e., can pass the company's requirements for insurability. Agents are trained to give careful attention to the needs of the individual prospect, so that he and those he wishes to provide for will be protected by that plan of insurance best suited to his particular needs. In exchange or in return for their successful sales efforts, agents receive compensation, usually by means of commissions, which are percentages of the gross premium.

Operation of the agency system does not end with the sale of the policy. Frequently thereafter agents serve policyowners in numerous matters of importance to them and their beneficiaries. These include: urging payment of renewal premiums, arranging for policy loans, changing the beneficiary designation, changing the mode or frequency of premium payments, adding new benefits not available or not desired at the time the policy was issued, processing disability and death claims, explaining and recommending the type of settlement of policy proceeds, etc. Partly as compensation for these and other services, partly as additional, deferred compensation for the original sale, agents receive renewal commissions and service fees on renewal premiums.

Thus, the term "agency system" is a comprehensive one. Its scope extends beyond that of only agents and their activities. If agents are going to do all the things we have described, other people must first recruit the right men and train them properly for careers as life insurance agents. These "other people" are, first of all, the agency heads, known as general agents and branch managers. And supporting the general agents and branch managers must be an effective home office agency department that understands the philosophy of good field organiaztion, knows what its objectives are and what it must do to attain these objectives.

Systems of Distribution

Historically, life insurance companies have used several arrangements or systems to distribute their product, i.e., to sell policies.[2]

1. General agency
2. Branch manager, also known as branch office or managerial
3. Debit or industrial
4. Group

General Agency

Of the two major systems of field organization in use—general agency and branch manager—the former is the older. Today the differences between these two systems are much less distinct than they once were. However, in its original or "pure" form the company gave exclusive franchise for a geographical territory to a person known as a general agent, whose status was that of independent contractor.

The general agent organized a sales force by appointing and contracting with agents for whose activities he[3] was primarily responsible. They were under contract to him rather than to the company whose policies they sold. He established and maintained at his own expense the office organization necessary

---

[2] Traditionally, life insurance has been divided into three broad forms: ordinary, debit or industrial, group. This division will be used in this text. Actually, though, both ordinary and debit involve the issuance of an *individual* policy on *each* life, whereas group insurance involves the issuance of a *single* contract to cover a *number* of lives. For this reason, it has been suggested that there really are two broad forms of life insurance rather than three—individual (consisting of ordinary and debit) and group. Virtually all companies sell ordinary, but many sell no debit and some sell no group. The discussion in this and remaining chapters will concern ordinary business only, unless otherwise specified.

[3] While there are relatively few female general agents or branch managers, soliciting agents include a considerable number of women in their ranks. To avoid repeating expressions like "men and women," "he and she," etc., the masculine form will be used throughout.

to run his agency, such as office rent, furniture, clerical salaries and telephone and telegraph. So long as his services were satisfactory, he was subject to relatively little home office control.

The general agent received compensation, known as overriding or overwriting commissions, in both first and renewal years, for all business written by men under contract to him as well as renewal commission on that business. He also received collection fees for premiums paid on business produced by his agency after the renewal commission period had expired. Usually he did, and frequently was expected to, sell a certain amount of life insurance himself, i.e., "personal production."

This may be an appropriate place to point out that those who sell life insurance earn commissions for *paid-for* business. Getting a man to sign an application does not necessarily mean that the home office underwriting department will approve that application. Further, approval by the home office does not assure that the applicant will pay the initial premium when the agent calls on him to deliver the policy. On the other hand, terms like selling, delivering, producing and placing mean that the prospect not only signed the application and was accepted by the company but that he paid the first premium, so that a contract went into force.

Branch Manager

This system, also known as branch office or managerial, came into being in the 1890s (the exact year is believed to have been 1896) as a result of the desire of some companies to exercise greater control over their agency operations. In its original or "pure" form the agency head, known as the branch manager, was (and still is) an *employee* of the company he represented, rather than an independent contractor. He recruited, trained, supervised and motivated agents. The agents' contracts, however, were not with him but with the company, so that the home office had final say as to whether an agent was acceptable. He was compensated by a salary and, usually, a bonus reflecting the size and success of his agency. He executed the instructions of the home office concerning all agency activities. The company paid all expenses of operation of the agency including the salaries of office personnel.

Comparisons of the Two Major Systems[4]

Today there are few examples of either system in the "pure" form. Practically, the general agency system has moved much closer to the managerial system. The primary reason has been a severe shortage of men who combine the (1) financial resources to be independent contractors with the (2) qualifications to be sales managers. Companies have been assuming increasing responsibility for the financing and operation of their general agencies, especially new ones. Substantial funds are required to open a new or "scratch" agency; money is needed to pay the rent, buy furniture and typewriters, install telephone service and the like, and provide financial assistance to new agents to help them get started in a life insurance selling career. Further, many general agency companies supervise recruiting and training activities in the field.

The general agent usually receives allowances or reimbursements for operating expenses. Collection of premiums and related activities may be under home office control, and the agency cashier may not even report directly to his general agent.

Many companies have felt it desirable to place some control on the recruiting practices of their general agents. Contracts the latter make with soliciting agents usually require home office approval. Some general agency companies are now contracting directly with the soliciting agents even though the agent works under the general agent. Some companies have also required

---

[4] In some companies, because of their small size, the home office acts as a kind of general agent until there has been enough growth to set up regular general agencies. The home office appoints agents who are supervised by it and report to it. Such representatives may or may not be assigned exclusive territories, i.e., a geographical area in which no other agent of the same company may solicit business. Contracts are directly between the company and the agents. Such an arrangement is sometimes known as "direct agency."

their general agents to subordinate extensive personal production to the building of an effective sales organization in their territories.

On the other hand, it has long been common for companies operating on the branch office system to offer their managers some financial incentive to devote themselves wholeheartedly to agency building. By placing increasing emphasis on agency success as a factor in compensating managers, these companies have given them a personal stake. And like general agency companies, they have measured such accomplishment in terms of volume and persistency of new business paid for, increase in the amount of insurance in force, economy of operation and the development of new and successful agents.

Some general agencies have acquired branch office characteristics to a greater extent than others. Even within the agency organization of a single company there may be shades of difference. Thus, the designations of general agency and branch office are less self-explanatory or self-defining than they once were. To compare them intelligently, we need to know not only that a particular field office is called a general agency but also its exact characteristics.

There are two chief differences between the two systems today. First, although subject to considerable home office direction, the general agent is still considered an independent contractor with a franchise (frequently not exclusive) authorizing him to develop business from a certain territory, whereas the branch manager's status is that of an employee on the company payroll. The general agent has a wider range of financial outlook. He has, on the one hand, more opportunity to make a large amount of money and, on the other hand, a larger risk of failing financially because of poor business management of his franchise. Second, the general agent has a vested (guaranteed) interest in commissions in the event his contract with his company is terminated. This situation does not apply in the case of a branch manager.

Under the branch office system the home office is in a somewhat better position to move agency personnel from one city to another as circumstances may require. Such transfers include the manager himself. Frequently a company recognizes a manager's superior performance by transferring him to a larger or more desirable territory.

RELATIVE COST. The average policyowner is not likely to be concerned with the merits of these two systems of field organization—if in fact he is even aware that there are two systems—unless he has to pay a higher premium for a given policy under one system than under the other. On this point there is little to choose between the two. In the overall, both systems perform the same functions at approximately the same ultimate cost to the companies. There are, however, significant differences in the incidence of that cost.

PREVALENCE. Some companies have both types of field organization. With respect to United States companies, therefore, accurate statistics as to which system is more prevalent are not easily determined, although the general agency system probably is still more common.

Canadian companies use managers virtually exclusively in their Canadian field offices. However, their compensation is largely dependent on the success of their agencies as reflected by increase in volume of new business, increase in business in force or agents' earnings, first-year and renewal. There has been some experimentation with general agents who are primarily, if not exclusively, personal producers. Canadian companies use both systems for their United States operations.

To avoid constant repetition of "general agent and branch manager," the single word "manager" will have a special meaning for the remainder of these chapters. Unless otherwise indicated, "manager" will be used to refer to the executive head of a life insurance agency irrespective of whether it is a general agency or a branch office.

Brokerage

Not all of a life company's business need *originate* with its regular sales organization. Some applications may be originated by men known as brokers, who then submit these applications through one of the company's general agents or branch managers.

"Broker" is not a precise term. Even the legal definition[5] is only slightly helpful, because "broker" is used so loosely in practice. Some brokers are engaged primarily in the general insurance business, selling fire and casualty lines; with many of them, life insurance is a sideline. Others are exclusively life insurance brokers; they have contracts with two or more life insurance companies and may produce a substantial volume of business. In Canada, regulations concerning the licensing of agents govern brokerage contracts. Every province except Quebec requires that a single company sponsor the application for a life insurance agent's license, and no other company is permitted to make a contract with that agent or broker. However, the Insurance Act of each province except Quebec permits a broker, or an agent for that matter, to place business with another company, provided he has the written permission of his own or sponsoring company.

While relatively few applicants are uninsurable, not all are insurable on the same terms. Hence some applications are harder to place than others, especially when larger amounts are involved. Some companies are more liberal than others with respect to impairments such as overweight, history of diabetes and unfavorable family history. A broker under contract to several companies may "shop around" for the best terms for his client and, also, himself.

Generally, brokerage is a supplementary means of obtaining life insurance business. Few companies rely exclusively on brokers to bring them sufficient persistent business for satisfactory growth. However, many companies actively solicit brokerage business. Some establish a "brokerage division" in their agency departments to develop such business

---

[5] An insurance broker has been defined as one "who for compensation acts or aids in any manner in the negotiating of contracts of insurance or reinsurance for a person other than himself, and not being the appointed agent or officer of the company in which such insurance or reinsurance is effected."

and to facilitate handling it. Other insurers advertise their interest in brokerage.

At one time a number of leading companies declined to consider applications known to have been submitted through or originated by brokers. Today most companies believe that carefully underwritten brokerage business will compare satisfactorily in experience with business originating with their own field forces.

OTHER FORMS OF INSURANCE SOLD BY LIFE INSURANCE COMPANIES

Most companies sell one or more lines of insurance in addition to ordinary. These include health insurance, debit (or weekly premium or industrial) insurance and group insurance. They will be discussed in more detail in chapter 15 bearing the above title, but a few general observations may be appropriate at this time.

Health Insurance Organization

Health insurance is a natural companion to life insurance. Many ordinary companies sell it, and the method of distributing health insurance is very similar to that for distributing life insurance. Hence, much of what follows with respect to ordinary also applies to health insurance.

Debit Insurance Organization

Most companies selling debit insurance operate mainly on the managerial system. The total geographical territory in which such a company operates is divided into districts. At the head of each is a manager or superintendent, who is usually aided by one or more assistant managers. The home office pays all expenses and controls virtually all activities of each agency or district. All personnel from the manager down are appointed by the company.

Group Insurance Organization

This form of protection may be distributed by the company's regular agents. Usually, though, companies actively soliciting group insurance consolidate substantially all group operations in a single department with its own sales and administrative divisions.

DISTRIBUTION OF LIFE INSURANCE ACCORDING TO "PRODUCT" LINES

When the branch manager system originated during the 1890s, and for a number of years afterward, lines of distribution were substantially more clear-cut than they are today. Group insurance was not introduced until 1911–12. Multiple-line companies, i.e., those selling both life and nonlife, were few. General agencies and managerial agencies were "easy to tell apart." There has been a steady evolution, however. Traditional terms like general agency and branch office are still used, but lines of demarcation are much less sharp than they once were.

For many years a life insurance company's "products" consisted of policies and annuities. More recently a substantial number of companies have added noninsurance activities to their "product" line in the form of mutual funds and equity products generally. These will be treated in more detail in chapter 16.

SUMMARY

The term "agency system" in life insurance embraces the concept of a body of men who are under contract to an insurer through a general agent or a branch manager. Involved are not only the company's agents and branch managers and general agents, but also the home office agency department.

Life insurance companies have used a variety of systems to sell their products. The general agency and the branch manager systems are the most common.

At one time these systems were quite different. As they evolved these differences have greatly diminished. Today the chief difference is that the general agent is still an independent contractor, while the branch manager is an employee of the company he represents. Advantages attributed to the general agency system are likely to be considered disadvantages attributed to the managerial system, and vice versa.

Many companies obtain some business through men known as brokers.

QUESTIONS FOR REVIEW

1. Traditionally, life insurance has been divided into three broad forms; name them. State briefly the reasoning for considering life insurance as consisting of two rather than three broad forms.

2. Compare the essential features of the general agency system and the branch manager system as originally constituted. What are the chief differences between the two systems today?

3. Describe briefly two systems, other than general agency and branch manager, for distributing life insurance.

4. Explain or define the terms "broker" and "brokerage business." Is such business a substantial proportion of your company's sales? Has any trend manifested itself?

4 | *The Agency Department*

Insurers seek to bring their products to prospective buyers in such a way as to make and keep them satisfied policyowners. On page 23 we first stated the objectives of the agency department, the sales department of a life insurance company. They are important—and worth restating:

1. To sell good business in adequate volume and at reasonable cost so as to show a profit to the company whether stock or mutual[1]
2. To develop and expand the company's territory intensively or extensively or both
3. To furnish field service to policyowners (and their beneficiaries)

What must the agency department do to achieve its objectives? Almost anything that will increase the effectiveness of sales and service will be the concern of the agency department. Most of the remainder of this book will be devoted to

---

[1] In a mutual company, the profits are paid to the policyowners in the form of policy dividends.

explaining what the agency department has to do—what its duties are—to attain its objectives. Offhand and superficial answers might be "to build a good sales organization" or "to hire a lot of good salesmen." Certainly finding men who can sell or can be trained to sell is a vital duty of the agency department. However, it cannot discharge its duties that simply.

HOME OFFICE AGENCY ORGANIZATION

The work of the agency department can be divided into two parts, that of the home office and that of the field. Overall management and control of agency activities are in the home office. The field carries out most of the work involved in new-business production and service to policyowners. It is up to the home office to assure itself that its objectives are being attained throughout the territory in which the company operates. The home office part of the work will now be described in greater detail.

Organization and Personnel

Home office agency organizations vary from the simple to the complex, depending on the size of the company and the various types of protection sold. A small company may have no more than an agency officer with one or two assistants. The home office agency organization in a large company may consist of a hundred or more persons organized into numerous sections or divisions. Compared to general agency companies, branch manager companies tend to have more employees in their home office agency departments; because of centralization of authority and control, their supervisory organizations are usually more extensive. A few large companies have regional agency vice presidents, sometimes known as regional superintendents. A simple form of agency organization chart for a company writing only ordinary business is shown in figure 2.

FIGURE 2

Example of an Agency Department Organization Chart

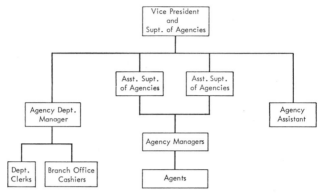

Terminology or nomenclature varies among companies. For example, the duties of the policyowners' service bureau in one company may differ considerably from those of a division of the same name in another company. Similarly, the duties of persons with such titles as agency secretary or even superintendent of agents are not standardized. Because of such variations, we will try to explain *what* the agency department does and *how* it does it rather than use titles of persons and divisions to explain *who* does *what*.

Like other major activities of a life insurance company, the agency department is under the direction of a senior officer. Usually he has a title like agency vice president or vice president and manager of agencies. Like other senior officers, the chief agency executive is responsible for carrying out the policies approved by the board of directors for the general management of the business.

Actually, few members of the board are likely to be agency or sales people. The majority are from other fields such as law, banking, industry and education. While the directors approve (or occasionally disapprove) the broad agency policies of the company, they expect the chief agency executive to submit effective plans for their consideration. They rarely originate sales policy themselves.

Usually the chief agency executive will have had sales

experience, either in insurance or elsewhere. A man who has never sold may have difficulty in stepping convincingly into the role of chief sales executive. However, the chief agency executive is valuable for his services as a skilled administrator and organizer even more than for his services as a sales expert. A number of men have become agency executives by coming up through the administrative or other departments rather than through the sales end of the business.

If the chief agency executive has had insurance background, he will usually have been a successful salesman and, frequently, manager of an agency. But he need not have been a leading salesman; other qualities, especially management capacity, are also important. Neither does it necessarily follow that a successful manager will be a successful agency executive, any more than it follows that a successful agent will be a successful manager.

To discharge properly the duties we are about to describe, the chief agency executive needs competent assistants both in the home office and in the field. Because of variations among companies, specific titles may not be too helpful—and probably they are not too important in a general text of this kind. What is important is that the agency department has certain duties to perform and that certain people perform them. Common titles used to designate senior home office agency department personnel include: superintendent of agencies, assistant superintendent of agencies, director of agencies (and assistant directors), director of marketing (and assistant directors), supervisors and assistant supervisors, agency secretary, educational director, training director.

With this background we are now ready to answer more specifically the question of what the agency department must do to achieve its three objectives. These duties will be listed, not necessarily in order of importance, but rather to present the overall picture at a glance:

1. To determine, together with the actuarial and law departments, the company's products, the line of policies that will be sold

2. To determine the territory in which the company will operate
3. To set, together with the actuarial and law departments, managers' and agents' rates of compensation
4. To control agency costs
5. To obtain and develop the right manpower: recruiting, training, supervision, motivation
6. To develop sales promotion techniques
7. To develop *office* organization in the field
8. To conserve business
9. To keep and analyze records of operations
10. To coordinate its activities with those of other home office departments
11. To perform a number of other duties

Some description of these duties may be appropriate at this point.

1. *To Determine the Line of Policies That Will Be Sold—* Vendors generally must decide what their stock of goods or merchandise will be. For example, one service station proprietor may sell only the basic gasoline and oil and perhaps tires and tubes. Another may offer in addition batteries and other accessories, car wash, wrecker service, complete garage mechanic service and even soda pop, ice cream and suntan lotion.

A life insurance company's "product" is a service, a promise to perform at some future date. The agency department must decide what its "stock" will be. First, it must help to decide what broad types it will offer—ordinary, debit, group, health,[2] annuities. Nearly all life insurance companies write some ordinary business. Even among many so-called debit or combination companies, the amount of ordinary insurance sold annually is now greater than the amount of debit. In most combination companies the ratio of ordinary to debit is increasing each year. Since the end of World War II more and

---

[2] Also known as accident and sickness, sickness and accident, accident and health, and health and accident.

more ordinary companies, including some of the largest, have entered the fields of group or health insurance, or both. A considerable number of Canadian companies have begun selling health insurance within the past few years.

Second, each agency department must decide how extensive a "portfolio" it will furnish its agents. While most companies offer a variety of whole life, endowment and term contracts, some limit themselves to only a few "standard" forms of these contracts. Some companies sell no yearly renewable term other than as group insurance. Most companies that once issued continuous installment contracts have discontinued doing so. On the other hand, the agency department must be prepared to capitalize on current economic, social and industry trends. Juvenile insurance, family income and mortgage redemption policies—and, more recently, the family policy—have become very popular. Also, business insurance plans and pension trust contracts have been added to many company portfolios. (As will be developed in chapter 16, a number of companies have begun to sell mutual funds, although these are not an "insurance" product.)

A company's insurance "portfolio" may depend on its particular goals. Some companies aim to solicit within a relatively narrow market; for example, they may concentrate on estate planning, and the amount of their average policy may be $15,000 or more. Others aim to meet the human needs and desires for personal security of all persons; they serve the entire market and offer all common life insurance coverages.

Related to the duty of determining the line of products that a life insurance company will sell is "marketing." This term has become increasingly common in life insurance companies in recent years. Like the expression "agency system" (introduced in chapter 3), "marketing" is frequently used but less frequently defined or explained.

Sometimes the term is used almost interchangeably with "sales." However, marketing may be defined as the program —plans, machinery, activities—with which an organization accomplishes the distribution of the goods and services it produces. Marketing in life insurance includes not only the usual person-to-person selling but also research, advertising, sales promotion, direct mail. In other words, marketing involves the discovery and definition of consumers' needs, the translation of these needs into product (policy) or service specifications, and the delivery of these products and services to the insuring public. Thus some companies, usually the larger ones, have established the title of marketing vice president (or an equivalent) as the senior executive to head all agency-related activities *including* sales.

2. *To Determine the Territory in Which the Company Will Operate*[3]—The total territory in which a company operates is usually divided into agencies or districts with a general agent or branch manager in charge of each. Sometimes territories are divided along state lines. Various factors such as population, amount of industry and facilities for service to policyowners and agents affect territorial division. A map will show that it may be more convenient for agents and policyowners in southwestern Illinois, for example, to deal with an agency in St. Louis than with one in more distant Chicago. Hence, a company operating in Missouri and Illinois may assign southwestern Illinois counties to its St. Louis office. In the large cities a company may have several agencies whose agents are free to write anywhere in the city.

Some companies operate in only one state or province. The larger the company, the more extensive its operations are likely to be. Some of the largest transact business in all the states, whereas others limit themselves to 40 or less. Most large Canadian companies operate in all provinces; some operate in many of the states as well. Some smaller companies have agencies from coast to coast; others thrive in a half-dozen states or less. Logically, it would appear that problems

---

[3] "To operate in" and "to be licensed in" are not necessarily synonymous. A company is *licensed* in a state (or province) if it has complied with the legal requirements of that state and is authorized to engage in the business specified. A company *operates* in a state if, in addition to being licensed, it has a sales organization that actively solicits business. Sometimes a company obtains a license in a particular state for future use or because an agency in an adjoining territory may occasionally solicit across the boundary.

of field supervision are simplified when the territory of operation is fairly compact. A company operating in widely separate states has a greater supervision problem than one whose territory is compact New England and a few of the mid-Atlantic states. Again, supervision of operations in California may be disproportionately costly and time-consuming for an eastern seaboard company, all of whose other agencies are east of the Mississippi.

Determination of territory of operation, particularly with respect to expansion, depends on several factors:

a.   Availability of an adequate field force, especially managerial talent, to exploit a broad territory. Manpower building is a never-ending agency problem. No company ever has enough managers and agents whom it considers satisfactory, let alone a surplus of them. Well-qualified representatives are especially needed to develop new territory. Having or not having the right quality and quantity of manpower is likely to mean the difference between success and failure of a new field office. Can the agency department obtain the necessary manpower for new agencies without seriously weakening its existing field organization?[4] Also, is the present agency manpower in the home office adequate to cope with the problems of such expansion?

b.   The expense involved in establishing an extensive organization. Can the company, especially a young one, afford it? We need not treat in detail the expenses involved in establishing a new agency. In the case of a managerial company all such costs are paid out of the company's surplus. Since policyowners' or stockholders' funds are at stake, the management must avoid any excessive drain on surplus as might be caused by the addition of several new agencies at about the same time. A company may incur substantial expenses even if it uses the general agency system. Depending on the circumstances and the terms of

---

[4] Of course, if a company wishes to open new offices but does not have the necessary manpower in its own field organization, it can, and often does, seek men outside its own ranks interested in becoming managers and agents.

its contract with the general agent, the company may defray all or a major part of the initial organizational expenses entailed in the establishment of a new general agency, such as furniture, rent, advertising and printing. It may also provide temporary financial assistance for the general agent himself, as well as his agents.

c. Prospects for success, i.e., the prosperity—present or prospective—of the area under consideration, and the extent of competition. Prudent management would hesitate to open an agency in a territory where population and economic activity are declining. For instance, there has been little expansion of agencies in coal mining and some rural areas for a number of years. On the other hand, there has been a notable shift of population, especially since the end of World War II, along with a significant increase in industrial activity, to the Pacific coast and to some of the southern and southwestern states.

The 1970 United States census shows that the coastal regions and the "sunshine states," especially California and Florida, continue to attract a high proportion of Americans. To quote from the census report itself: "Migration patterns continued much as in the past . . . from midcountry out, from rural to urban; coastal areas continued to grow . . ." Residents of the suburbs now outnumber those who live in the central cities. The farm population continues to decline, dropping about one-third since 1960, or from about 15 million to 10 million.

While agency activities have expanded in many states, the establishment of new agencies has been greatest in the areas where population has been growing. Like other industries, companies go "where the action is," i.e., where the people and the business are.

Competition is also involved. Theoretically, perhaps, there is always room for one more agency, and some companies have opened sales offices in areas that appeared saturated. However, not all agencies prosper, and sometimes a company will close one or more of its field offices.

d. Intensive versus extensive development. Although a company may derive some prestige from the fact that it operates in a large number of states or provinces, such a distinction really is of minor importance. Some managements favor intensive rather than extensive development of territory, at least until sales operations are well established. They feel that a smaller company should especially cultivate its home office area and limit itself to a small number of geographically accessible states that can be supervised effectively and economically. There are times when a company will withdraw from, or at least become inactive in, cities and states where past results and current prospects do not seem to warrant further efforts.

e. Legal aspects, including deposit requirements and taxation. To obtain a license to operate in a new state, a company must comply with the legal and other requirements of that state. Examples of requirements are premium tax legislation and limitations on expenses of doing business. Some states impose investment regulations that companies may consider onerous.

3. *To Set Managers' and Agents' Rates of Compensation*[5]— Life insurance salesmen are compensated by means of commission based on a percentage of the premiums paid. The terms of such compensation are spelled out in contracts with their companies or, perhaps in the case of general agency companies, with their general agent. General agents themselves are under contract, as are branch managers, even though the latter's status is that of employees. In almost all companies, contracts between general agents and their subagents are subject to home office approval. In most companies compensation plans for general agents embrace both commission schedules and expense allowance arrangements.

All such matters are the responsibility of the home office. In collaboration with other home office departments, the agency department draws up contracts for managers and

---

[5] This subject is considered in more detail in chapter 5.

agents. Commission schedules and other provisions of agency contracts will be revised as changing conditions indicate.

A special phase of field compensation is financing. Getting started in life insurance selling is not easy. Few *new* salesmen are self-supporting in less than two years—during which time their regular living expenses continue. *Established* agents occasionally suffer a slump and, despite their income from renewal commission, the need for some temporary financial assistance may arise. Even general agents sometimes find themselves in somewhat straitened circumstances, perhaps through no fault of their own.

The home office agency department determines the rules that apply to financing—whom to help when, how much and how long. Branch managers, being salaried personnel, would not be considered for assistance themselves, although their agents would be. General agents may be eligible for assistance. Many general agency companies have financing plans for their new agents, usually cooperative plans with their general agents.

4. *To Control Agency Costs*[6]—The duties of the agency department must be discharged within proper cost limits, or its basic objectives will not be attained. As in other business enterprises, volume of sales and profit are not necessarily synonymous.

5. *To Obtain and Develop the Right Manpower*[7]—After the agency department has adopted its "portfolio" of policies, determined the territory in which it will operate, decided which system of agency organization it will use and set bases of compensation, it must appoint managers to direct its sales activities in the field. They in turn appoint agents who solicit people to buy the company's "products"—insurance and annuities.

Life insurance is a business of people—policyowners, home office and field office personnel and sales personnel. It has no manufacturing plants, no machines or production line, no visible or tangible goods for sale. That kind of selling is hard.

---

[6] This subject is considered in more detail in chapter 6.

[7] This subject is considered in more detail in chapters 7, 8, 9, 10 and 11.

Even men who have sold various other commodities success-fully will not necessarily succeed as agents.

Obtaining the right sales manpower is often considered the agency department's most important duty. Certainly no other duty is more important in attaining its objectives. The agency department may have a competitive "line" of policies, operate in desirable territory, offer attractive sales contracts to managers and agents, have a well-conceived and compre-hensive sales promotion program, keep useful records, have an effective conservation procedure, and get along well with other home office departments. If the right manpower is lacking, though, there won't be much progress. The few com-panies that have tried to get along without *any* sales man-power have shown little growth. Those without the *right* sales manpower haven't shown much more.

The agency department must obtain the right manpower in three areas: agency managers, soliciting agents and other agency personnel both in the home office and in the field. Obtaining the right agency heads is definitely the agency department's direct concern. It must decide whether to use general agents or branch managers or both. It must recruit, train, supervise and motivate[8] managers. An essential corollary to the duty of obtaining the right manpower is the elimination and replacement of managers and agents who, because of lack of ability or unwillingness to cooperate, are not achieving satisfactory results.

In many agencies, especially larger ones, there are assistants to the manager. Usually, the home office determines whether, and how many, such assistants should be engaged and has final say as to who will be hired or contracted.

The agency department is also concerned with the recruit-ing, training, supervision and motivation of the soliciting agents. These activities are conducted primarily by the field

---

[8] Sometimes obtaining the right manpower is considered as involving five activities rather than four: recruiting, selection, training, supervision, motiva-tion. The first and second are so closely related that "recruiting" will also include "selection" in this text. Even among four activities there is some blending or overlap—the lines of demarcation are not always sharp.

offices. Standards and methods, however, originate in the home office. Further, whether or not the home office always exercises its authority, it may approve or disapprove placing under contract the soliciting agents recommended by the branch managers. Even in the case of salesmen engaged by general agents, today the agency department usually has the right to reject such recommendations.

To perform its various home office and field office duties, the agency department also needs qualified personnel not directly engaged in selling. They assist the chief agency executive in performing the various duties necessary to achieve the department's objectives. Some of the home office agency staff are specialists in certain areas; frequently they are men transferred or promoted to the home office after experience as agents or managers, or both.

Field operations must be supervised. The home office must assure itself, by means of an effective supervisory staff of representatives under its direction, that the field is performing its duties and executing home office plans. Field managers are expected to devote considerable time to supervision of their agency forces. But they look to the home office for assistance and, in any event, the home office must supervise the managers. Effective supervision requires well-planned field visits by members of the agency department. These men are required to perform many exacting duties and must be on the road much of the time.

6. *To Develop Sales Promotion Techniques*[9]—There is no substitute for a good agent and the services he provides. People are more insurance-conscious than they were, say, 40 years ago. Also, most people know, either from their personal experience or from the experience of a friend, what a boon life insurance can be or, conversely, what the lack of adequate life insurance can mean to a family. Nevertheless, few apply of their own accord, and even the superior agent sometimes needs help to get prospects to recognize their needs for life

---

[9] This subject is considered in more detail in chapter 12.

insurance. Sales promotion work will not make sales without salesmen, but it will *facilitate* sales. Sales promotion will make it easier for agents to find prospects and to convince these prospects of their need for life insurance and thus enable the salesmen to sell more insurance to more people.

7. *To Develop* Office *Organization in the Field*[10]—Successful agency operations require a substantial number of field *office* personnel to process applications and policy loans, receive premiums paid in person or by mail and give service to policyowners and agents. In managerial companies all such persons are employees of the home office, which must approve the hiring of cashiers and clerks. Normally, the manager's personnel recommendations will be approved. There is less uniformity in the case of a general agency company. In many cases today, the cashier or branch secretary is an employee of the company and is not directly or exclusively under the jurisdiction of the general agent.

8. *To Conserve Business*[11]—Literally, this duty means to keep the company's business in force insofar as "preventable" terminations—lapses and surrenders—are concerned. Broadly, this duty also embraces effective selling that will reduce such terminations and efforts to reinstate such policies that do lapse.

9. *To Keep and Analyze Records of Operations*—The agency department needs numerous records to measure the progress of its operations. It seeks answers to many questions. Is the agency operation as a whole doing well? What about production, premium income, renewals, in-force figures—in terms of the entire company, the individual agency, the individual agent? How do these figures compare to one year ago, two years ago, five years ago? Are any trends discernible? If so, are they significant? If any of the trends seem adverse, what can or should be done to change them?

Mere volume of business sold each year is less indicative of

---

[10] This subject is considered in more detail in chapter 13.
[11] This subject is considered in more detail in chapter 14.

a company's progress than its yearend in-force figures, but even the latter may be deceptive. Since the end of World War II almost all companies have shown substantial increases for business in force each year. So growth alone shows only part of the picture. Management also wants to know: How are we doing compared to other companies? Is our company keeping pace with its competitors? If not, there may be entirely satisfactory explanations—mergers of other companies, entry of straight ordinary companies into health, group or juvenile, variable annuities, etc. Such expansion of activities may well account for the more rapid growth of some competitors.

Analysis by types of and amounts of policies is also valuable. People may have been buying a higher proportion of term insurance in recent years. In its place, term is useful and desirable. But are agents selling a higher proportion of term each year? Is the proportion of term to whole life and endowment increasing? Is the proportion of group to ordinary increasing? How are sales of permanent plans holding up? Is the amount of the average policy increasing? The trend for most companies has been upward in recent years, because people's disposable income has increased.

Are the company's agents getting enough new business from present policyowners, sometimes known as repeat business? A man already converted from prospect to client should be easier to sell the next time he needs more life insurance. In some companies the amount of new business that agents place on the lives of their present clients is substantial; in others, it is negligible. Why?

What about the sale itself? What proportion of business is sold "cash with application"? Such business shows less NTO (not taken out, i.e., the agent does not collect the first premium at the time the applicant signs the application and the latter declines to pay this premium when the agent calls to deliver the policy) and better persistency. What about the frequency of premium payments? There has been a trend to monthly payments, but are they always necessary? Some agents sell annual or semiannual. Perhaps more could.

10. *To Coordinate Its Activities With Those of Other Home Office Departments*—The agency department must maintain liaison with other departments. It is up to the chief agency executive to assure that the viewpoint of his department receives due consideration before his fellow executives reach decisions that affect the agency department. (Conversely, the viewpoints of his fellow executives should be considered before he reaches decisions that affect other departments.)

Differences of opinion and outlook between the sales division and the various home office departments are common to industry generally. Life insurance companies are not immune to this friction. An effective sales organization is essential to the very existence of a company. To cite an extreme case, if the field force should disband and if no replacements were hired, eventual liquidation of the company would follow. However, the course from application, to issued policy, to maturity as a death claim or otherwise, involves many departments. To mention only two: The home office underwriting department must be able to do its job properly if the company is to experience favorable mortality; and the investment department must put the company's funds, largely premiums, to work prudently if a satisfactory rate of interest is to be earned and, even more vital, if safety of principal is to be assured.

In most cases, misunderstandings result from unfamiliarity or inadequate familiarity with the work of other departments. It has been said that insurance agents and other salesmen are averse to detail. Whether or not they really are, the agent may certainly wonder why a case, approval of which means needed protection to an applicant and his family (it also means food and rent money for the agent and *his* family), should be delayed because he neglected to record on the application information as to former addresses and former occupations. The home office underwriter may wonder whether such omissions were deliberate. Did the applicant formerly engage in a hazardous occupation—to which he may return? The home office underwriter needs complete information before he acts. The agent should furnish it.

Field forces tend to question the necessity for rules and for adherence to them. It is easy for agents to feel that a home office department cites a rule or requirement without enough recognition of their own problems. Understandably, the agent looks at a given situation from his own viewpoint; in his view *his* cases are the most important ones, if not the only cases, because *his* prospects or *his* clients are involved. For instance, if a policyowner tells him that he just hasn't the money for a premium due March 1 but will have it May 1, why can't the agent grant such an extension without bothering the home office for forms of one kind or another? Home office departments have to be concerned about discrimination, "custom and usage," etc. Serious difficulties, legal and otherwise, have arisen when companies have appeared to countenance such modifications of the customary policy provision that "no agent or other person except the president, a vice president, or a secretary of the company has power on behalf of the company to bind the company by making any promises respecting benefits or accepting any representations or information not contained in the written application for this policy, or to make or modify this contract, or to extend the time for payment of a premium, or to waive any lapse or forfeiture or any of the company's rights or requirements."

Managements are constantly trying to promote better understanding between home office and field. Many companies bring managers and agents into the home office for training and information, part of which consists of meeting with representatives of various departments to ask questions and exchange ideas. In turn, representatives of home office departments, particularly the underwriting and the claim, visit agencies to discuss and explain problems of concern to managers and agents. Regular company sales conferences afford other opportunities for meetings of field and home office minds.

Such meetings can go far to impress on both the field and the home office that they are both working toward the same objectives (and for the same company). As the result of such exchanges or contacts, often certain requests from the field are modified or withdrawn, and certain home office requirements are modified or discontinued.

11. *To Perform a Number of Other Duties*—In addition to the foregoing, an agency department may have other duties. One example is research. While many companies rely exclusively on the research facilities of an organization like the Life Insurance Agency Management Association for assistance with their agency problems, some of the larger ones supplement such research by special divisions of their own. The agency department also sets sales goals and establishes procedures and rules for each phase of its operations.

·   ·   ·   ·

Chapter 3 indicated the increasing role of the home office in the direction of field activities in recent years. Electronic data processing seems to have accelerated this trend. Hence, some reference to the impact of EDP on *agency department* activities is in order at this point. (Since its place in the organization structure of a life insurance company varies, the EDP division does not appear in Figure 1.)

There will be no attempt here to explain just how the computer is used to develop desired data. Briefly, the computer receives and processes data and reports the results extremely rapidly, usually more rapidly than by other means.

Some agency departments have been using EDP almost from its beginning; others have been doing so only recently. Some have been using EDP to a much greater extent than others. With respect to agency departments their basic objective in the use of EDP is to improve service to policyowners, field underwriters and agency managers by making service faster, more accurate and more reliable. Through EDP agency departments seek to provide:

1. Faster and more significant information to field agents, especially in such areas as prospecting and planning of insurance programs for prospects
2. Information for better marketing research

3. Information for better development of new insurance products
4. More and better information for sales management
5. Better control over billing and posting premiums, calculating commissions, cash values, loans and so forth

| SUMMARY

The work of the agency department can be divided into two parts, that of the home office and that of the field. Essentially, the home office is policy-making; the field is policy-executing.

Home office organization of the agency department may vary from simple to complex, depending on the size of the company and the types of protection sold. To achieve its three basic objectives, the home office agency department must discharge numerous important duties that involve activities in both the home office and in the field, including close relationships with other departments.

QUESTIONS FOR REVIEW

1. List the duties of the agency department in attaining its basic objectives. Describe each duty.
2. Discuss the factors involved in determining the territory in which a life insurance company will operate. Has the number of agencies in your area increased or decreased during the past 10 years?
3. Why is the development of the right manpower such an important duty of the agency department? Describe the three major areas in which the right manpower must be obtained.
4. Outline the useful information that the agency department can derive from keeping and analyzing records of its operations.
5. Account for differences of opinion and outlook that sometimes arise between the agency department and other departments. How can company managements promote better understanding between home office and field?

5 | Contracts and Compensation

Life insurance agents receive their compensation in the form of commissions. When they sell, they earn; when they don't sell, they don't earn. However, the sale of a policy usually provides an agent with some annual income, on a reduced basis, long after the first year.

Many persons unfamiliar with the work of a life insurance agent have erroneous ideas as to the basis of his bread and butter. There is some resentment that he gets paid for getting men to do what they should do for themselves—protect themselves and their dependents. Their attitude is frequently based on incomplete and inaccurate information. They know of an agent who "got a big commission for a half-hour's talking." What they don't know is how many other hours the agent may have worked on this particular case before the final, successful half-hour. And few members of the general public realize that the competent life insurance salesman has spent and is spending many hours in preparing himself for his work and in keeping himself occupationally fit—hours that are usually self-financed. Neither do others always know of his many hours of work that do not result in sales and therefore do not result in any income. Not everybody is insurable, and few of those who are will apply without urging.

Earnings of general agents, branch managers and soliciting agents depend largely upon their successful sales efforts. Rates of compensation are contained in the contracts with the company they represent. Accordingly, contracts and compensation will be discussed together.

CONTRACTS AND COMPENSATION— GENERAL AGENTS

General agents and branch managers work under certain conditions of employment or association. Whenever one person performs work for another in any situation—contractual or otherwise—a clear understanding of the obligations of each is desirable if not essential. In the case of general agents and branch managers, these understandings are formalized by means of a contract or agreement.

What a general agent is and does was explained in chapter 3. Actually, the life insurance general agent is not a "general agent" in the legal sense of the term, because he is not empowered to do all that his principal could do if the latter were present. The life insurance general agent's powers are strictly defined by contract. They concern primarily the sales end of the business, although service to policyowners may be specified in the contract.

The contract is a signed, legal document between the company and the individual confirming that the former appoints the latter as one of its general agents. As such, it must embody the several requisites of any valid contract. Subject matter will include:

1.   Statement of appointment as general agent
2.   Description or definition of his territory, whether ex-

clusive or otherwise. (In some large urban areas, two or more general agencies may represent one company and share the same territory. In such a situation, none will have exclusive rights to any one area.)

3. Statement of the general agent's powers and duties. (The general law of agency governs any situation not specifically covered by the contract, such as the power to appoint soliciting agents, with or without formal home office approval, as the case may be.)

4. Authorization to the general agent to submit for home office consideration applications for life insurance obtained by himself and his agents and to deliver policies and premium receipts.

5. Statement or schedule of rates of commission he will receive on gross first-year and on renewal premiums of his agency. Specific schedules state the commission rates applicable to various policy plans; for example, ordinary life, various limited-payment contracts, endowments of various durations, and term policies.

6. Allowances to the general agent to defray part of the expenses of maintaining his agency. Companies use three bases to compute such expense allowances:

   a. A formula that sets the maximum expense allowance in each field office in terms of quantity of business done, i.e., new and renewal business

   b. Direct payment of or reimbursement for certain actual agency office expenses incurred—for example, rent, clerical salaries, postage, telephone and telegraph, agency promotion, supervisors' salaries, new-agent financing losses—without regard to formula

   c. Some combination of a and b

7. Provision for life insurance, disability and retirement benefits, if any

8. Provision for termination of the contract and statement of the rights of both parties in that event

Commission Schedules

On business the general agent writes himself, the entire first-year and renewal commissions are his.[1]

He receives the company's established commission rates on business paid for by its agents. On business that his agents write, he retains the overriding commissions on both first-year and renewal premiums. Such overriding commission may be the difference between the commission the general agent receives from the company and the amount to which the soliciting agent is entitled under his own contract, or it may be set forth separately.

At this point the term "vesting" should be considered briefly. As used in life insurance sales compensation, vesting may be defined or explained as the right of a general agent or of a soliciting agent to receive all or part of his accruing commissions, even if his contract with the company has been terminated. The general agent's overriding commissions for both first and renewal years are usually fully vested, as are also first-year and at least some renewal commissions on his personal production. Vesting may be unconditional, or it may depend on the general agent's or the soliciting agent's period of service or amount of production. Vesting may vary according to the cause of termination—whether by death, disability, retirement, or decision to discontinue the general agency relationship by either the general agent or the company.

The schedules on pages 59–61 show, as percentages of gross premiums, first-year and renewal commission rates for ordinary life, 20-payment life, 20-year endowment and 10-year term policies under the general agents' and soliciting agents' contracts of four representative United States companies. Companies A and B operate in New York and therefore are subject to the statutory commission rate limits of that state (see pages 97–98); C and D do not. In each case the general agent's com-

---

[1] Some companies, however, pay only the soliciting agent's compensation to a general agent on his personal business.

mission rates shown are those he receives for *business he writes himself, i.e., his personal production.*

There are many ramifications to compensation plans. Those that follow outline only the bare essentials of commission schedules. Contracts contain many provisions that increase or decrease these commission rates. For example, so-called

Schedules of Commissions

Company A

General Agent

Policy Plan	1st Year	2nd to 10th Years†	11th Year‡
Ordinary life	55%*	7½%	3%
20-payment life	42*	7½	3
20-year endowment	35*	7½	3
10-year term	38	7½	—

* This rate is paid on policies of $5,000 or more.
† Rates shown include 1% service fee.
‡ Service fees are paid in 11th and subsequent years.

Soliciting Agent

Policy Plan	1st Year	2nd to 10th Years	11th Year†
Ordinary life	55%*	5%	2%
20-payment life	42*	5	2
20-year endowment	35*	5	2
10-year term	38	5	—

* This rate is paid on policies of $5,000 or more.
† Service fees are paid in 11th and subsequent years.

Company B

General Agent

Policy Plans	1st Year	2nd Year	3rd Year	4th and 5th Years*	6th to 10th Year*	11th Year†
Ordinary life	55%	22½%	12½%	10%	5½%	3%
20-payment life	40	22½	12½	10	5½	3
20-year endowment	30	22½	12½	10	5½	3
10-year term	40	17½	12½	10	5½	—

* Rates shown include 7½% service fee in policy years 4–5 and 3% in years 6–10.
† Service fees are paid in 11th and subsequent years; collection fee not included.

Soliciting Agent

Policy Plans	1st Year	2nd Year	3rd Year	4th and 5th Years*	6th Year*
Ordinary life	50%	15%	10%	7½%	3%
20-payment life	40	15	10	7½	3
20-year endowment	30	15	10	7½	3
10-year term	35	15	10	7½	3

* Service fees are paid in fourth and subsequent years.

Company C

General Agent

Policy Plan	1st Year	2nd to 10th Years	11th Year*
Ordinary life	78%	7%	4%
20-payment life	78	7	4
20-year endowment	66	7	4
10-year term	48	7	—

* Service fees are paid in 11th and subsequent years.

Soliciting Agent

Policy Plan	1st Year	2nd to 10th Years	11th Year*
Ordinary life	65%	5%	2%
20-payment life	65	5	2
20-year endowment	55	5	2
10-year term	40	5	—

* Service fees are paid in 11th and subsequent years.

Company D

General Agent

Policy Plan	1st Year	2nd Year	3rd Year	4th to 7th Years	8th Year*
Ordinary life	60%	20%	10%	5%	2%
20-payment life	49	20	10	5	2
20-year endowment	36	20	10	5	2
10-year term	60	10	5	5	2

* Service fees are paid in eighth and subsequent years.

Soliciting Agent

Policy Plan	1st Year	2nd Year	3rd Year	4th to 7th Years	8th Year*
Ordinary life	60%	20%	10%	5%	2%
20-payment life	49	20	10	5	2
20-year endowment	36	20	10	5	2
10-year term	60	10	5	5	2

* Service fees are paid in eighth and subsequent years.

Supplementary notes:

Company A and Company B.   General agent receives the same commissions as the soliciting agent, plus an overriding commission in the second and subsequent policy years on his personal production.

Company C.   General agent holds a soliciting agent's contract, and he receives overriding commissions in the first and subsequent policy years on his personal production.

Company D.   General agent receives the same commissions as soliciting agent but does not receive an overriding commission policy years on his personal production.

"quality bonuses" may be added, or reduced rates may be paid in cases of replacement of existing insurance by new insurance.

Collection Fees and Expense Allowances

Usually a general agent's contract allows him a collection fee of, say, 2 percent on each renewal premium paid through his agency after the end of the renewal commission period. The distinction between a commission and a collection fee or expense allowance is often a fine one. The same compensation may be designated as a commission in some contracts, and as an allowance in others. A common distinction is that a commission belongs to the general agent who was in charge of the agency when the business was produced; a collection fee or expense allowance belongs to the general agent in charge when the fee or allowance becomes payable.

The expense allowance paid to a general agent may be either of two kinds, or a mixture of them:

1.   It may be related to the *results* that the agency achieves. For example, it may be a percentage of gross premiums

of the agency, or a dollar amount per $1,000 of production or of business in force.

2. It may be related to the *expenses* that are incurred. For example, one allowance might be a percentage, such as 50 percent, of the rent payable by the general agent for his office.

Security Benefits

Many companies offer their general agents some form of security or welfare benefits. Thus, a general agent may be eligible for certain security benefits *entirely apart* from and in addition to those he receives as a result of his personal production. These programs vary widely. The most common of such benefits is group insurance, either life insurance or a combination of life insurance and health insurance. Programs may also provide for certain benefits if the general agent becomes totally and permanently disabled while under contract. Some companies provide retirement benefits for general agents. However, these cannot be "qualified" under federal income tax regulations if, as is usual, the general agent has the legal status of an independent contractor.

Commonly the company and the general agent share the cost of security benefits. Some companies pay the entire cost.

CONTRACTS AND COMPENSATION— BRANCH MANAGERS

Although branch managers are employees, their compensation depends in large measure on their success in building agency organizations that will produce a quantity and quality of business satisfactory to the company. The formal agreement under which a branch manager represents his company is usually referred to as a "contract" or "manager's contract." Much of its subject matter is similar to that of a general agent's contract:

1. Statement of appointment as branch manager
2. Description or definition of his territory
3. Statement of powers and duties; specifically, the power to appoint soliciting agents, subject to home office approval
4. Authorization to submit for home office consideration applications obtained by his branch office
5. Statement of compensation, including salary arrangements and personal production, if permitted
6. Reimbursement for business travel expenses
7. Provision[2] for disability and retirement benefits, if any
8. Provision for termination of the contract and statement of the rights of both parties in that event

Details of company plans for compensating branch managers vary. Representative elements of such plans will be considered under the following headings:

1. Factors determining managerial compensation
    a. Overall agency factors
    b. Flat salary
    c. Incentive bonuses and allowances
2. Frequency of payment of compensation
3. Operating expenses
4. Compensation for personal production
5. Group insurance coverages
6. Retirement provisions

1a. Overall agency factors concern particularly new business. A manager's income will reflect the amount of new business paid for by his agents. Compensation factors may be related to persistency as well as quantity of business. Contracts may provide that the manager will also receive a percentage of gross renewal premium income or agents' renewal commissions paid. Thus, a manager's pay frequently consists of two parts—current income and deferred income.

---

[2] Sometimes this provision is included in the home office pension plan.

1b. Most compensation plans provide for a flat or guaranteed salary to the manager. Depending on the size of the agency, the salary may range from about $5,000 to a maximum of about $15,000 annually.

1c. Managers generally are eligible for additional incentive bonuses and allowances. These take various forms. A manager may receive compensation for each agent who was placed under contract in his agency during the past calendar year or two and who is still with the agency and producing some specified minimum amount of new business. (Some companies pay their managers such compensation only if the new agents have *not* sold life insurance before, i.e., if they are new to the business.) There is also financial recognition for attainment by the agency of production requirements and quotas set by the home office. Sometimes the manager receives a bonus for each of his agents who qualify for the company's field club or production club. Some companies pay a bonus to a manager if the expenses of his agency are low as compared with the company average or some other standard of expense measurement.

2. Branch managers are usually paid once a month. Such payment includes both their flat salary, if any, and any additional items such as described in 1.

3. Broadly speaking, the company pays agency operating expenses. These include payments for financing new agents in excess of the commissions earned by those agents.[3] The home office pays most or all of the compensation of supervisors whom it employs, subject to some variations. The home office likewise usually pays for travel expense on company business (for other than personal production) if outside the city in which the agency is located.

4. In general, branch managers are expected to devote considerably more time to agency building than to personal production. Usually a manager receives commission in accordance

---

[3] Sometimes the contract may be modified so that a manager receives a bonus for successful recruiting and is charged for unsuccessful recruiting on some basis that provides for sharing financing losses with the company.

with the company's regular *agent's* contract for the business he writes himself, when the latter is permitted.

5. Managers are representatives with employee status. Therefore, subject to the company's requirements, they are eligible for such group insurance coverages as it offers. These include one or more of the following and may be contributory or noncontributory:

    a. Group life insurance
    b. Group disability benefits
        1) Temporary disability benefits
        2) Long-term disability benefits
        3) Hospital and surgical benefits
        4) Major medical expense benefits

6. Branch managers' compensation plans generally include provisions for retirement. Among the common features covered are these:

    a. The manager's contract for personal production may or may not be continued.

    b. Group insurance coverages that the individual enjoyed as manager are affected in various ways. For example, in some companies they are continued wholly or partly indefinitely; in others they are discontinued at once or after some specified period.

    c. Pension benefits, usually some form of life annuity, may be contributory or noncontributory. The amount of retirement benefit payable will depend on such factors as length of service and amount of manager's total annual basic compensation (from which his commissions for personal production may be excluded).

    d. The most common normal retirement age is 65. Whatever the retirement age is, it sometimes may be advanced at the option of the manager or the company, or it may be postponed at the option of the company.

    e. Retirement provisions are predicated on the assumption that a manager will be in his post until he reaches retirement age. Situations may arise before attainment of retirement age, however; a manager may die, become totally and permanently disabled, return to the status of soliciting agent or leave the company's service. Clauses in the manager's compensation plan will state what benefits, if any, are granted in such cases.

CONTRACTS AND COMPENSATION— SOLICITING AGENTS

Before this subject is discussed, statement of a few basic principles may be in order.

1. The agent who does a creditable and *successful* job should be enabled to earn an adequate living. Compensation plans should provide (a) income commensurate with the quality and quantity of work performed as well as (b) retirement benefits to the agent who has served his company satisfactorily over some minimum period of time. Plans should yield the agent a larger return on business with good persistency than on business with poor persistency. Further, the agent should receive reasonable compensation in some form for service that he renders his policyowners while he is active in the business.

2. No compensation contract that is sound for the company and fair to the policyowner can possibly pay a living wage to the agent whose quantity of production remains low. Qualified men will do well under almost any system in use; unqualified men will fail.

3. Compensation plans should be such as to attract—and retain—desirable and promising candidates for careers in life insurance selling.

History

Remuneration of men for the sale of life insurance has had an interesting history. The soliciting agent's contract used in

1845 by one of the earliest companies provided in part that first-year commissions would be at the rate of 5 percent of gross premiums. This company, still in operation, fairly soon thereafter amended its contract to pay 10 percent first-year commissions with 5 percent renewals so long as the policy remained in force. (For many years, of course, its commission rates have been comparable to those of other companies.)

Granted that the sale of life insurance was a part-time activity with most men in the early days of the business, such a scale was not likely to attract many prospective agents. Gradually, initial commissions increased to 75 percent and more of the premium. As a result of legislation in New York State following the Armstrong Investigation in 1905 and 1906, a first-year commission of either 50 percent or 55 percent with nine vested renewals of 5 percent was widely adopted as the soliciting agent's remuneration for a whole life contract. Thus an agent would receive approximately a full annual premium as commission, spread out over the 10-year period, for selling a whole life contract, upon which nine renewal premiums were paid. Commission rates for other plans were in proportion. This legislation, now contained in Section 213 of the Insurance Law of New York, applies only to companies operating in that state, but it applies to all United States business of those companies, not just to business sold in New York state. Thus these limitations established a widespread pattern influencing the actions of many companies not subject to that law.

Vesting

In the preceding paragraph the word "vested" was used. Renewal commissions may be vested or nonvested. As explained on page 58, they are said to be vested if payable to the agent who wrote the policy, irrespective of whether he remains with the company while it is in force. They are nonvested if the agent loses his right to them in the event he leaves the company. Under a contract providing for nine vested renewals, an agent affiliated with company A at the time he wrote the policy would be entitled to nine renewal commissions even though he terminated long before the policyowner paid all of the nine renewal premiums.

The question of vested versus nonvested commissions has been widely debated. Much depends on the whole concept of renewal commissions. According to one view,[4] they are a form of deferred compensation for the sale; as such, they are earned if the renewal premium involved is received by the company. Hence they should be vested, and the agent who originally sold the policy is entitled to the renewals irrespective of whether he remains with the company or even in the life insurance business. Inherent in this view is the belief that *all* commissions are paid as compensation for production, i.e., for selling, and that renewals are not to be considered as remuneration for service to policyowners.

According to the second view, renewal commissions are a kind of service fee paid to the agent to induce him to do his best to keep the business on the books and to provide the customary services to policyowners. Inherent in this view is the belief that such commissions should be paid to the agent who is called on to furnish the service rather than to the man who wrote the business originally but has since terminated. Hence they should be nonvested.

Vested renewals to soliciting agents were not common before the Armstrong Investigation. In the absence of a vesting provision, agents no longer under contract were not entitled to renewal commissions on business originally written by them. However, if the agent sold for a general agency, such commissions reverted to the general agent rather than to the company. For many years after the investigation vesting provisions in soliciting agents' contracts were quite general. More recently there has been a trend toward nonvested renewals, with the company using reversions or commission recoveries to increase commission rates or to help provide for security benefits or

---

[4] This is the view held by the United States Social Security Administration. Some companies consider their agents employees for purposes of workmen's compensation and unemployment compensation. New agents on salary plans are considered employees.

service fees. Most commission schedules for full-time agents now state that some or all of the renewal commissions shall be nonvested. Many contracts provide for a so-called service fee after all renewal commissions have been paid. Such fees usually are a small percentage of the premium, such as 2 percent (see schedules on pages 59 and 60.) These fees likewise are nonvested.

Even today there is considerable opinion that the salesman's chief duty is to sell, and that other persons, such as cashiers and their assistants, should furnish most of the service on existing policies. Thus there is a third view that renewal commissions are a kind of reward to the agent who remains under contract and whose policies stay in force. Inherent in this view is the belief that renewal commissions should be nonvested but should be paid to the surviving agent on the surviving policies, even though he provides little or no service to his policyowners.

The majority view, however, is the second: Service is one of the agent's important duties and thus he should be directly compensated for furnishing it. *Theoretically,* renewal commissions should be paid *only* if the agent gives service; if that agent leaves, any remaining renewal commissions payable should be paid to another agent of the company, provided that other agent actually furnishes service. *In practice* it is often difficult to define just what "service" embraces and to determine whether the agent is or is not furnishing such service.

The foregoing discussion shows that in the development of a compensation plan a company has a choice. Its soliciting agents' contracts may offer vested renewal commissions at some specified rates; or they may offer *higher* rates of *nonvested* renewal commissions. The latter approach to compensation pays more to the agent who stays by paying less to the agent who leaves.

Trends in Agents' Compensation

The remuneration of agents has undergone important changes in the past quarter of a century. The traditional basis was a high first-year commission followed by a number of small renewals. This basis has certain advantages from the standpoints of both company and agent. For the company, the traditional basis produces a direct relationship between the remuneration it pays an agent and his success both as to production and maintenance of business in force. Also, the traditional commission basis limits the company's cost, assuming that the commission stated in the contract is all that is being paid for the business. As for the agent, his earnings directly reflect the success of his efforts. The traditional commission basis gives him freedom of action with relatively modest obligation to fulfill any set requirements; he is his own boss.

But there are disadvantages along with the advantages to both company and agent. Vesting has already been discussed. Further, because of a large first-year commission, the traditional basis creates for the company a much higher expense rate in the first year of each policy than in other years. There are also disadvantages to the agent:

1. Even the most outstanding agents need time to get established. Particularly, men with families have difficulty making ends meet while getting started, since sales are likely to be few and for relatively small amounts. (Today any ordinary policy for $5,000 or less would be considered small.)

2. Sales tend to be emphasized to the detriment of service. With 75 percent or more of their income coming from new business, many agents do not feel they can afford to spend much time on service. Moreover, when commissions do not run beyond 10 years, an agent has little financial incentive to service business more than 10 years old, since his clients may well have reached an age when they will buy little additional insurance.

3. Earnings are likely to fluctuate considerably from year to year, even from month to month. Also, if a man's production declines, a common occurrence as he grows

older and becomes less active, or in times of economic recession, his income may drop sharply.

Even in the heyday of the "55 and nine 5s" scale there was little evidence that this schedule had any scientific basis. However, it seemed to work reasonably well for a number of years. Two important developments gave impetus to reexamination of this basis. One was the depression of the 1930s. During that period many prospects just did not have the money to purchase the protection they needed; in fact many were obliged to surrender much or all of the insurance they had bought in earlier years.[5] These were difficult years for many able agents whose contracts placed topheavy emphasis on the production of new business.

A second development was the decision of most companies that service to policyowners was a proper duty of their salesmen. A natural consequence of that decision was compensation to agents for furnishing such service.

Companies that have modified their commission plans of compensation have recognized that agents were not overpaid and that they should be enabled to earn at least as much under any new plan as under the traditional one. Most of the changes that have occurred in agents' compensation plans in recent years have involved one or more of the following:

1. Payment of *service fees* to agents after they have received all renewal commissions provided for in their contracts.

2. Nonvesting of some or all of the renewal commissions. The amount saved has been used either to increase the renewal commission rate or to provide a service fee to the original agent or to the successor agent to whom the policy is assigned for service.

3. Moderate reduction of first-year commission rates with somewhat higher renewal commission rates than the

---

[5] Such a situation may be hard to conceive for those reading this text now, many of whom were not born at that time. But it certainly existed.

traditional in the second and third (or even later) years of the policy.

The first two factors have already been explained. As for the third, one modification of the traditional "55 and nine 5s" for a whole life contract was illustrated in soliciting agent's plan B on page 60. It will be seen that renewals are paid for only five years. This type of renewal compensation is sometimes referred to as "heaped renewals" or "telescoped renewals."

In addition to the foregoing a number of companies are paying some form of performance bonus for production or persistency or both. Sometimes compensation plans recognize length of service as a factor. With more than 1,900 legal reserve life insurance companies in the United States and Canada, numerous variations in commission scales exist. Because of competition and the necessity for financial soundness, no one plan of remuneration is superior by *all* standards. Some are more favorable to agents in some respects; some are more favorable in others.

As stated in chapter 3, under the general agency system the life insurance salesman's contract may be with the general agent, although practically always subject to home office approval. Under the managerial system the agent's contract is with the company.

Soliciting Agents' Contracts

Any corporation may be legally liable for the acts of those who represent it. In life insurance the contracts spell out as specifically as possible the legal relationships between the companies and their general agents, branch managers and soliciting agents. Powers of soliciting agents are considerably less than those of general agents and managers. Nevertheless, because of their many contacts with the public as representatives of their companies, soliciting agents' powers and limitations thereon must be carefully defined. Provisions in soliciting agents' contracts commonly cover the following subjects:

1. Statement of existence of a contract
2. Powers of agent, primarily to solicit applications, collect premiums and issue receipts
3. Obligation to remit promptly any premiums he collects
4. Territory in which he may operate
5. Limitations or prohibitions, especially modification of policy contract (see page 52), rebating and twisting
6. Compensation
   a. First-year commission scale for company's various policy plans
   b. Renewal commission scale for company's various policy plans
   c. Additional incentives, e.g., a bonus based on the amount and the persistency of the agent's production
   d. Requirements for agent to maintain his contract (certain minimum production standards are often set)
7. Vesting provisions
   a. On termination other than by death or disability
   b. On termination by death
   c. On termination by total and permanent disability
8. Security benefits
   a. Retirement plan, if any
      1) Contributory or noncontributory
      2) Benefits provided[6]
   b. Group insurance coverages, if any (these benefits frequently are separate from the agent's contract itself)
      1) Life
      2) Hospital
      3) Surgical

---

[6] Full-time agents are eligible for Social Security benefits.

    4)   Medical
    5)   Major medical
    6)   Indemnity
    7)   Other
9.   Provision for termination of the contract

REBATING AND TWISTING. These terms were mentioned in section 5, "limitations or prohibitions." Rebating has been called price-cutting of premiums. It is the return to the applicant by the agent of all or a part of the premium—or the offering of any other valuable consideration, such as a radio or a camera—as an inducement to apply for life insurance.

Twisting is misleading a policyowner to drop existing insurance and replace it with new protection. Usually, the term is applied to the act whereby agent A persuades his prospect B to drop his coverage in B's company and replace it with new insurance in A's company. Twisting is nearly always disadvantageous to B. To quote a slogan used by a major company for many years: "Do not lapse your policy with any other company to take one with us. Do not lapse your policy with us to take one with any other company. You lose in either case."

If not forbidden by the agent's contract, rebating and twisting are usually prohibited by company rules. These acts also are illegal in most states and provinces, although such acts are not easily proved, because *replacement* of one policy by another is not twisting unless the transaction involves loss to the insured. Neither party to an act of rebating or twisting is likely to publicize it.

Soliciting Agents' Commission Schedules in Canada

The schedules for general agents and soliciting agents on pages 59 and 60 were limited to the United States because Canadian companies use the managerial system for their agencies in Canada. In the main, agents' commission rates are quite similar in the two countries. Companies quite generally pay up to 60 percent first-year commissions for ordinary life, followed by 10 percent or 15 percent in the second year and eight renewals of 5 percent. Service commissions of 2 percent or 2½ percent are frequently paid beyond the 10th year. In many Canadian companies the commission scale for participating business is 5 to 10 percent higher than for nonparticipating business. There has been a growing trend among Canadian companies to the "heaped renewal" type of compensation, to a greater extent than in the United States.

Agents' Earnings

An illustration may help show what agents can earn. To keep the example uncomplicated, let us assume an agent pays for $300,000 of whole life in his first year and increases his annual production at the rate of $100,000 annually, until he pays for $800,000 in his sixth year. Let us also assume that the average premium per $1,000 of insurance is $25, that all premiums are paid annually, that first-year commission is at the rate of 50 percent of the premium per thousand, or $12.50, that the renewal commission rate is 5 percent or $1.25 and that 80 percent of each year's new business remains in force in the second year and in each subsequent year. The table below shows for each of the six years the first-year commissions, total renewal commissions and total commissions for this business.

	Amount Sold	First-year Commissions	Total Renewal Commissions	Total Commissions
First year	$300,000	$ 3,750	$ —	$ 3,750
Second year	400,000	5,000	300	5,300
Third year	500,000	6,250	700	6,950
Fourth year	600,000	7,500	1,200	8,700
Fifth year	700,000	8,750	1,800	10,550
Sixth year	800,000	10,000	2,500	12,500

In the interests of simplicity, this illustration has been limited to ordinary business. If his company sells annuities, health and group insurance, an agent may also derive income from these sources. Further, an agent under contract to one company is sometimes in a position to place a policy with another life company or to sell a nonlife policy, such as automobile or fire. And as will be touched upon later, some life insurance companies sell mutual funds, another potential source of income for the agent.

FINANCING OF AGENTS

Closely related to the subject of agents' compensation is financing. The word embraces the various forms of dollar assistance that the new agent receives from his manager and/or company to help him meet his necessary living and operating expenses while he is getting established as a life underwriter.

Up to the late 1920s, organized financing of agents was uncommon. Agency people generally took it for granted that new men probably would not be self-supporting right away but felt that the prospect of a substantial income from commissions made a career in life underwriting attractive. For a long time agents and their sales techniques developed in a highly individualistic way. Men were paid for what they sold. If they did not sell enough to live as they felt they should, they left the business.

As indicated earlier, the depression of the 1930s was a difficult period even for many able, experienced, life insurance agents. It was still more so for new men without income from renewal commissions and with few prospects for insurance. Without supplementary financial assistance, only the most exceptional beginner was able to earn enough in the early years of his career to support himself and his dependents.

Attractive as are the long-range earnings prospects for the qualified life insurance salesman, the *immediate* returns are not likely to be large (see example on page 75). In fact, they are likely to fall short of maintaining the agent and his family satisfactorily without additional financial assistance from some other source. Further, the time he spends in basic training and early prospecting reduces his immediate opportunity to earn.

Some financial assistance may come from the new man's own

resources, from friends or relatives or from a loan. Usually, however, it comes from the manager and/or company (most often the latter) in the form of a financing arrangement that will make up the difference between the income the new man needs and the income he can earn under his company's standard basis of compensation. In this way the manager may be able to bring into the agency desirable men who otherwise could not afford to try life insurance selling as a career.

Financing plans vary widely. Broadly, they are of two types, advances and subsidies. Under the advance or loan type, the new agent receives payments at regular intervals, usually monthly. Such payments are charged against the agent's account, and are repaid out of future commissions as these are earned. Depending on the terms of the plan, the agent may or may not be required to liquidate any outstanding balance in the event of termination.

Under the subsidy type, the new agent also receives monthly payments. However, he does not incur indebtedness for the financial assistance he receives. Therefore, the subsidy type of financing is more liberal if the amounts paid are equal. Of course the agent who terminates before repaying his advances is not likely to repay after he leaves the company or the business.

The *median* for monthly payments to new agents under financing plans is believed currently to be about $550; some companies go to $1,000 monthly, occasionally higher. Payments may run from three months to three years, or even longer. A common feature of financing plans, whether they involve advances or subsidies, is a clearly defined schedule of expected performance on the part of the agent. The heart of a financing plan is the validation schedule, i.e., the performance the company requires if the financed agent is to continue to receive the stated monthly income promised under the plan.

Financing is a *long-term* investment, one which will require capital to be tied up for a considerable period of time. An example will illustrate what can happen. Let us suppose that a new man will produce $450,000 of volume per year starting with the first year and that he has been granted a *nonsubsidized* advance of $500 per month. Assuming reasonable commission rates, persistency of business and distribution of business by plan and mode of premium, the debt charged against this agent at the end of three years (on a cash commission basis) will amount to approximately $5,700. If we assume that he will produce $450,000 his first year, $540,000 his second and $600,000 his third and subsequent years, he will be in the red about $3,900 at the end of three years and won't break even until part way through his sixth year.[7]

Even if the men financed have been carefully recruited and selected, a company cannot avoid paying large sums to some men who do not succeed. Although selection and aptitude tests can screen out men whose failure is highly probable, so far no test has been devised that will predict *success*. Almost any reasonable plan can finance the qualified agent. However, no plan has yet been developed to finance the unqualified agent. There still is no substitute for proper recruiting, training, supervision and motivation on the part of the manager and hard work and enterprise on the part of the agent. Without these ingredients a man cannot be financed into success.

In fact, although at least 90 percent of the new men now entering the field of life insurance selling receive some form of financing from their companies or managers, opinion is not unanimously in favor. Opponents of financing believe that in competing for prospective agents, recruiters should sell the opportunity, the agency and the company—but not bid for them financially. Opponents of financing object especially to advances, arguing that a man cannot borrow himself out of debt, that advancing him money to pay off his existing debts merely transfers the creditor status to manager or company, and that most men resent owing money to either manager or company.

There is a danger that generous financing plans may tempt drifters and "leaners." Managers must be on guard against men

---

[7] Example taken from *Managing an Agency* (14th printing, 1969)

who choose to move from agency to agency in order to obtain new financing, at substantial cost to the companies involved. It is essential that new men be sold on the *career* in life insurance selling rather than on the *financing* available. The business has sometimes been criticized for what some consider overly liberal arrangements. Financing, however, has become one of the factors in manpower building.

SALARY PLANS

Under the commission form of remuneration, the man—the agent—who determines the success of his company to a substantial degree and tries to provide security for the families of others is less certain of a regular income than any other group of life insurance personnel.

Some companies have experimented with salaried compensation of life insurance agents. Most salary plans embody the following features: (1) payment of the salary depends on fulfillment by the agent of certain conditions, such as the number of his calls and interviews, the number of hours worked during the period and the amount of business sold; (2) the amount of salary the agent receives is based on minimum living requirements; (3) if the agent's earnings on a commission basis exceed his salary, he receives the excess, but his salary is not reduced if the reverse is true; (4) the salary plan is superseded by a regular commission basis of compensation after two or three years; (5) continuance on salary during this period requires that the agent sell at least a specified minimum amount of life insurance each month.

As indicated by No. 4, most salary plans in effect to date are temporary in nature. A very few companies have adopted permanent salaried compensation plans, agents' earnings being directly related to the results they achieve. (In some cases the agent may transfer to a regular commission contract if he wishes.) Permanent salary plans usually include group insurance, hospitalization, disability and retirement on the same basis as the salaried personnel in the home office.

Obviously, managers whose companies operate on either a temporary or permanent salary plan should recruit agents extremely carefully; because of the substantial sums involved failures must be kept to a minimum. A salary plan will help attract desirable men. However, as already stated, it may also attract men who are more interested in the salary opportunity of agency work than its career opportunity. To be successful, a salary plan requires close and thorough supervision of agents' activities.

SUMMARY

Life insurance agents receive their compensation in the form of commissions rather than salary. The more successful their sales efforts, the greater their earnings, and vice versa.

The bases on which general agents, branch managers and soliciting agents are compensated are stated in agreements or contracts, which also spell out their specific authority and duties. The company pays the general agent commissions on business paid for by his agency and by himself. He may also receive certain allowances to defray part of the expenses of maintaining his agency.

A branch manager is an employee of the company he represents. Although he receives a salary, his overall compensation depends largely on the success of the agents working under his direction.

The soliciting agent usually receives a number of annual commissions for each policy he sells, provided it remains in force. The first-year commission is almost always the largest, and many variations of compensation plans have been devised over the years.

Apart from their regular compensation, an ever-increasing number of companies grant various benefits to their general agents, branch managers and agents. These include one or more of the following: group life insurance, group disability benefits and retirement plans.

Today about 90 percent of new agents receive some financial

assistance from their companies to help them meet their necessary living and operating expenses while they are getting established as life underwriters. A very few companies have experimented with salaried compensation of their salesmen, usually on a temporary basis.

QUESTIONS FOR REVIEW

1. Outline the subjects usually covered in a general agent's contract. Which of these are also found in a branch manager's contract?

2. Discuss the various factors that underlie company plans for compensating branch managers.

3. What is vesting? Develop the merits of vesting in relation to three basic concepts of renewal commissions.

4. State the advantages and disadvantages of the traditional basis of agents' compensation to the (a) company and (b) agent. What features are reflected in most of the changes that have occurred in agents' compensation plans in recent years? What modifications, if any, has your company introduced?

5. Is there general agreement that financing of new agents is (a) necessary, (b) desirable? Explain.

6. Outline the essential features of a salary plan for compensating life insurance agents. If you were a new agent, which basis, commission or salary, would you prefer? Explain why.

6 | *Agency Costs and Their Control*

O_{ne} of the objectives of the home office agency department is "to sell good business in adequate volume and at reasonable cost so as to show a profit to the company whether stock or mutual."[1]

In business operations, whether large or small, control of costs is important to success. In the case of a life insurance company it is necessary to know the costs of various operations, sales and other. With particular reference to the agency department, efficient management wants to know, among other things, how much money is being spent for various agency activities and where and how effectively it is being spent. For example, can present costs be reduced? Or can more be accomplished with the same amount of money? Or can additional money be fruitfully spent?

Selling a large volume of business does not by any means

---

[1] As previously explained, the profits in a mutual company belong to the policyowners in the form of policy dividends.

assure that a life insurance company is operating profitably. In fact, some companies measure growth in terms of premium income rather than volume of new business. Losses may arise either from premiums that are unrealistically low or from poor experience in one or more of the basic operating factors—mortality, investment earnings, persistency and expense. In this chapter we will discuss what in most companies is the largest category of expense—agency costs.

In most companies today management seeks to exercise budgetary control over both the overall costs of its sales operations and individual items of cost. However, the entire area of agency costs is quite elusive. It has been the subject of continuing study and investigation, but few solutions have been found. Sometimes a company may not even be able to say with certainty whether a particular agency is operating profitably. Hence this discussion will necessarily be general; it will be more of an exposition of the problem than an attempt to suggest solutions.

Costs are of vital concern to a life insurance company. First, they affect the level of premiums it must charge or the policy dividends it can afford to pay and, therefore, its standing in competition with other companies. Second, companies recognize their position of stewardship to the public and try to provide protection at low cost. Third, the life insurance business must compete in effectiveness with other institutions that offer savings plans, such as banks, savings and loan associations and mutual funds. Fourth, if the company operates in New York state, Illinois or Wisconsin, it must comply with the existing statutory cost limitations.

Categories of Agency Costs

Since agency costs constitute a major portion of total operating expenses in a typical company, a large part of any effective attempt to control costs must be directed toward agency costs. Broadly, there is current cost—money spent to keep the agency plant operating today; there is also capital investment—money spent to make the agency operation larger and more effective tomorrow. Examples of capital investment are new-agent financing, appointment of a supervisor, travel costs for developing outlying territory, alterations to improve working conditions or utilization of space in a field office.

In the specific measurement and control of agency costs, four categories may be distinguished:

1. Home office agency department expenses, including salaries, traveling expenses, agency conventions. The term "salaries" is self-explanatory. The nature of traveling expenses and agency conventions will be considered in chapter 12.

2. Compensation and security benefits for general agents, branch managers and soliciting agents. These were developed in the preceding chapter, "Contracts and Compensation."

3. Operating expenses *in agencies* associated with new-business activities, i.e., recruiting and maintenance of agents, obtaining new applications and collecting first premiums.

4. Operating expenses *in agencies* for collection of renewal premiums and giving service on existing policies.

In each of these four categories, control requires determination by the company of suitable standards, and then the measurement of costs in relation to these standards. In all categories it is possible to err in the direction of spending too much or too little. Low cost can be false economy, although in practice mistakes in this direction are less common than those involving overspending.

Furthermore, the cost—when it has been measured in dollars—must be related to the value received. It is common, and relatively simple, to measure new-business cost per thousand of the amount of new business. But measurement in this manner may prove unsatisfactory because:

a. Expenditure that appears large in relation to the volume of business currently obtained may be money well spent if it builds a strong and durable agency force that will produce a large future volume of new business for the company at reasonable cost.

b. Blocks of business of equal *size* are not by any means equal in their capacity for returning the initial investment to the company. This aspect will be treated in chapter 9 under the heading of "Quality Business."

OPERATING EXPENSES IN AGENCIES

Category 1 of agency costs is treated in chapters 3 and 12; category 2, in chapter 5. Because of their interrelationship categories 3 and 4 will be discussed together.

The Manager as a Businessman

Running a field office costs money. Aside from commissions and allowances, each agent is a cause of expense as well as a source of business. He must be recruited, trained, supervised, motivated and helped. The manager's (or an assistant's) time so expended has a cash value. And as explained in chapter 5, the new agent today usually must be financed.

Maintenance of an agent costs money. Maintenance includes desk and other space made available to him, equipment and services furnished him, sales aids used, etc. Clerical work also costs money. Various operations are required in the agency to transform applications into policies. And if the result is a declined or not-taken-out case, expense has been incurred nevertheless, even though in vain. As for old business, expenses are incurred to collect renewal premiums, to keep such business in force and to furnish service such as arranging policy loans, processing changes in beneficiary designations, effecting reinstatements and handling death and other claims.

A truly successful agency head must be a good business manager or businessman as well as a good sales manager or director of salesmen in his agency. If the manager can't bring in sales, he can't succeed. But even if he does bring in business, it still must be written and maintained at reasonable cost if he is to succeed. Volume achieved without regard to costs usually means unprofitable operations.

How does the home office provide the money for running an agency? The same principles underlying agency costs apply to both general agent and branch manager. (As explained in chapter 3, there are virtually no pure general agencies today.) Commonly the company pays an expense allowance, which may be a flat amount or a portion of total expenses. Sometimes the company advances money to the general agent which he is to repay. With some of his own money invested, the general agent has a very direct interest in trying to keep operating expenses down. The company is also concerned, however, because it has a stake in the financial soundness of its general agents, because rising expenses in agencies usually lead to requests for larger expense allowances, and because when the general agent leaves for any reason, the company will find itself confronted with any existing problem of excessive expense.

Agency costs may seem of less concern to the branch manager, since the home office pays the expenses of his agency. However, he too must adhere to the basic principles of agency financial management. Excessive costs may reduce his own income as manager. Further, since the home office does pay all expenses, it keeps agency costs under close scrutiny. A managerial company cannot subsidize its field operations above the general agency level if its product is to compete effectively with what general agency companies have to offer.

Types of Expenses in an Agency

Agency expenses are divided into two broad classes—new business and renewal. To facilitate allocation to these two classes, agency expenses can be itemized under the following headings:[2]

1.   Clerical salaries
2.   Rent

---

[2] This breakdown has been used in LIAMA literature.

3. Postage and express
4. Stationery, printing, supplies
5. Telephone and telegraph
6. Travel
7. Advertising and sales promotion (of a local nature)
8. Compensation of agency supervisors attached to the agency (as distinguished from those operating out of the home office)
9. Losses on financing of agents
10. Miscellaneous

To some extent these headings are self-explanatory. Some enlargement will indicate the basis of allocating such items to (1) new business or (2) renewal business expense.

1. *Clerical Salaries*—Analysis of each clerk's time will disclose what percentage of his (more often her) time is spent on each class. Each clerk's salary is then apportioned according to this percentage. For example, assume that 40 percent of one clerk's time is spent on new business, 60 percent on renewal and that she earns $90 a week. Then $36 would be apportioned to class 1 (new business), and $54 to class 2 (renewal business).

2. *Rent*—The actual monthly rent for the agency office is known, as is also the total square footage occupied. Total rent divided by total number of square feet of space equals rent per square foot. The footage—and rent—to be allocated to each class of expense can then be determined. Charges to class 1 include space occupied by salesmen, the manager and his supervisors. Clerical space is divided and charged in the same proportions as the salaries of the personnel who occupy it.

3. *Postage and Express*

4. *Stationery, Printing, Supplies*

5. *Telephone and Telegraph*—Normally, the aggregate of numbers 3, 4 and 5 is small in proportion to the total expenses of an agency. Actual tests conducted during a representative but limited period will produce sufficiently accurate percentages for separating these items. Without such records these items are estimated, or they may be charged in the same proportion as the total clerical salaries in heading 1.

Postage for renewal premium notices, conservation letters and various policy changes would be charged to renewal business. Postage for new applications mailed to the home office, for correspondence regarding new business, for direct-mail sales letters and for new policies sent out by the agency would go to new business. Expenses for stationery, printing, supplies, telephone and telegraph are apportioned along similar lines. The expense is charged according to the purpose for which the particular item is used. For instance, most telephone calls by agents concern class 1 (new business expense). Calls reminding policyowners of overdue premiums go to class 2 (renewal expense), while those involving home office underwriting matters are charged to class 1.

6. *Travel*—This item applies to the agency manager or to his supervisor and usually involves class 1, being money spent for new business or for working with present or prospective agents. Occasionally travel expense, such as to prevent the lapse of, or to reinstate, a policy of substantial amount, is incurred on old business.

7. *Advertising and Sales Promotion*—This item is normally a new-business expense and is distinct from national advertising and sales promotion from the home office. It includes local advertising, agency meetings, sales helps developed in the agency, subscriptions to insurance magazines, etc. In some companies outlays for advertising and sales promotion by the agency would be negligible, because both are directed and controlled almost entirely by the home office.

8. *Compensation of Supervisors Attached to the Agency*— Except for supervisors' time spent on occasional service to policyowners and conservation work, this is also a new-business expense. It includes all salaries, bonuses and extra commissions paid to supervisors.

9. *Losses on Financing of Agents*—Not all agents succeed. When agents who have received advances against commissions prove to be unsuccessful, such advances usually are uncollectible and are charged off. (In such cases agents' contracts commonly provide for offsetting against the debt the renewal com-

missions that become payable after the unsuccessful agent has left the agency.) This item likewise goes under class 1 (new business expense).

10. *Miscellaneous*—This item includes expenses that do not fit any of the foregoing, such as furniture, equipment and alterations. Usually, approximations based on the relationship of the charges of the two classes will suffice.

Comparative Statistics for Individual Agencies

Statistical ratios for a particular agency provide a useful guide to the results it achieves. Let us assume that the data for a hypothetical agency[3] shows the following:

First-Year New Business

	Number of policies	Amount of insurance
New paid business, excluding annuities and single premiums	838	$4,043,212
Terminated during calendar year of sale	7	25,876
In force as of Dec. 31	831	$4,017,336
New premiums, excluding annuities and single premiums		$ 111,148
Number of premium collections first year	1,275	

Renewal Business

	Number of policies	Amount of insurance
Total insurance in force Dec. 31	9,216	$41,592,682
Less new business in force	831	4,017,336
Old business in force	8,385	$37,575,346
Less paid-up business	1,095	3,622,468
Old premium-paying business in force	7,290	$33,952,878
Renewal premiums collected		$ 1,093,911
Number of premium collections	14,169	

[3] Most of these figures are based upon LIAMA studies of some years ago. The *methods* used to determine these ratios are applicable to today's economy. Because of the lower purchasing power of today's dollar, some of the figures are somewhat low. The reader should bear in mind that the amounts used are illustrative only.

From the foregoing the following data for new or first-year business can be developed directly:

1. Average-size policy ($4,043,212 ÷ 838) $4,824.84
2. Average premium per $1,000 of insurance
    ($111,148 ÷ $4,043,212 × 1,000) $27.49
3. Average premium per policy ($111,148 ÷ 838) $132.63
4. Average premium per collection ($111,148 ÷ 1,275) $87.17
5. Collection frequency (1,275 ÷ 838)   1.52
6. Collections per $1 million of insurance
    (1,275 ÷ $4,043,212 × 1,000,000)   315.00

Similar data can be developed for renewal business:

1. Average-size policy (on which premiums are
    being paid) ($33,952,878 ÷ 7,290) $4,657.46
2. Average premium per $1,000 of insurance
    ($1,093,911 ÷ $33,952,878 × 1,000) $32.22
3. Average premium per policy ($1,093,911 ÷ 7,290) $150.06
4. Average premium per collection ($1,093,911 ÷ 14,169) $77.20
5. Collection frequency (14,169 ÷ 7,290)   1.94
6. Collections per $1 million of insurance
    (14,169 ÷ $33,952,878 × 1,000,000)   417.00

The foregoing statistics for first-year and renewal business provide valuable comparative data for the agency manager and the home office. Once established, they can be calculated annually to measure the agency's current performance against that of former years, and to determine its standing in relation to other agencies of the company and to company or industry norms. The home office agency department that collects such information for all its agencies can find the relative standing of each field office in these 12 areas and can then determine where improvements are needed. It does not follow, of course, that the highest (or lowest) value in any of these 12 items measures the best (or poorest) performance.

Furthermore, such data do not consider the essential aspect of agency costs. What does it cost to achieve certain results? If a particular agency shows satisfactory overall results in the various areas of first-year and renewal business described, it is still necessary to relate these results to the costs of achieving them.

Cost Ratios

As explained on page 84, cost figures, even when measured in dollars against the company's standards, are not a complete answer to control of agency costs. Nevertheless, cost figures for an individual agency can be compared to other agencies of the company and the company averages. Such figures can also show the trend of cost within an individual agency from year to year.

The foregoing data can be used to develop important cost ratios. In the example cited, new and renewal expenses for the year were as follows:

		Total	New	Renewal
1.	Clerical salaries	$15,637	$7,349	$8,288
2.	Rent	3,863	3,168	695
3.	Postage and express	1,485	223	1,262
4.	Stationery, printing, supplies	423	190	233
5.	Telephone and telegraph	1,181	767	414
6.	Travel	1,769	1,769	—
7.	Advertising and sales promotion	5,422	5,422	—
8.	Compensation of supervisors attached to the home office	3,665	3,665	—
9.	Losses on advances to agents	560	560	—
10.	Miscellaneous	1,529	693	836
	Total	$35,534	$23,806	$11,728
	Percentage	100%	67%	33%

Total first-year expenses include all expenses for ordinary insurance and ordinary annuities for the agency irrespective of whether such expenses are paid by the general agent or by the home office.

FIRST-YEAR EXPENSE. To find the first-year expense per $1,000 of insurance, we divide total first-year expenses by the amount of new business, excluding annuities and single premiums:

$$\frac{\text{First-year expenses}}{\text{New business}} = \frac{\$23,806}{\$4,043,212} \times 1,000$$

$$= \$5.89 \text{ expense per } \$1,000$$

RENEWAL EXPENSE RATIO. To find the renewal expense ratio, we divide renewal expense by renewal premiums:

$$\frac{\text{Renewal expenses}}{\text{Renewal premiums}} = \frac{\$11,728}{\$1,093,911} = 1.07\%$$

or in more detail,

$$\frac{\text{Cost per collection} \times \text{collection frequency}}{\text{Average policy in thousands} \times \text{average premium per \$1,000}}$$

$$= \frac{\text{Cost per policy}}{\text{Premium per policy}} = \text{Renewal expense ratio}$$

COST PER COLLECTION. All values in the first foregoing word fraction are known or have already been computed (see p. 90) with the exception of "cost per collection," which equals:

$$\frac{\text{Total renewal expense}}{\text{Number of collections}} = \frac{\$11,728}{14,169}$$

$$= \$0.83 \text{ cost per collection}$$

We can then substitute in the first foregoing word fraction for the renewal expense ratio as follows:

$$\frac{\$0.83 \times 1.94}{4.657 \times \$32.22} = \frac{\$1.61}{\$150.06} = 1.07\%$$

A low renewal expense ratio is an important factor in the profitableness of an agency's operations, provided there has been no postponement of essential, normal agency expenses. Each of the four values in the detailed equation is significant. Assuming the other three values remain constant:

1. The lower the cost per collection, the lower the renewal expense ratio.
2. The lower the collection frequency, the lower the renewal expense ratio.
3. The larger the average policy, the lower the renewal expense ratio.
4. The larger the average premium per thousand, the lower the renewal expense ratio.

Conversely, the higher the cost per collection, the higher the renewal expense ratio, etc. Changes in one value may offset changes in another. Each calculation of this ratio reemphasizes that good business costs less than poor business.

Production Expense Ratio[4]

This is another useful cost ratio. It gives a quick picture of the relationship between the production expense for new life insurance business and total first-year premium income. If these figures for the Y agency are $45,000 and $220,000 respectively, then the production expense ratio is

$$\frac{\text{Total first-year expenses}}{\text{Total first-year premium income}} = \frac{\$45,000}{\$220,000} = 20.5\%$$

Functional Costs Analysis

A promising step in the area of cost determination is the "Agency Activity Analysis" published in 1965. Developed by the Life Insurance Agency Management Association, the analysis aims to provide the basis for improving supervision of agencies by the home office. It is a management tool to determine for each agency how the manager, his supervisors in his agency and his clerical staff distribute their time among various agency activities. To develop the necessary data, each member of the agency staff *other than the agents* keeps a daily record of his or her activities for a period of 5 to 13 weeks.[5]

A total of 34 agency functions are defined and identified to cover all activities in an agency. These 34 functions are grouped under the following major headings:

1. Recruiting and selection
2. Manpower development

---

[4] Armand Stalnaker, *Life Insurance Agency Financial Management* (rev. ed.). Richard D. Irwin, Inc., Homewood, Ill. (1965).

[5] Instructions emphasize that the purpose of having each participant record how he spends his working time each day is to enable the home office to determine the total time devoted to each agency activity; the purpose is not to check on an individual's performance.

3. Sales assistance and other new-business activities
4. Insurance maintenance
5. General administration

As stated above, the major objective of the analysis is to provide the basis for improving the supervision of agencies by the home office. However, valuable cost data can be derived from use of the analysis. These include:

1. Directing agency activities into the most profitable areas by determining
   a. The cost of business in relation to the production level of the agent
   b. The cost of business from different types of producers—full-time, part-time, brokers
2. Evaluating and interpreting the cost efficiency of different agencies
3. Setting up budgetary controls for agencies
4. Evaluating the differences in activity and cost patterns in one region as compared to another: comparing large city agencies with relatively rural territories, successful agencies with less successful agencies, expanding agencies with stable or agencies being liquidated and main offices with suboffices
5. Developing time and cost factors for agency-simulation studies
6. Assessing the cost implications of transferring certain functions to the home office

Importance of the Agent in Agency Costs

Generally, productivity of the agent is the most significant single item in controlling agency costs. This statement applies particularly to new-business costs. Agents writing good business with a high average policy make for low agency costs, and vice versa. Unprofitable agents include the following:

1. Those who do not remain under contract long enough to repay their induction costs

2. Those who produce unprofitable business
3. Those who stay but do not produce enough business to cover their maintenance costs

CHARACTERISTICS OF LOW-COST AND HIGH-COST AGENCIES

Low-Cost Agencies

Genuine, efficient low-cost agencies[6] show a profit, whether they are large or small organizations. Such agencies possess most or all of the following characteristics:

1. The agency head is a personable combination of businessman, salesman and sales manager.
2. These agencies have a stable sales force with a high average production per man.
3. These producers obtain good business, business that shows a low lapse rate.
4. These agencies are the results of sound growth and intelligent planning—not of high-pressure methods.
5. The agency head is not overworked and does not attempt to do more than he can do well.
6. Recognizing the value of an effective cashier's or office division to the success of his agency, the agency head staffs accordingly and makes this group feel part of the team.
7. Because his agency is doing well, the agency head can recruit and select the best men available as he needs them.

High-Cost Agencies

Aside from agencies entirely in the development stage, high-cost agencies are likely to show characteristics that are the converse of those of low-cost organizations:

---

[6] These do not include agencies temporarily able to show low costs because manpower development and other essential activities are being neglected or deferred.

1. The agency head lacks one or two of the three essential qualities of businessman, salesman and sales manager.
2. Turnover of agents is high and average production per man is low, with few consistent producers.
3. The agents sell business marked by poor persistency, many policies for small amounts, low premium per policy, high collection frequency.
4. Excessive reliance is being placed on high-pressure methods to produce volume.
5. The agency head depends too much on poorly conceived sales helps and other forms of stimulation.
6. The agency head is indifferent to, or unable to understand the importance of, the cashier's or office division, so that this group is characterized by high turnover, low efficiency and low morale.
7. Because his agency is not doing well, the agency head's efforts to solve his chronic manpower and financial problems are often misdirected, resulting in excessive and ineffective recruiting and the hiring of unqualified supervisors.

Deceptive Nature of Low Costs

Deferring necessary expenditures is not avoiding them. As pointed out earlier in this chapter, expenditures that appear large in relation to the volume of business currently obtained may actually be money well spent. The cost of restoring a house or rehabilitating expensive machinery whose maintenance has been neglected is likely to be higher than regular annual care would have been. Similarly, an agency may deteriorate because of false economies. Rehabilitation is likely to be expensive. Examples of such false economies include:

1. Inadequate office facilities for agents. Facilities need not be lavish, but salesmen should have sufficient desk space for their paperwork and a suitable place to talk with their clients. Agents may lose sales if interviewing facilities are inadequate.

2. Inadequate clerical salaries. Such compensation must be reasonably competitive for the area, or low morale and poor-grade office staff will result, and turnover will be high.

3. Financing new agents on the basis of "breaking even" rather than attracting and building outstanding men. The latter are likely to go elsewhere, whereas less desirable men may be more interested in some form of financing, which they look on as a temporary salary, than in a life insurance sales career.

4. Neglecting manpower building. Recruiting and training costs money. But the manager who fails to recruit continuously will find he has an acute manpower shortage that requires expensive rebuilding all at once.

5. Failing to appoint a supervisor when one is needed. The manager himself may not have enough time to give his men the help they need. If there is no one else to help them, they and the agency will suffer.

| LIMITATIONS ON AGENCY EXPENSES

Prudent management in the home office agency department and on the part of the field managers will attempt to control agency expenses. Three states have sought to control these expenses by statute.

The well-known Section 213 of the New York insurance law is an outgrowth of the Armstrong Investigation. The section in its entirety is quite complicated and need not be considered in detail here. Briefly, it imposes on companies *operating* in the state of New York (whether domiciled there or not) certain limits upon acquisition costs, i.e., costs of acquiring new business, and upon total agency operating costs. Specific restrictions are also imposed on the compensation that may be paid to individual agents and general agents. For example, no company, no matter how economically operated, may pay more than a 55 percent first-year commission to a soliciting agent. Since most of the largest companies operate in New York, its regulations affect directly a very substantial proportion of the total life insurance sold and in force in United States companies (very few Canadian companies operate in New York).

Section 213[7] has been both assailed and defended for many years. Although it has been modified from time to time, its essential features remain in effect. It has been attacked on the grounds that companies affected are placed at a competitive disadvantage in obtaining and keeping field manpower, and that agents are underpaid for their work.

Advocates of higher field compensation limits argue that life insurance agents need more inducement to solicit actively among those persons whose needs for protection are substantial but whose means are limited and whose purchases therefore will be for modest amounts. It is said that Section 213 commission restrictions encourage agents to concentrate their soliciting among prospects who are financially able to apply for substantial amounts of insurance. The same amount of sales effort, if successful, will yield much larger first-year and renewal commissions.

Section 213 has been defended, or at least explained, on the ground that companies not subject to this restrictive legislation have pretty much the same problems regarding agency costs. It is interesting to note that the number of companies domiciled in New York grew from 19 in 1941 to 60 at the end of 1970. Apparently the organizers of the companies established since 1941 did not consider Section 213 an insurmountable handicap.

It should be observed that Section 213 has been revised frequently since original enactment of an expense limitation statute. Wisconsin and, more recently, Illinois have also enacted legislation to limit companies' agency and other expenses.

SUMMARY

Costs are of vital concern to a life insurance company; a large volume of business alone does not assure that it is operating profitably. Agency costs make up the largest part of company costs.

---

[7] Section 213-A of the code applies to debit (industrial) insurance.

Four categories of agency costs may be distinguished:

1. Home office agency department expenses
2. Compensation and security benefits for the field forces
3. Operating expenses in agencies for new business
4. Operating expences in agencies for renewal business

Each of these must be analyzed carefully, and the results must be interpreted and understood. Genuine, efficient low-cost agencies show a profit. However, while control of agency costs is important, deferring necessary expenditures does not avoid them. Sometimes, seemingly large agency expenditures may be decidedly worthwhile. Three states, New York, Wisconsin and Illinois, have enacted laws to limit companies' agency and other expenses.

QUESTIONS FOR REVIEW

1. List and describe briefly four categories of agency costs.
2. Discuss the importance of agency costs to the company, the general agent and the branch manager. State the two broad classes of agency costs and prepare a list of expense items suitable for allocating agency expenses to each class.
3. Comment on the benefits and the limitations of comparative cost statistics for individual agencies.
4. Elaborate on the statement: "Agents writing good business with a high average policy make for low agency costs, whereas agents writing poor business with a low average policy make for high agency costs."
5. If your company is not domiciled in New York, does it operate in that state? If not, is Section 213 one of the reasons?

7 | Getting the Right Manpower: Managers

In chapter 4 we indicated that probably the major duty of the agency department in attaining its objective is getting the right manpower to represent the company in the field.

Briefly, a company's field organization consists of its various agencies in the territory in which it operates. Large or small, each agency performs both production and office or clerical functions. Each is under the direction of a manager, who may be assisted by one or more assistant managers, sometimes called supervisors.

The objectives of the home office agency department restated on page 36 also apply to the field, but with this difference —the field *executes* agency department policy rather than *makes* it. The home office determines what contracts are to be sold, in what territories the company will operate, what agents' contracts will provide and what agencies are expected to do in the recruiting, training, supervision and motivation[1] of agents

---

[1] Not all companies have a clearly defined policy regarding recruiting, training, supervision and motivation. Many of those that do, allow a good manager considerable leeway, even if some of his activities do not conform to home office policy 100 percent.

and service to policyowners and beneficiaries. Thus, the home office agency department determines the overall policies and plans that will govern *all* its agencies in order to achieve the three objectives. It will also set up the necessary machinery to see that these policies and plans are executed.

The responsibility for executing the plans and policies of the home office falls primarily on the head of each agency. It is the agency manager who is the main contact between the agency department and the agency. To the extent that any one individual is responsible for the success or failure of an agency, the manager is that individual. What sort of a person is likely to be a good manager?

Listing of essential qualities may vary somewhat, depending on who is doing the listing. But practically all would agree that a manager should be friendly and have a good memory for names and faces; he should be sincerely interested in the welfare of his men, listen to his men's problems—occupational and personal—and do what he can to help solve them. In short, he should have a good personality, be a faithful friend and a wise counselor.

Specific Qualities or Characteristics of a Good Manager

We all know people who possess these general qualities. It does not necessarily follow, however, that they would be successful managers of life insurance agencies. Conversely, some of the most effective managers would be considered deficient in some of these general qualities. More *specific* descriptions of qualities or characteristics are required. Among them are:

1. *Constructive Leadership*—A leader is a person other people follow. It has been said that the degree of leadership is the essential difference between successful agencies and mediocre ones. Considerable evidence shows that agents esteem this quality in their managers above most others. Leadership is a broad word. Here it includes agency building, whereby he develops *and* maintains a good organization, and enthusiastic motivation of his men so that they *want* to do a good job, i.e., succeed in proportion to their capacity. If a manager has this

quality, he will be able to make willing followers of his men and develop them so that they will do their best.

2. *Unquestionable Integrity*—To earn and keep the respect of his associates, the manager's reputation must be above reproach. Those who deal with him must be able to feel that they can rely on him and his word completely.

3. *Enthusiasm*—None of us, no matter how much we like the work we are doing, are always at our peak. Life insurance salesmen are no exception. Sometimes they get in a rut. In fact, the nature of their work is such that the danger of a letdown is greater in their case than in the case of an office employee with established work hours and duties. How often agents get into a rut and how quickly they get out of it may depend in no small measure on the ability of the manager to inspire and refire.

4. *Salesmanship*—The manager must know and understand life insurance. He should be able to show as well as to tell how the job of selling is done. He need not have been his company's top salesman while an agent. Nevertheless, he should have been sufficiently successful so that he can, if necessary, practice effectively what he preaches. He should generate the confidence that comes from having done, himself, the job he is now teaching others to do.

5. *Executive and Business Ability*—Another term might be vocational competence. This quality includes the manager's capacity to direct the sales and office staff, large or small, as well as a desire to train and supervise. Not only is he the sales manager for his agency, but also its administrative head. As such he must really manage, by coordinating the work of his salesmen, office force and himself, so that his agency will progress in all areas. Successful coordination is essential to the profitable operation of his agency for his men, for his company and for himself.

6. *Right Attitude Toward His Company*—While this quality may be implied in one or more of the foregoing, it merits specific mention. The manager should be able to take as well as to give instructions. Quite apart from his other qualities, his

attitude toward home office direction will affect strongly the attitude of his sales and clerical staff. If the manager himself is casual about instructions from the home office, he can hardly expect members of his organization to be responsive. Cooperation on his part will not necessarily insure success of his agency —it may be weak in other respects. But if his own attitude is one of indifference, prospects for success are rather dim.

Duties of the Manager

Most of these may be fairly apparent. The manager is both a sales manager and a business manager. As distinguished from qualities or characteristics, his major duties are:

1. To build and maintain sales manpower, unquestionably his major duty. It is up to him to develop a force of career salesmen who will sell a sufficient volume of good business at reasonable cost to help attain the agency department's objectives and the quota assigned his agency by the home office. The manager must obtain, train, retrain and retain a strong sales organization.

    All phases of this major duty come under the heading of manpower-building. This duty requires careful planning, including the building of sound human relations and the development of men not only for advancement but also for the replacement of other men who leave his agency for any reason.

2. To manage all activities of his agency, sales and office. There has already been some indication of the scope of his sales duties. As the agency head, he is also responsible for service to policyowners in his territory. Worthy of particular mention is control of costs. As stated in the preceding chapter, large volume does not assure profitable management. The manager must keep operating costs within the bounds established by the home office or by the expense margins in his contract.

3. To represent the company in his community—to his sales

and office force, to policyowners and to the general public. With respect to his sales force, the manager *is* the company. Many an agent never even sees the inside of his home office, especially if it is a long distance from his territory. It is the manager who must interpret and implement home office policies and instructions. It is the manager who hears the grievances and problems of his agents and who must seek to solve them in line with company policy and instructions. To *some* extent the manager may also be the company in relation to policyowners in his territory. Although the average policyowner looks first to his agent, if he feels that the agent has not given him satisfaction, or if the agent has left the company, the insured may wish to "go higher up"—to the manager—with his complaint or problem.

To a considerable degree, the manager is also the company in the eyes of the community where the agency office is located. True, the community is composed of individuals who consider the agents to be the company. However, on a more official level, civic and other groups are likely to take their cue from the manager and from what he says and does.

Personal Production

The extent to which a manager devotes his energies to personal production depends considerably on his company's wishes. Apart from this aspect, authorities differ as to whether a manager, given his choice, *should* sell much life insurance himself, even if his contract with his company permits him to. Those who argue against substantial personal production maintain:

1. The manager is paid to help others; he should spend his selling time where it will do the most good, and not where it pays him the largest commissions.
2. By doing less personal selling, he has more time for manpower or agency building and for administering.
3. Managers engaging in personal production may some-

times actually be competing with their own agents, particularly for good prospects.

Proponents of substantial personal production by the manager maintain that it:

1. Enhances his position as a leader when he demonstrates that he can "practice as well as preach."
2. Enables him to keep his finger on the life insurance market.
3. Results in better public relations when prospects can deal with the "boss" now and then.
4. May be necessary to "make ends meet" in some general agencies, particularly new or small ones.

As already stated, the branch manager is usually not expected to write a large amount of business himself. Rather, he is expected to be a good administrator and to carry out the instructions of the home office agency department. He will concentrate on agency building, so that he will have a well-trained staff of successful producers. As occasions arise, he will accompany his agents to help "close" difficult cases, and he will spend considerable time demonstrating and observing in the field.

The general agent is in a somewhat different position. As an independent contractor, he is more or less in business for himself. He may write a substantial volume of business himself. He receives commissions on his personal production. Further, he receives overriding or overwriting commissions on business written by his agents as well as on his own personal business. Such overriding commissions naturally are a much lower rate than regular first-year commissions on business he writes himself.

Hence, the general agent may sometimes run into a conflict of interest. Suppose he learns that Mr. A. is a prospect for a sizable policy, say $25,000 or more. If he goes out on the case himself, the chances of making the sale may actually be better than if one of his agents called on Mr. A. Further, the general agent's immediate commission as the salesman may be as much as $500. If one of his agents makes the sales, the general agent's first-year overriding commission may be about $50.

This example is not meant to suggest that general agents make a practice of thinking of themselves first. If they did, the general agency system would have disappeared long ago. There is an element of conflict, however, and there may be times when some general agents will resolve the doubt in their own favor. Of course, if a general agent cannot resist competing with his men, probably he would be happier and more successful as a personal producer than as the head of an agency. (There are some personal producer general agencies, where the general agent constitutes the entire sales force.)

Another aspect may be mentioned as a factor in translating the home office's instructions into action. Not infrequently a well-established general agent becomes less active as he grows older. He has a substantial income from his renewal commissions and allowances and from overriding commissions on business produced by well-established agents. This income, together with what he produces personally, may be more than enough to take care of his needs. Theoretically, the general agent should continue to build manpower for the future for his agency and for his company. But from a purely personal standpoint, why should he risk more of his own money? Recruiting and training of new agents may not hold the appeal they once did, so why should he expend time and money when his successor rather than he himself stands to benefit? Such cases are not uncommon, and frequently little can be done to rehabilitate such an agency until or unless the general agent retires or is replaced.

Need for Managers

As a life insurance company prospers, it usually wishes to open additional field offices. For these, managers are needed. Even without an increase in the actual number of sales offices, a company constantly needs managers for replacement. Openings occur for a variety of reasons, be it death, retirement because of age or disability, demotion, discharge, promotion or transfer to home office staff or voluntary resignation. All but the last are self-explanatory. A manager may resign to go with another life insurance company or to enter another business. Occasionally, a manager decides that the substantial responsibilities of the job are not for him. In that event, he may voluntarily relinquish his managerial post to "return to personal production." From a purely financial standpoint, working exclusively as a salesman may be more rewarding.

SOURCES OF MANAGERS

Where do agency departments look for prospective managers possessing the necessary qualities for success?

Selling a relative intangible like life insurance is quite different in many respects from selling tangibles like machinery, chemicals, textiles, etc. Hence, it is not often that a sales or district manager for some tangible commodity is appointed directly to the managership of a life insurance agency.

We have already indicated that the manager of a life insurance agency will usually have been a successful agent at some time in his career (although not necessarily a leading salesman). So a deceptively easy answer to the foregoing question might be to "take the best salesmen you have and appoint them managers." At one time it was customary to fill the ranks of managers in this way. Even today some agency executives subordinate other qualities to sales ability when seeking men for managerial posts.

Granting that a prospective manager should have been a good agent, not every successful salesman is a good executive. Attention must be paid to all the characteristics that the job requires. Experience has shown the drawbacks of appointing branch managers or general agents largely or entirely because of their success as salesmen. The most that can safely be said about this practice is that sometimes such men succeed as managers and sometimes they don't. When they don't, all concerned suffer—they themselves, their agents, their company, the insuring public and thereby the business as a whole. Sometimes they themselves recognize that their forte is not management; sometimes the agency department suggests or even directs the change.

Whenever possible, most companies will draw on their own organizations for managerial talent. A company looks first among its supervisors or assistant managers, then among agents[2] and members of the home office agency staff. So-called management trainees are becoming an increasingly important source of managers for many companies. Under this arrangement a company brings prospective managers, usually successful agents who show evidence of executive potential, into the home office for training for the position of manager. Such programs vary in content and duration; they may cover a period of a year or more. Then, as managerial vacancies occur, these trainees return to the field as managers. Other companies are working through the field to select men who will be trained in their agency offices to become managers.

Less frequently companies will seek the services of representatives of other life insurance companies. Sources of managers appointed from other companies include managers or general agents, supervisors or assistant managers, and agents.

MANAGERS AND TRAINING

Historically, training of agents preceded training of managers. In retrospect that sequence was probably a mistake—not that training of agents was wrong but rather that training of their managers first would have been better. However, at the time companies first began to recognize that their field forces needed training to do a proper selling job, the agents' needs seemed considerably more acute. For one thing, agents were far more numerous than managers, and many men under con-

---

[2] Devices such as the "Career Analysis Procedure," developed by the Life Insurance Agency Management Association, are helpful in predicting whether a particular agent's long-range prospects for success are likely to be greater in management or in selling.

tract knew little about either life insurance or life insurance selling. Further, companies had not yet realized that outstanding salesmen would not necessarily become outstanding managers. Virtually all managers were being drawn from the ranks of big producers; success as an agent was by far the major prerequisite for a man who aspired to become a manager. Even though a manager might be neither a businessman nor an administrator, at least he could sell.

Also, not having been trained themselves and having succeeded as salesmen despite inadequate training, such managers frequently were unable to train their agents satisfactorily. The remedy seemed to be for the home office itself to do the job of training agents. Consequently, over a period of years many agency departments took over recruiting and training of agents, thereby doing much of the work that more appropriately was the managers'.

Today many agency departments, especially those of large companies, believe that the best training of agents is done in the field. Hence they are developing programs to train managers to train their agents. We have already referred briefly to the management trainee arrangement. In the field of institutional or noncompany programs are the Life Insurance Agency Management Association Schools in Agency Management, and the Round Tables in Agency Management under the sponsorship of the General Agents and Managers Committee of the National Association of Life Underwriters. Such training programs for managers vary as to mechanics, scope and duration, although recruiting and training of agents are basic elements. The "curricula," in general, include such topics as the following:

Objectives of the manager
Management planning
Agency cost analysis
Profitable company operation
Agency business management
Planning for growth
Analysis of the agent's job
Leadership

Presenting the career
Training of new men
Group training methods
Principles of supervision
Motivating men
Continuous training of experienced men
Financing

Market conditions and problems may differ between agencies classed as urban, suburban and rural. They may also differ within agencies in one class or type. For example, a particular company may have agencies in Baltimore and Seattle. Both are urban, but the company's market conditions in the two territories may be quite different. If circumstances permit, a man's preparation for assuming a managership in a new city should include some background study of the territory in which he will have to recruit, train, supervise and motivate his field organization.

Why Manage?

There is a vast difference between assuming the responsibility for a group of agents and being responsible for oneself alone. The life of an agent may seem rather uncomplicated by contrast. Insofar as income is concerned, the agent's practical ceiling is limited only by his ability and industry. In fact, many successful agents earn a higher income than their manager, and sometimes even more than the president of their company. Why, then, should a successful soliciting agent, whose contract provides for retirement and other benefits, want to be a manager? Some agents have answered that question by remaining in personal production without the responsibility of becoming the go-between for the home office and the agents. The manager must represent the company to his men, and his men to the company; it may sometimes be impossible to please both. More than a few men return voluntarily to agent status after having had a fling at being a manager.

Nevertheless there are a number of reasons why men want to be managers:

1. If the agent has management ability, his income eventually may be greater as a manager. Naturally, he would have to build a corps of able men to attain that objective.

2. Sometimes a good teacher decides that he would rather get into the administrative side of his profession. Similarly, a good agent may find that he has a real urge to organize and manage.

3. Today many men are hired as managerial trainees. Hence their service as soliciting agents is likely to be incidental to their eventual goal of general agent or branch manager. Other men like the actual sales work but do not care for some of the other tasks they must perform to earn a living as agents. Such men are attracted to management.

4. An aspect of prestige and rank is involved. It sounds better to be a manager than an agent. (Sometimes women are involved; some would rather be the wife of a manager than of an agent.)

5. Finally, if an agent has set his sights particularly high, there may be another reason for wanting to become a manager. He may consider the position as a stepping-stone to executive status. From the ranks of managers have come most agency vice presidents and other senior agency department executives, as well as some company presidents. Although the odds are long, the fact that some managers have become part of top management may be enough motivation for some especially ambitious and capable agents.

SUMMARY

The responsibility for executing the plans and policies of the home office agency department falls primarily on the head of each agency. Certain general and specific qualities go into the makeup of a manager if he is to discharge his duties successfully. Sales ability is important, but he need not have been a leading (outstanding) producer.

Various programs, company and institutional, have been developed to prepare men for the job of manager. It should be noted that a successful agent will not necessarily increase his earnings if he becomes a manager. In fact, he may earn less. Nevertheless, for a variety of reasons the prospect of a managership exerts a strong appeal for many agents.

QUESTIONS FOR REVIEW

1. What are some of the common qualities or characteristics of successful agency managers? List a manager's main duties.
2. Discuss the pros and cons of personal production by the agency head. What is the rule or practice in your company? Who is more likely to be a substantial personal producer, a general agent or a branch manager? Why?
3. Outline the usual sources of agency managers. Where do most of the managers in your company come from? Evaluate the desirability of drawing primarily on successful (a) life insurance salesmen, (b) salesmen in other lines of business.
4. Enumerate the subjects commonly included in a training program for agency managers.
5. What factors prompt men to want to become agency managers? In what respects is the work of a manager more complicated than that of an agent?

8 | Getting the Right Manpower: Agents

The home office, its field managers and its agents all have relations with the insuring public. Managers are closer to this public than the home office. However, agents stand closest of all. Few people purchase life insurance entirely voluntarily, even when they recognize that they need it—and many do not recognize that they need it. Only the agent, with his personal solicitation, is in a position to explain to prospects how they can provide adequately for themselves and for those dependent on them.

Everybody has some ideas as to what an agent is and does. Unfortunately, those ideas are sometimes somewhat distorted. To some, a life insurance agent is a man who nags or hounds other people to buy life insurance so that he can earn a large commission.

Granted that most persons require some urging before they will apply for the life insurance they need, such a concept is inaccurate and unfair. Even today, though, such misconceptions of what an agent is and does are all too prevalent. A good agent is more than just a salesman. He is a person under contract to a life insurance company—directly or through a general agent—and is under the direction of a field manager. Today's agent has been recruited and selected with considerably more care than was formerly the case. He has been trained to recommend the right plans of insurance to persons who need life insurance and can afford to pay for it. His work is not over when he has sold and delivered a policy. Service as well as sale is involved, and sometimes continues until the death of the policyowner and beyond. The insured may wish to assign his contract, change the beneficiary designation or obtain a policy loan. In each instance the agent can be of assistance. If the insured does not pay a premium within the grace period, the agent may have to try to resell him so that premium payments will continue and the life insurance will fulfill the purpose for which it was purchased. Further, a good agent keeps abreast of changes in the policyowner's situation and in applicable laws, especially tax laws, to assure that the insurance continues to meet his needs. As the occasion arises —and it frequently does—he recommends additional protection to his client. He also calls his client's attention to new benefits that may be added to existing insurance.

These and other activities involve the agent—through his agency office—with various home office departments, even though he himself may rarely or never set foot inside the home office building. The agent may not consider that he is representing the various departments of the company when he deals with the insuring public. Nevertheless, serving his clients will bring him into indirect contact with a number of home office departments, such as loan, accounting, actuarial, mode of settlement, claim, law and tax. Even though he considers himself to be primarily, if not exclusively, a representative of the X agency, he really symbolizes home office activities. Insofar as the insuring public is concerned, the agent *is* the company.

An explanation of just what is meant by the term "agent" is in order at this point. While there are part-time men and brokers, it is not feasible to include them in this discussion. Unless otherwise specified, the term "agent" in the remainder of this book will be a so-called full-time life insurance salesman, one who devotes most of his time to, and/or derives most of his income from, representing one company and who is publicly identified with that company.

Thus "full-time" is not interpreted literally. Where *time* is the basis of the definition, a full-time agent is one who is expected to devote some minimum percentage, such as 75 percent, of his time to selling his company's products.

Where *income* is the basis, a man is defined as a full-time agent if his total income is not more than some percentage, e.g., 120 percent, of his income from his company. Thus, if a man reports $12,000 income from his company and $13,920 total (16 percent excess), he is classified as a full-time agent. If the total is $15,000 (25 percent excess), he is classified as part-time. Agents under contract to one company sometimes are in a position to place a policy with another life company or to write, say, an automobile or a fire policy.

Qualities or Characteristics of a Successful Agent

The agent plays a vital role in attaining two of the agency department's three objectives. He does not directly control development and expansion of his company's territory. But he certainly is the one to accomplish the other two objectives: selling good business and rendering field service to policy-owners. The agent sells and services.

What are the characteristics or qualities of a successful agent? As in the case of the qualities of a manager, many of them apply to other occupations as well. Common ones include:

1. Personality—This is an overworked word. Nevertheless, it connotes a generally outgoing type of person who meets people easily, who is a good mixer.
2. Motivation or ambition—A man must really want to

succeed; he must have personal drive. Even men with adequate motivation have not always succeeded as life insurance salesmen. However, a man content with merely getting by will not go far.

3. Perseverance—Closely related to motivation, this quality has sometimes been the butt of jokes and cartoons. Many a sale would be lost, though, and many a family would be unprotected if an agent accepted the first or even the second turndown as final. Perseverance also enters into the important job of continuous prospecting.

4. Self-confidence—As in other worthy endeavors, the agent must have a bone-deep rather than a skin-deep feeling that he will make the grade.

5. Unselfishness or interest in others—This quality does not mean that the successful agent must be a conventional backslapper, first-namer and hail-fellow-well-met with everybody with whom he comes in contact. However, to succeed he must have a genuine desire to help others solve their personal and business problems through what he has to offer—life insurance.

6. Enthusiasm—A good agent must have the fervor warranted by what he has to sell. If he has trouble getting excited about the life insurance business, he probably should not be in it.

7. Integrity—Just as the manager's associates must be able to rely on him, so must those who come in contact with the agent be able to have confidence in his integrity, including his manager and the public.

8. Intelligence—He should master training material readily, respond effectively to supervision, and have a sufficient mathematical turn of mind to grasp the complexities of life insurance policies.

While most successful agents possess most of these qualities, there is sometimes only moderate correlation between possession of such qualities and subsequent success in a career in life insurance selling. It is difficult to develop tests that measure such qualities accurately. Sometimes some of these qualities develop *with* success.

Duties of the Agent

These are more specific. They can be summarized in three broad categories:

1. To sell the right kind of life insurance to those who need it and can pay for it, basing selling on the needs of the prospect.
2. To keep that insurance in force. Sometimes the agent must resell a policyowner on the importance of continuing premium payments.
3. To give satisfactory service. The agent should keep in frequent touch with his clients' personal and business situations as they relate to life insurance. (Not all agents do. There are still men who "sell them and leave them," as some studies have shown.) He will then be in a position to arrange loans, settlement options and other changes; inform policyowners of new benefits available or new policies available; assist in the completion of disability and death claim papers, etc.

RECRUITING

The building of career agents can be considered to consist of four basic steps: recruiting, training, supervision, motivation. While reasonably distinct, these steps actually constitute a continuous activity. The first of these will be considered in this chapter.

As applied to agents, recruiting[1] is the process of finding and hiring new men. It is the process of finding men who can

---

[1] Sometimes recruiting and selection are considered separate steps. Also, sometimes recruiting, in the broad sense, is considered to include prospecting (for agents), selection, presenting the career, financing, training. Supervision is then considered to include motivation as well.

become interested in life insurance selling, selling them on the career and selecting those who seem likely to succeed. Standards and methods of recruiting usually originate in the home office, so that some degree of uniformity is achieved, but the actual work of finding and hiring is done primarily in the field, generally by the manager or one of his assistants.

Problems of Agent Manpower

There always has been and probably always will be a shortage of good life insurance salesmen. Just as hardly any company ever feels that it has enough good managers, so hardly any manager ever feels that he has enough good agents. New agents are needed for the same reasons that new managers are: death, retirement because of age or disability, discharge, promotion to position of manager or assistant manager, promotion or transfer to home office staff or voluntary resignation.

Further, if the agency is to grow, i.e., increase the amount of business sold from year to year, one way is to increase the number of good men under contract. Hence, the need to recruit is continuous. It must be done regularly as part of the manager's job, not as the spirit moves him. Otherwise, he may suddenly find that attrition for various reasons has left him with a serious manpower problem. Rebuilding is slow and hard. Prevention is more effective and easier than cure.

Few potentially successful salesmen apply to agency managers of their own accord and ask for the opportunity to sell life insurance. Companies, through their field managers, must find and attract promising men and create interest in the job.

How, then, do managers obtain new agents? Who should be an agent? Not every intelligent person is cut out to be an electrical engineer, or a lawyer or a diamond-cutter. Neither is every intelligent person cut out to be a life insurance agent. Most companies and managers recognize the need for competent agents. They strive to hire only those men who are likely to achieve success in the business and to stay in it, and to avoid those who are not likely to be successful.

Like any other occupation, a career in life insurance selling has some features that do not appeal to everyone. To repeat, there are still people who think the agent's job is an easy and lucrative one, especially if they hear that agent Jones has just sold a $50,000 policy and earned a $1,000 commission "for a half-hour's work." They don't know how long Jones may have been working on the case; neither do they know how many hours Jones has worked on cases where he did not make a sale.

Disadvantages to a Career in Life Insurance Selling

There definitely are some. Among these are:

1. The difficulty of selling a service, a piece of paper, a promise of future benefits in exchange for present financial sacrifices on the part of the purchaser, frequently for the benefit of somebody else.
2. The many disappointments when, for one reason or another—many of them beyond the agent's control—prospects do not become policyowners.
3. The inability of the agent to blame anyone but himself if he does not succeed; buckpassing is difficult.
4. The irregularity of working hours—agents seldom succeed by adhering to a 9-to-5 day five days a week. Many work at their jobs evenings, Saturdays and Sundays, especially during the early phases of their careers.

Advantages to a Career in Life Insurance Selling

If the product is so hard to sell and there are other drawbacks, what are the advantages? Why should anyone want to be a life insurance agent? Here are some of the reasons:

1. The opportunity for greater income. Many sales lines in effect divide the market for their goods or services. The

total market is limited. For example, if one automobile tire manufacturer increases his sales, other manufacturers will sell less. The life underwriter rarely runs into such direct competition. He creates in the prospect's mind recognition of a life insurance need, which the prospect usually was not aware of before. For the outstanding man the income ceiling is high.

2. The desire for a considerable measure of independence, "being one's own boss." Most agents are on their own to a considerably greater extent than are persons paid by the hour or by the week.

3. The desire to meet and work with other people. Life insurance selling offers a satisfying outlet for the energies of the gregarious type of individual.

Literature and speeches sometimes suggest that the opportunity for service to others is an important factor in influencing men to *become* agents. The validity of this statement is at least open to question. A person who has not yet sold life insurance is likely to have little appreciation of the satisfaction that comes from rendering service to policyowners and beneficiaries. *After* he has been in harness for a while, there is considerable evidence that the experience of rendering valuable services to his fellowmen is a substantial factor in *keeping* an agent in the business. In fact, it has been said that an agent is not really a life insurance man until he has delivered his first death claim check, particularly on a policy he sold himself.

Sources of New Agents

There is no one single source of new agents. Representatives of practically all major occupations are included in the ranks of today's successful agents: office workers, bank clerks, lawyers, accountants, teachers, government employees, factory workers—to name just a few. Some have come from the ranks of agency cashiers and home office employees of life insurance companies. Recent college graduates, especially those who have prepared for a sales career, are another source. Occasionally, a policyowner seeking service may get interested in becoming an agent.

Apart from persons just out of high school or college, i.e., those with little or no significant work experience, recruits for any legitimate type of work are likely to come from those who are somewhat dissatisfied with their present job. This statement is true of life insurance selling. Prospective agents hope to increase their earnings, and the idea of setting their own pace appeals to them. Some are attracted by the idea of a considerable degree of independence; they don't care to punch a timeclock, literally or figuratively. Others find inside work too confining. Still others have never sold and think they would like to try life insurance. Then there are those who have sold in other fields and think they would do better or be happier selling life insurance.

Although men enter the career of life insurance selling from many walks of life, recruiting must be planned. The manager should try to anticipate possible expansion of his sales force as well as replacements resulting from turnover because of retirements, promotions and otherwise. Most prospective agents, and of course actual agents, are obtained through the following channels:

1. The manager himself knows a number of desirable prospects personally. Further, as a fairly prominent individual in his community, he will have a wide circle of personal and business friends and acquaintances who may become valuable centers of influence, i.e., persons both willing and able to help him. These persons may not be interested in life insurance selling themselves. However, they usually have extensive contacts through church activities, clubs, service and fraternal organizations, PTA groups, charity drives and the like. These

centers of influence, also known as nominators or co-operators, may know of desirable men who would be interested and qualified.

2. The agency organization (assistant manager or managers, supervisors, agents, office staff) have contacts that often lead to men becoming interested in life insurance selling. The effectiveness of the agency organization in recruiting will depend in large measure on their confidence in and respect for their manager as an organizer and as a leader. Further, to help effectively, they need to be briefed specifically as to the general type of man their manager is seeking.

3. Satisfied policyowners frequently can furnish names of prospective agents. Many will if asked.

4. Local newspapers are another channel through which prospective agents may be obtained. First, managers may read the "employment wanted" columns. Second, they may run advertisements of their own. Sometimes managers will identify themselves; sometimes the advertisement will ask applicants to write to a post office box number. The latter device enables managers to screen replies before granting interviews.

5. Direct mail to selected persons can help in recruiting. It must be used discreetly, however.

6. Occasionally persons call at the agency office of their own accord to seek information concerning the possibility of a career in life insurance selling.

Selecting the Right Man

No universally successful plan for selecting the right agent manpower has yet been found—and is not likely to be in the near future. Successful men differ in so many respects that no one set of qualities will be common to all. There are usually more than enough men available *quantitatively* speaking, but their quality level for life insurance selling is likely to be low. Recruiting involves considering a large number of people, from whom a considerably smaller number is chosen to represent the company.

Placing a man under contract and training him are expensive if he succeeds, even more so if he fails. Today many life insurance agents are financed for a considerable period of time. It was estimated[2] some years ago that the cost of bringing one such agent through to his fourth year was $18,000. Training and supervision costs for three years amounted to $8,000; financing costs over and above commissions earned by the agent amounted to $10,000. These figures would be considerably higher now.

Relating this information to agent recruiting highlights the importance of preventing prospective failures from getting into the business and reducing the number of potentially successful men who leave it. Managers use several means to try to screen or weed out those whose prospects for success are poor. Among them are:

1. *The Interview*—Most managers will grant at least a short interview to practically anyone who expresses an interest in life insurance selling. Many managers will understate rather than overstate the advantages of a career as an agent. They know that selling life insurance is hard work and that little is to be gained from painting too rosy a picture, least of all for those who reveal that they probably don't have what it takes to make good. A few searching questions and an untinted picture will discourage many of the obviously unqualified.

2. *Testing*—With those men who show at least some promise and serious interest, the manager will proceed to the second step, which is usually testing.

Today preemployment tests are common for many jobs. There are tests designed to measure a person's interest for a particular kind of work, his mechanical skills, his general intelligence, his aptitude for certain activities, etc. By themselves tests are quite inadequate to predict success for any particular position. In conjunction with other selection tools

---

[2] *Proceedings*, Life Insurance Agency Management Association (1962), p. 15.

they can be very useful. Some tests are at least as valuable in indicating whether a person is likely to fail in a given occupation as whether he is likely to succeed. For this reason selection tests are sometimes known as rejection tests. Those using them are able to reject persons not likely to succeed. Even then, not all those accepted will be successful.

To select prospective life insurance agents, companies and managers have also used a number of general tests that have been shown to help select salesmen for other lines of endeavor. In general, selection tests are designed to obtain and appraise information concerning the following factors considered important for a good would-be salesman:

1. Marital status
2. Previous occupations
3. Formal education
4. Personality characteristics
5. Leadership or initiative
6. Enthusiasm or ambition
7. Gregariousness
8. Health and habits
9. Amount of life insurance owned
10. Cooperativeness
11. Acquaintances in his community

The Aptitude Index Battery—One test has been designed expressly for the life insurance business. This is the well-known Aptitude Index, now known as the Aptitude Index Battery, Form 1, first published in 1937 by the Life Insurance Agency Management Association. LIAMA developed it to assist companies and managers in the United States and Canada in selecting new, inexperienced men for their ordinary business—as distinguished from debit and group. (Subsequently, LIAMA developed the comparable Combination Inventory for debit agents.)

In 1965, after four years of research, LIAMA introduced its latest selection instrument. LIAMA designed it to enable companies to predict even more accurately the chances for success of ordinary agents and to increase the test's validity for prospective ordinary agents below the age of 26. Subsequent studies indicate that these objectives have been attained. Because LIAMA incorporated a number of tests in this latest revision, it was named the Aptitude Index Battery, Form 1.

The AIB Form 1 is not designed to disclose a prospective agent's intelligence or his personality quotient. Neither does it necessarily predict selling ability in general. But the AIB does predict the ability of an inexperienced prospective agent to sell life insurance. It cannot foretell definitely whether he can or will succeed as an agent; it will, however, state what his relative chances of success are. Prospective agents are thus assisted in deciding whether to try to enter a career of life insurance selling.

This test explores many facets of a man's makeup. Among them are:

1. Employment—past and present; number of employers during the past five years
2. Finances—net worth, annual income, amount of life insurance owned, overall living expenses, indebtedness
3. Educational background—high school; college, if any; scholastic standing; extracurricular activities
4. Marital and dependency status—job status of wife, number of children
5. Job attitudes—his and his family's attitudes toward present job and coworkers and career in life insurance selling

Available information indicates that managers earnestly desirous of building an effective agency force should hire only those men whose AIB ratings are high, because relatively few in the other categories will succeed. Each company can denote what score it will use for its "passing mark." Based on the average experience of large ordinary companies, even men with the best ratings or scores show only 50 percent success. Some men with low scores will succeed, but they are long shots. "If the man passes the test, forget the test; if he fails the test, forget the man."

3. *Application Blank*—If the prospective agent does well enough on his test, he will be asked to complete an application blank. This step is also followed in most other job situations. However, the life insurance form may include a greater number of questions designed to elicit information as to the applicant's personality, interests, introversion or extroversion and the like. Agents work with people, and the manager needs to know in advance all he can about how a man gets along with other people. Is he active in church or community affairs, fraternal, service or social organizations, sports, clubs? Has he held office in any of these? Has he ever sold before? Why does he think he would like to sell life insurance and why does he think he would succeed?

Information as to the personal and family situation is especially important. Is he mature? Considerable evidence indicates that the age group of from about 30 to 45 yields the most successful prospects. Apparently men under 30 are likely to succeed as much in spite of, as because of, their youth. Men above 45 are likely to have lost some of their adaptability for work that is completely different from what they have been doing. Also, many men 45 and over who would be desirable agents are sufficiently well established in their present work and so are less likely to be interested in a change.

What about the man's family? Married men tend to become better life insurance agents than do bachelors. The manager will be interested in the attitude of the wife. How does she feel about life insurance selling as a career? It is an adverse sign if a man's wife is opposed. Many agents have succeeded partly because of their wives, but very few have in spite of them.

Somewhere in the selection process, perhaps at this point, the manager will tell the prospective agent something of the nature of life insurance, of his particular company, of the potential long-range earnings. He will emphasize that earnings are likely to be modest for a considerable period, possibly not enough to live on without help from other sources. He will describe the company's training program as well as the essentials of its compensation plan. He will explain his company's financing arrangements clearly to minimize the danger of misunderstanding later. He will emphasize the disadvantages as well as the advantages of the occupation of agent. Specifically, he will outline clearly what the prospective agent would be called on to do should he be placed under contract.

4. *Investigation*—Frequently the prospective agent will be a stranger to the manager. The latter can learn something of a man's background by checking with his former employers and with others who know him. Usually, the applicant's situation and background should be verified through some reporting organization, such as the Retail Credit Company or the Hooper-Holmes Bureau. An inspection report will also cover a man's health history and apparent physical condition in a general way. Medical examination is often required.

5. *Further Interviews*—If the information developed through the initial interview, the selection test, the application form, and the investigation is generally favorable, further interviews may follow. The original interviewer should talk to the applicant again and take up points that merit additional discussion. Others in the agency may also interview the man to get their viewpoints. The manager will want to meet and talk with the man's wife, preferably at their home. The wife and her attitude are important factors in the success or failure of men in most occupations, particularly in one like life insurance selling.

6. *Analysis and Decision*—When the foregoing steps have been taken, the information from all sources should be carefully analyzed. On the basis of this analysis, the manager must decide whether or not to offer the man a contract to represent the agency and the company. (As previously explained, final approval of the applicant by the home office may be necessary, especially when, as is commonly the case today, company money is being used to finance new men.)

For the right man, the attractions of a career in life insurance selling are many. A good manager should be able to present this career effectively. At the same time, the manager should guard against overselling the career. No job should be oversold just to get a man to take it; neither should the job of life insurance salesman if disappointments are to be avoided, or at least minimized, later.

The offer of a contract to a prospective agent will not always be accepted. Just as companies in a recruiting procedure may decide not to offer contracts to some of the prospective agents they interview, some of the applicants also change their minds along the way. Among the main reasons for declination by applicants are competition from other sales jobs, and perhaps their belief that the job of agent is financially unattractive.

7. *Precontract Orientation*—Even among carefully recruited men a substantial percentage will fail as life insurance salesmen. The usual result is loss of time and money to the man and to the company. In an effort to eliminate more of those men who are likely to fail, a number of companies have adopted the technique of precontract orientation, also known as precontract selection and career orientation.

While there are numerous variations, precontract orientation fundamentally is an arrangement or "work sample" enabling a prospective agent to get some of the "feel" of life insurance selling *before* he is placed under contract. Sometimes he works with the manager on a trial basis. If he is currently employed elsewhere, the prospective agent may receive orientation evenings or weekends on a part-time basis. In other cases he receives study assignments covering the company's basic training program.

Studies indicate that precontract training possesses at least two important advantages. The chief one is that it improves selection by obviating the necessity to eliminate a considerable number of unqualified, uninterested men, even when they have shown up well in the other steps in the recruiting procedure. Some of these men will eliminate themselves. The second advantage is that men placed under contract *after* precontract orientation, having had a foretaste of their work, are likely to be off to a better start in regular training and will do a better job as agents.

Companies consider its time-consuming nature the principal disadvantage of precontract orientation. Thus it may have two major adverse effects: (1) tying up the manager's or the trainer's time, perhaps to the neglect of the existing agency staff; (2) losing potentially good men, either because of their impatience or necessity to get started or because of competition from other agencies.

8. *Signing the Contract*—Placing a new man under contract involves a number of administrative activities. His personal history is a matter of record. Details of his working arrangements are spelled out in his agent's contract. As already indicated, most new men today receive some kind of financing and this is formalized to some extent. Any "fringe" benefits will likewise be recorded. Placing of a fidelity bond is common in many companies. At this time the new recruit may also receive a sales kit containing such materials as application forms, the ratebook, sales presentation forms and sales literature.

The new man will have to be licensed. More than three-fourths of the states now require a new agent to pass a written examination before he can solicit business. In New York, one of the strictest states, the failure rate of those who have taken its licensing examinations over the past 20 years has been over 20 percent. Since 1970, all the Canadian provinces require candidates to pass a written examination before obtaining an agent's license.

After a man has been licensed, his manager will wish to announce his appointment as an agent. Appropriate letters are commonly sent to persons who the new agent believes will be prospects for life insurance and upon whom he will soon be calling.

General Comments on Recruiting

Not every manager is going to perform every step of the recruiting procedure that has been outlined. Even if he does, he may not follow the same order. And not every manager will evaluate the information he has about a prospective agent in the same way. Like other people, managers have their distinctive personalities. Certain qualities appeal to certain managers. Hence they will tend to surround themselves as much as possible with agents possessing these qualities. One manager will reject a man with certain qualities, whereas another will place that man under contract because of those same qualities. Further, an agent working under one manager may be only modestly successful. Working for another manager, one whom he understands and who understands him, that same man may hit his stride and become an outstanding agent.

No selection process has yet been devised which guarantees to select the right man for any given job. Tests for agents are not a panacea; their real value is in *helping* a manager reach a decision. The Aptitude Index Battery itself is primarily a device to screen or reject some men who may "look good" to the manager, but whose chances for success are slight. For maximum effectiveness this and other selection tests should be given before the manager has reached any decision that he hopes to prove or disprove by test results. If a man rates as desirable after such tests, he *may* be the man the manager is seeking.

SPECIAL ASPECTS OF RECRUITING

The foregoing discussion has dealt with recruiting in general. Some specific aspects of this activity will now be considered.

College Seniors and Graduates

More and more people are going to college every year; more and more are graduating. College graduates are found in all types of sales work. If they have entered life insurance selling, they have usually done so after significant work experience elsewhere. Many of them have become outstandingly successful.

According to a 1969 LIAMA survey,[3] nearly 30 percent of *all* new United States agents then being hired were college graduates. Most of them were men who, upon graduation, had gone into some other line of work and eventually had been recruited into life insurance selling. However, the same survey also indicated that very few new agents were being currently hired directly off college campuses.

What about the recent or the just-out-of-college graduate? How well does he fit into a selling career in life insurance? Companies in favor of recruiting seniors and recent college graduates advance the following reasons:

1. Graduation indicates that the individual has started and recently completed at least one important undertaking.
2. He should know how to study and where to look for information he may need.
3. It should be easier to hire a man for his first job than to attract him away from some other job later.
4. Presumably he is unmarried. Hence, his living expenses are likely to be lower than those of a man a few years older with a family. If financing is involved, the single man should require considerably less.
5. He may have access to a very desirable market, one that if cultivated should become increasingly worthwhile. Many of the people he knows will be young like himself, getting started in a career, getting married, having children, and starting their savings and insurance plans. As their economic lot improves and as their needs increase, their purchases of life insurance will increase also.

Among the reasons against recruiting recent college graduates are the following:

---

[3] "How to Recruit College Seniors to Life Insurance Selling."

1. Such a man is likely to be between 21 and 23 years old and therefore immature. Chances are that whatever his first job is, he will soon leave it, because he probably doesn't really yet know what he actually wants to do. (It is estimated that about half of all college graduates change jobs within five years after graduation.) Since training is expensive, why spend money, including financing, that probably will be wasted?

2. When jobs are plentiful, the prospect of living as a life insurance salesman on a commission basis has been considerably less inviting than the assurance of a guaranteed starting salary elsewhere. Recruiting takes time, so why waste it on people who are not likely to be attracted by the short-range prospects as against guaranteed starting salaries of $10,000 a year or more?

3. Many men just out of college are likely to look down on a program of training; some may even think it's too elementary. How likely and how soon are such men to buckle down to hard work? And even if they do, how likely are prospects for life insurance, particularly those who may be in the market for a substantial amount of life insurance, to listen to someone young enough to be their son?

The foregoing paragraphs reflect what have been the main considerations in recruiting agents among men with college background—seniors, just-out-of-college graduates and other graduates. In view of what is broadly called campus unrest, discussion of the current situation is difficult except to say that it is "in flux." Many in college today seem somewhat indifferent to business careers in general. Sales work, including life insurance selling, seems to attract them even less.

Just how soon this attitude will change is hard to predict. For the immediate future, though, it would appear that companies will have to convey the story of job opportunities in life insurance selling more effectively than heretofore, if they wish to interest substantial numbers of the current generation of college students.

Many companies recruit young college graduates into their home offices and train them to become group sales representatives. As will be explained in chapter 15, in group insurance the sales approach is quite different. Specifically, there is not the individual agent-to-prospect approach as in the sale of ordinary insurance.

Rural Agents

Most agency activity is in urban and suburban areas, so that the manager is in charge of a small, compact territory. Such a setup has obvious advantages. However, despite the shift of population to the cities and their suburbs, many areas of the United States and Canada will be rural for a long time to come. Such areas also need sales representation. How do companies and managers cultivate "the country"?

Some rural communities may not be large enough to enable a full-time agent to earn a satisfactory living. Hence he may conduct a general insurance business in addition. Also, in such areas men in occupations like law, banking, teaching, real estate and local government may devote some of their time to selling life insurance.

But many rural communities are large enough to support a full-time agent. The problem is to find such a man. Quite probably a manager will have fewer people from which to recruit. Greater expenditures of time and money are likely to be involved in visiting prospective agents where they live and in getting them to come in to see the manager in his office. Training is likely to be more costly, especially if a new agent lives so far from the place of training (usually the agency office) that he must obtain room and board for the duration of his indoctrination.

Supervision and motivation also are more difficult. The manager can see most of his urban and suburban salesmen almost daily, whereas weeks may go by between personal face-to-face contacts with some of his rural agents. He can write, of course, and he should. Use of the telephone can be even more effective. The agent can hear his manager's voice and ask questions as well as answer them. While not an adequate substitute for a personal get-together, a well-timed and well-organized telephone call from a manager to one of his rural representatives is the next best thing.

General Insurance Men

These are men who sell primarily lines of insurance other than life. Frequently they are brokers. The amount of life business they write varies from substantial to little or none. The importance of brokerage business to many life companies has increased greatly in recent years. Some general insurance men have become prominent life salesmen.

This may be an appropriate spot to mention multiple-line or "all lines" operations, also known as "one-stop selling," in which the same agent prescribes for all of a prospect's insurance needs—life, health, property, casualty. There have been *some* multiple-line companies for many years. Since about 1950 a number of nonlife carriers, including several of the largest, have entered the life field. Some have done so by creating a life insurance subsidiary; others, by acquiring control of an existing life company. Well over 300 life insurance companies in the United States are now either owned by, controlled by, linked for management with, or are owners of, property-liability insurance companies.

The laws of many states prevent life companies from entering the nonlife fields. A few life companies in these states have developed informal, noncorporate affiliations with property-liability insurers.

Some authorities have advocated that the competent insurance man handle all phases of his client's insurance instead of being a specialist in either life insurance or the nonlife field. Other authorities doubt that the time will come when all life agents will sell every form of insurance protection. In their opinion multiple-line activity is not desirable for either client or agent. They feel that life insurance is complex enough to require attention of salesmen who will concentrate solely on this one line.

When nonlife companies first began to enter life operations, there were enthusiastic predictions that one-stop insurance selling would soon be the order of the day. For some the venture has been successful. In the overall, however, nonlife companies and their agents have not become heavily involved in life insurance.

A few years ago the National Association of Insurance Agents, an organization of property-liability agents, conducted a study of its members. Nonlife sales are commonly measured in terms of premium income rather than face amount as in life insurance. Eighty percent of the general insurance agencies surveyed wrote life insurance for a face amount equal to less than 10 percent of their nonlife premium.

Suppose a general insurance agency writes $250,000 nonlife premium in a year; then its annual life production will usually be less than $25,000 in volume. If this volume involves an average premium of $20 per $1,000 of life insurance, the agency's total life premium will come to about $500 a year. Since two-thirds of the agencies studied write less than $250,000 of nonlife premium annually, these figures are significant for life insurance sales by general insurance agencies.

To many, multiple-line operations are still a valid concept. All-lines selling is a market technique that may serve the insuring public well. Whether a trend will develop remains to be seen.

TURNOVER

Not all people are fitted for some of the work they attempt, whether it be banking, clerking in a store or carpentry. People leave jobs for a variety of reasons. They get a better job elsewhere; they are not happy in their work; they can't stand the mental or physical strain; they don't get along with their associates or their superiors. They may be discharged or they may be asked to "resign." When people enter a line of work and then leave it, the result is known as "turnover."

While turnover is not a phenomenon peculiar to life insurance selling, companies recognize that excessive turnover is detrimental to all concerned—agents, companies, policyowners and beneficiaries. Despite companies' best efforts, the rate of agents' turnover continues to be a serious problem. Companies have been trying to reduce excessive turnover by means of better recruiting, better training, better supervision, better motivation and improved plans of compensation.

On the other hand, some turnover among salesmen is normal, inevitable and even desirable in *any* sales operation. Life insurance has attracted and held men because, among other things, it is a remunerative occupation; hence it may also attract some who are not qualified.

A recent LIAMA research report, "Where Do They Go?" (1970), casts some interesting light on turnover. The Association compiled data from the records of 1,500 terminated ordinary agents in 58 United States and Canadian companies.

Much of the so-called "high agent turnover" results from the moving of agents from one company to another. Specifically, in the United States:

1.   Forty-one percent of the terminators remained in the life insurance business but with another organization—23 percent as full-time agents; 8 percent as brokers; and 10 percent as managers, supervisors, or home office agency department personnel.
2.   Twenty percent chose selling of nonlife products.
3.   Only 39 percent left the business and selling altogether.

Percentages for these three categories for Canada are 25, 25 and 50 respectively. Thus the percentage of agents who leave life insurance for another business is considerably smaller than the termination rates reported by individual companies.

Proselyting

Some companies openly compete for agents from other insurers; some do so more discreetly. Opinions vary as to the propriety of one life insurance company's recruiting agents among the sales forces of other companies. Those who oppose criticize the practice as "proselyting" or "raiding." However, under an economic system that permits free choice of employer and occupation, people will change jobs. Home office personnel, including executives, even presidents, change jobs, not only in life insurance organizations but in business and professions generally. Hence a prospective employer has the right to offer, and a prospective employee or representative the right to accept, a new connection. The person approached does not have to accept. Apart from other considerations, a company that proselytes agents actively runs the risk of attracting men who are below the highest quality, and even some who are doing poorly in their present agency.

| SUMMARY

The effective agent sells life insurance, seeks to keep it in force and renders a variety of services to his clients. Insofar as the insuring public is concerned, the agent is the insurance company.

Competent persons are needed for such a career, and companies are increasing their efforts to *recruit* men (and women) who are likely to succeed. There are advantages to a career in life insurance selling, but many persons interested lack the necessary qualifications for success.

Many companies have developed fairly elaborate procedures to select only those persons whose prospects for success are good. One of the best known selection devices is the Aptitude Index Battery developed by the Life Insurance Agency Management Association.

Nevertheless, selection techniques are far from perfect. Not all persons selected and placed under contract are successful, and turnover continues to be a problem. But companies continue the search for better solutions.

QUESTIONS FOR REVIEW

1. Is it correct to say that "insofar as the insuring public is concerned, the agent is the company"? Explain.
2. Define recruiting. Discuss its importance in the development of an agency.
3. Enumerate the several steps in the recruiting process and explain each.
4. Discuss the considerations involved in the recruiting of college graduates for careers in life insurance selling. Describe the present practice of your company.
5. What is a multiple-line company? Is yours such a company? Was it organized as a multiple-line organization?
6. What is turnover? Is turnover undesirable? Explain. What significant information has recent research in the area of turnover revealed?

9 | Training the Right Manpower: Agents

*A*ssume the manager has selected, i.e., contracted, a a number of men who he believes are likely to succeed as agents. They have been recruited from several walks of life. Some have had no selling experience of any kind; few, if any, have sold life insurance before. These men must be prepared for the vocation of life insurance selling—they must be trained. Proper selection is important; so is proper training. One cause of new-agent failure and agent turnover may well be inadequate and improper training. Many agents leave their first company; yet they remain in the life insurance business. If their second agency affiliation finds them acceptable, perhaps the original selection was all right but the original training was not.

There probably was a time when it was generally believed that "salesmen are born, not made." Even today there is general agreement that some men possess more aptitude for selling than others. However, there is also general agreement that many men can learn, can be trained, to sell successfully.

One definition of training is "the process of guiding and assisting individuals to develop skill and proficiency in their jobs." In the more specific field of life insurance, training is the preparation for a successful career of those men who have been recruited and selected as agents. Training involves imparting the necessary knowledge and the skills to apply that knowledge correctly, effectively and conscientiously.

WHY TRAINING IS NECESSARY— THE NEGATIVE SIDE

When agents were either not trained at all or inadequately trained, results were less than satisfactory to the salesman himself, his agency and his company, the insuring public and the entire business.

Few occupations satisfy unless those engaged in them are able to earn an adequate living. The untrained agent usually ran into financial difficulty early. Even with the best of intentions he was unable to prescribe intelligently for the needs of those he called on. After he had "sold" friends and relatives, he frequently reached a dead end—no more prospects. If he sold a few additional policies to other persons, his sales talk frequently appealed to the sympathy of his prospects; instead of explaining why *they* needed life insurance, he would explain why *he* needed the commission. Without an adequate income, the majority of such agents soon gave up the struggle and drifted out of the business pretty much as they had drifted into it.

Unqualified men were also unsatisfactory from the standpoint of the agencies and their companies. For quite awhile the fallacy persisted in some quarters that so long as such men produced some business they could reasonably be kept under contract; after all, the company did not pay them any commissions unless they sold, and some business was better than no business. This reasoning failed to recognize that every agent under contract cost his company something—materials, service, office space—whether he sold or not, and that the business such men produced usually showed poor persistency.

Then, as now, the public needed life insurance. Not being versed in what life insurance could do, people sometimes were persuaded to buy plans not best suited to their needs. Also, such policyowners rarely received the service to which they were entitled.

Cumulatively, the effect of untrained or poorly trained agents on the entire business was adverse, and the prestige of life insurance suffered. Aside from the dollars-and-cents cost of unqualified representatives, the cost to the business was substantial in ill will on the part of the public. Fortunately, the situation is greatly improved today.

WHY TRAINING IS NECESSARY— THE POSITIVE SIDE

As companies began to realize the significance of inadequately trained representatives, they decided to do something about the situation. The *widespread* use of training programs, as they are understood today, is a development of the early 1930s.[1]

The well-trained agent is more likely to sell good business, and selling such business means better earnings for himself, because it is likely to remain in force. An agent who sells good business also helps his agency and his manager. By meeting or exceeding his own quota, he helps meet and maintain the agency's quota. Also, the well-trained agent requires less supervision and motivation himself, and thereby he leaves the manager more time to concentrate on those members of the agency sales force who do need more help. And in addition, the well-trained agent is more likely to prescribe adequately for the needs of his clients.

The problems of agency management would be simplified

---

[1] Even today there are a few companies and agencies willing to take a chance on men for whom every available bit of information predicts failure. Apparently they feel that some of these agents will make good, and that almost all of them will produce some business. And even today some training programs are only modestly successful.

considerably if all business were good business. There would still be the problem of getting agents who would and could sell good business. However, companies could pretty much feel that once their agents had put the business on the books, persistency and related matters would take care of themselves.

Quality Business

Up to now we have talked of "good business" rather than "quality business," because of the somewhat nebulous concept that the latter term conveys. Nevertheless, "quality business" has been used so commonly in agency work and agency literature that some attempt to define or explain the term is appropriate at this point.

Quality business has been defined as policies that have good persistency, satisfactory mortality, low acquisition cost and low maintenance expense. Some enlargement may be in order.

1. *Good Persistency*—Life insurance contracts terminate for several reasons: death, maturity, expiry, lapse and surrender. (Strictly, a policy *lapses* only when it goes out of force before it has a nonforfeiture value. However, "lapse" often is used to include all types of *voluntary* terminations, either by surrender for cash or by change to reduced paid-up or to extended term insurance, as well as genuine lapses.) The first three are unpreventable terminations, beyond the control of agent or company, and are not involved in measuring persistency.

Business has satisfactory persistency if terminations because of lapse or surrenders are few. Perfect persistency would mean that all policies would remain in force until they terminated by death, maturity or expiry. However, a policy that is surrendered after it has been in force for many years has usually accomplished its purpose and cannot be said to contribute toward unfavorable persistency.

2. *Satisfactory Mortality*—Premiums and policy dividends are calculated on the assumption that death claims will be at a level estimated by the actuary. Mortality is satisfactory if it is at that level, favorable if it runs below it.

3. *Low Acquisition Cost*—Acquisition costs include such items as first-year commissions, other first-year field expense, inspection report, medical examination (if used), home office underwriting expense and policy issue expense. These nearly always total more than the entire first year's gross premium on a policy. A new contract usually does not "pay its own way" for several years. The higher the acquisition costs, the longer it takes a policy to go on a paying basis.

4. *Low Maintenance Cost*—Companies should give service to policy owners; in fact, to give such service is one of the objectives of the agency department. Conditions arise that necessitate policy transactions such as change of beneficiary, change of mode of premium payment, reinstatement, assignment and policy loan. Business involving excessive requests for such changes can be very costly to the insurer. Business properly sold originally will entail fewer requests for service.

Amount of Policy and Quality Business

A larger-than-average policy is sometimes considered a fifth characteristic of quality business. Quality business does not necessarily contemplate only policies for large amounts. If the institution of life insurance is to justify its existence, it must be prepared to offer its services to all those eligible, whether for small, medium or large amounts. Many agents sell quality business even though the amount of their average sale is not more than $5,000. On the other hand, there are advantages to both agent and company in the sale of larger amounts of insurance to persons of higher income. Some expenses, such as commission to agents, increase with the amount of the premium. Others are less related to the amount of the premium. These include the general administrative expenses of the home office and the cost of keeping policy records. For example, the cost of handling a policy loan is likely to be the same irrespective of whether the face amount of the policy is $2,000 or $20,000. Furthermore, today companies grade premiums according to amount of policy; as the amount of the contract increases, the premium per $1,000 decreases. Thus, smaller insurance policies have relatively larger provision for expense.

Thus the trained agent is more satisfactory to his agency and his company. He costs them less, he earns more, he produces more business and more good business, his morale is higher, he requires less supervision and motivation, he builds a favorable company reputation.

Quality Business and Persistent Business

The terms "quality business" and "persistent business," i.e., business that stays in force, are often used almost interchangeably. "The business that stays is the business that pays." Probably, "persistent" is somewhat more specific and therefore more meaningful.

Just what makes for quality or persistent business is somewhat difficult to say. There is general agreement, though, that the agent who sells a particular contract to an applicant is an important, if not the most important, factor in the persistency of that contract. The first year or two are the most critical for the persistency of a policy. There is also evidence that a policy is more likely to remain in force if the agent who sold it remains under contract with the company. Among other factors associated with good persistency are annual or semiannual premium payments, insurance on persons with higher incomes, previous ownership of life insurance in the same company, insurance on professional men and women, and insurance on older persons. (According to LIAMA's *Markets in Life Insurance* (1966), income of the policyowner and mode of premium payment are the most important factors.)

The trained agent is more satisfactory to the insuring public. We all prefer to deal with people in whose ability we have confidence—whether physician, plumber, dentist or life insurance agent. The trained salesman can be of great service to prospects and clients by analyzing and prescribing for their life insurance needs. The entire life insurance business benefits from having well-trained salesmen. Its public relations improve, its prestige grows and its acceptance increases.

Training Versus Education

These terms are related but not synonymous. Education is the imparting of knowledge and information; it is background and understanding. Training is the acquisition of the know-how, the skill and the facility for using knowledge. Education produces knowledge but not necessarily action. Training produces action.

An agent will acquire considerable knowledge in the course of his training, but he is not expected to be a "walking encyclopedia" on every detail of life insurance; in fact, he probably should not be. It is hardly possible for a salesman to know too much about his product, but he should usually refrain from imparting all his knowledge to his prospects. The average car buyer is usually not too much interested in "what is under the hood." He may want to know the number of cylinders and the horsepower, whether the car has power brakes, power steering and air conditioning, but he rarely is interested in—and probably would not understand—just how these features are constructed and operate.

The situation in life insurance is similar. A prospect is interested in what a particular policy will accomplish for him and his dependents, what the important provisions are, what it costs, how long premiums are payable—and the agent should be trained to give him this information. Also, the salesman should have a general understanding as to how premium, cash value and dividend rates are determined. But he need not—and probably should not try to—overwhelm his prospect with details of "what is under the hood," such as the actuarial principles involved, development of a particular clause, etc. Excessive detail by the agent may obscure "the forest for the trees" for the prospect and may confuse rather than clarify.

WHAT TRAINING PROGRAMS INCLUDE

Many agencies will have men of various degrees of experience or seasoning: the newest recruits, the recent additions and men with two or more years of service. Training is a continuing process and experienced men need to review and keep up to date. At this time, however, we shall be concerned only with new agents. (Even if company A contracts an agent who has had experience with company B, the former will usually wish to put him through its regular program for new men in order to familiarize him with its own policies and practices.)

The term "training" takes in a lot of territory. Conceivably almost anything relating to the work of an agent could be considered as part of his training. To limit the discussion, we will treat what is included in a training program for *new* agents under three broad headings:

1. Basic knowledge of life insurance
   a. What it does for people
   b. Various policy plans and important provisions
2. The company's contracts and practices
   a. General information about the company
   b. Its portfolio of policies
   c. Its rules and regulations, including the ratebook
3. Sale of life insurance
   a. Prospecting
   b. Approach
   c. Sales presentation
   d. Answering objections
   e. Close
   f. Planning or personal work habits

Basic Knowledge of Life Insurance

An agent should be able to answer clearly and intelligently the usual questions prospects are apt to ask. He should know that permanent life insurance for the individual involves a savings plan that creates an immediate estate on payment of the first premium. He should have a fair idea of the level-premium system involving the reserves and nonforfeiture options. He should know the difference between ordinary, debit and group. He must understand the common needs of prospects for life insurance. Most literature stresses the family situation with husband, wife and children. Other people need protection also, but the bulk of personal life insurance is sold to husband-fathers. These needs are usually analyzed and prescribed for from the standpoint of cleanup fund, readjustment income, cost of educating children, mortgage redemption if applicable, emergency fund, savings and retirement income.

To prescribe intelligently for the above needs, the agent must know the various common policy plans of insurance and how they are adapted to these needs. He should also know and be able to explain the various provisions included in most contracts. As a minimum he should be able to explain: nonforfeiture options, policy loans—regular and automatic premium—grace period, modes of settlement, policy dividend if applicable, disability benefits and accidental death benefits. As soon as possible he should master *all* policy provisions.

Company Contracts and Practices

This heading embraces (a) background information about the agent's own company, (b) his company's portfolio of policies and (c) his company's "rules and regulations." Under (a) he should know something about his company's history, age, relative size, amount of insurance in force, extensiveness of operations (number of states or provinces operated in). Under (b) the agent should be thoroughly conversant with his own company's "products." Few companies issue *all* forms of policies; on the other hand, many companies offer one or more contracts, sometimes with a distinctive name, that they consider specialties; or they may emphasize pension business or credit insurance. If his company issues policies which it calls "Executive Protector" and "Lifeguard," the agent should know how they differ and the particular features of each.

All companies promulgate "rules and regulations" to achieve a maximum degree of uniformity in their field operations and sound underwriting. Sometimes these are contained in the ratebook, and sometimes in a separate manual. It will take time for an agent to master them. And even when he does, unusual situations will arise that may have to be submitted to higher authority for a decision. However, this part of the training of the new agent will usually cover *his* company's rules on such subjects as the following:

1. Minimum and maximum ages at which various coverages will be issued
2. Minimum amounts of insurance or premium, if any
3. Insurance on minors
4. Nonmedical insurance
5. Substandard insurance
6. Disability and accidental death benefits coverage
7. Differences for female lives, if any
8. Procedures for completion of applications and other forms, and delivery of policies
9. Settlement options

Training of the new man will include a certain amount of what has been called "office instruction": use of the ratebook, proper completion of application blanks and agents' report forms to the home office, building of prospect files and the like. The ratebook is the main or primary source of information concerning the company's field activities. It is a catalog telling the agent just what his company carries in stock—its inventory. It lists premium rates for all ages of issue for the company's various policy forms, together with tables of loan and surrender values. Premium rates usually are shown for annual, semiannual, quarterly and, sometimes, monthly payments. Any agent who aspires to give sound advice and competent service to policyowners must become proficient in the use of the ratebook.

Sale of Life Insurance

The information concerning basic knowledge of life insurance and company contracts and policies, important as it is, will sell few policies. It is closer to education than to training. Companies must train agents to approach the public and sell to them according to their needs.

A mechanical definition of selling is the solicitation of orders for merchandise or services. As applied to life insurance, such a definition would be seriously inadequate. More expressive definitions would be: "The art whereby one person presents the advantages of an offer in a way that appeals directly to, and tends to prompt action by, a second person." Or: "Inducing people to want what you have—products or ideas. Selling is a dual instrument of discovering and persuading—discovering human needs and wants, and persuading people to meet them with your products or service."

Training men for life insurance selling will be considered under these headings: (a) prospecting, (b) approach, (c) sales presentations, (d) answering objections, (e) close, (f) completing application, (g) planning or personal work habits.

PROSPECTING. This phase of selling involves finding purchasers for life insurance. Loosely used, a prospect is almost any insurable person that might have a need for and buy some protection. More specifically, the prospect is an individual about whom an agent knows the approximate age, income, marital status, number of children, occupation and resident status (tenant or homeowner); further and importantly, he is an individual that the agent can get to see under circumstances *conducive to a good interview.* A most favorable circumstance would be a personal introduction to a prospect by a mutual friend who is already a client of the agent. A card or letter of introduction would also be favorable.

It has been said that a *prospect* is someone an agent has not sold; a *policyowner,* someone he has sold at least one policy; a *client,* someone he has sold more than once and for whom he has arranged a program and who is willing to listen to his advice throughout life.

The main sources of prospects for *established* agents are: persons they have previously called on and who are likely to buy; clients, i.e., present policyowners they have sold; policyowners in their territory who are not their clients; friends.

The first two sources are not available to the *new* agent; he has neither called nor sold yet. As explained in the next paragraph, the third group, friends, may be a source of prospects. In fact, many companies require the new man to prepare a list of 50 or more names of persons whom he knows and considers prospects for life insurance. Friends may or may not buy. If they do, they usually are limited sources of direct sales, although they may refer him to other persons who are prospects. But if these do not materialize, where else are the new man's prospects coming from, at least until he has made a few sales? There are several sources.

1. One source is the agency itself. Each field office comes into possession of a certain number of "leads," i.e., names of persons who *may* be prospects for life insurance. Usual practice is to apportion these leads among the salesmen in that agency. New men will receive some of them. Also, each agency has a number of so-called orphan policyowners. These are persons who bought their protection through agents no longer with the company. Some of these names may be assigned to new agents.

2. Newspapers, conversations and personal observation can be sources of many rewarding leads. Through any or all of these three sources even a new agent may recognize life insurance needs occasioned by such events as:
    a. A birth
    b. A graduation
    c. An engagement
    d. A marriage
    e. A death
    f. An inheritance
    g. A promotion
    h. Arrival of a new family in the neighborhood
    i. Purchase of a home or other property
    j. Sale of a home or other property
    k. Various business transactions, including:
        1) New incorporations, partnerships and one-man enterprises

2) Enlargement of existing enterprises
3. Various lists or directories may also be valuable as sources of names of prospective purchasers of life insurance. To mention just a few:
   a. Membership lists of various business, social, fraternal and service clubs and other organizations
   b. Lists of patrons for charitable and other events
   c. City and telephone directories
   d. Occupational directories

Suppose we analyze briefly two examples and explain how each may be a valuable lead to a new agent (and also to an established agent). "A birth" (2a) may be as good as any. An addition to the family unit means another mouth to feed, another life dependent on the breadwinner. Should the husband and father die, the widow and mother will need a greater income to provide for readjustment until such time as she can become a breadwinner herself, assuming she is able. Here is an obvious need for protection, a need that can best be met by life insurance.

Patrons of various activities (3b) in a community usually are prominent and prosperous. If the agent can find a need, presumably they would be in a position to pay for the added insurance.

It will be seen that persons located through the sources just discussed measure up pretty well to the first part of the definition of prospect: "an individual about whom an agent knows the approximate age, income, marital status, number of children, occupation and resident status." They are less likely, however, to measure up to the second part: "an individual the agent can get to see under circumstances conducive to a good interview." In many cases the agent will not know the prospect or even anyone who does know him. Frequently, however, some mutual contact can be developed. Even without such a contact, many sales have resulted from just such impersonal leads.

There is also "cold canvass," which is usually the least efficient method of prospecting, if in fact, it should be called prospecting at all. The agent calls on a person, knowing little more about him than his name, perhaps not even that. There is nothing scientific about "cold canvass"; studies show that the ratio of interviews obtained to calls (a call is an attempt to obtain an interview) made is low, and that the ratio of sales to interviews is also low. Thus "cold canvass" is likely to be costly to the agent from the standpoint of time and therefore income. From the standpoint of the *new* agent, it is discouraging besides.

THE APPROACH. After the new agent has been trained in prospecting, he must be trained to approach his prospects, preferably under the most favorable circumstances, to obtain an interview so that he can present his case for life insurance.

People do not all react the same way to approaches, whether they are being asked to contribute to a worthy charity, or to accept an assignment in their church, club or community. Some appeals or approaches rub them the right way; others don't. Some people are more receptive in the morning, others in the afternoon, still others just after lunch or after dinner at home. Anybody trying to get somebody else to do something—even if that something is very worthwhile and if that something will benefit that somebody else—needs to consider carefully such traits of human nature.

The foregoing applies particularly to the sale of life insurance. It certainly is most worthwhile and necessary to the prospect and to his family. Few husbands and fewer widows have regretted the purchase of life insurance. Nevertheless it does involve present sacrifice for future benefits. Further, in the case of a new car, television set or house, the salesman can say in effect: "Enjoy now and pay later." The life insurance agent, on the contrary, not only has to try to sell something less tangible; he virtually has to tell his prospect: "Pay now and you (or your beneficiary) will enjoy later." There is little demand for life insurance for its own sake. Agents create demand by pointing out needs to prospects, showing them how life insurance can meet those needs, and motivating them to apply.

It is important for all agents, especially new men, to develop the most effective approach possible. Of course, the agent should be neatly dressed and be courteous and tactful in his conversation. He should also be poised, confident and friendly rather than diffident or apologetic. His opening remarks should be such that they will gain the prospect's favorable attention. He should master a number of well-planned openings to fit varying circumstances.

SALES PRESENTATION. In the presentation itself, the agent should strive to introduce the subject of life insurance at the proper moment, although that is something that will come with experience. He will use reason to convince his prospect that the needs uncovered are real and important and that they can best be met by life insurance. At the same time, he should recognize that most persons in a sales situation are influenced by emotions as well as by reason. What a prospect *thinks* is important; what he *feels* is sometimes more important. Hence the agent will compliment and praise judiciously and thereby capitalize on the basic human desire for "ego recognition." He will also recognize and appeal to such human traits as personal pride, love of family, the acquisitive instinct, the desire for personal security, the desire for peace of mind. In addition he will be a good listener, will try to avoid argument and will secure agreement on as many points as possible as the interview progresses.

ANSWERING OBJECTIONS. When we are asked to do something we think we do not want to do, we try to get out of doing it. The fact that what we are asked to do may be for our own good or for the good of our families usually makes little difference in our reaction. Our doctor may tell us that we are overweight and should go on a diet. What do we do? We rationalize that we really do not eat very much, or that overweight runs in our family, or that the extra pounds don't bother us.

The situation in life insurance selling is similar. Many people honestly do not recognize that they need protection or, if they are already insured for some small amount, that they should have more protection. Even when an agent calls the need to their attention, their first reaction is to think of some pretext for disagreeing with him. Nevertheless, the longer a man goes without life insurance, the more he needs it, the less chance he has of getting it, and the larger the annual outlay if he does get it. Hence, companies train their agents to meet the various common objections offered by prospects.

Frequently so-called objections to the purchase of life insurance are little more than evasions—the prospect just doesn't want to say yes. Sometimes the prospect sincerely believes that his objections are well grounded. But sincere or not, objections are advanced and the new agent should be trained to answer them convincingly. Let us again assume that our typical prospect is a man with a wife and one or more children. The agent may then expect the typical prospect to offer one or more of the following objections. The first nine apply to the prospect alone; the remainder concern his family as well.

1. I can't afford it.
2. I have all the insurance I want or need. (Objections 1 and 2 are most often stated by nonbuyers.)
3. I don't believe in it—you have to die to win.
4. I'm not ready to decide yet.
5. I can meet my needs better through investments—I have a friend who can give me good tips on the stock market.
6. I've heard a lot about mutual funds—I think they're a better bet for me and I can get life insurance that way too.
7. I have a friend who is an agent, and I'd buy from him.
8. Life insurance isn't such a good buy today with the declining purchasing power of the dollar.
9. Some other company's rates may be lower—I want to shop around first.
10. I want to talk it over with my wife.
11. My wife doesn't believe in it.
12. My wife had a good job before we were married; she

could go back to work and provide for herself and the children if necessary.

13. Why should I leave a lot of money for some other man to spend?

14. Parents do too much for their kids these days. Let mine make their own way—I had to.

The foregoing list includes most of the objections that an agent is likely to encounter. There are appropriate rebuttals to all of them, and the new agent should learn them as soon as he can.

A brief reference to objection 6 may be in order. Simply or perhaps oversimply stated, a mutual fund is an investment company. The money of the investors is pooled with that of other individuals who have invested in the fund. Managers of this fund invest these sums, for a fee, in a diversity of corporations for the benefit of the fund's participants. (Some life insurance companies have arrangements whereby their representatives sell shares in mutual funds as well as policies of life insurance. This will be considered in chapter 16.)

Occasionally, something new or at least something different in the way of objections will come up, something that conventional answers will not quite fit. Such atypical "curves" require skillful handling and are real tests of an agent's imagination, knowledge and resourcefulness.

THE CLOSE. Assume an agent has been trained in the fundamentals of life insurance, in prospecting, in approach and presentation, and in answering objections. He has visited a likely prospect whom he seems to have persuaded and whose objections, if any, he seems to have answered. Yet the sale may not materialize unless he has mastered the close, the final and necessary step in selling that will convert a man from prospect to policyowner, provided, of course, he is insurable.

For some, that part of the interview in which the agent gets the prospect to apply formally, to answer the questions in the application and "sign on the dotted line," is a kind of crisis. The situation has been likened to one in which most of us have found ourselves at one time or another—asking the boss for a raise. We may have determined a receptive time of the day or week and prepared our approach well, extolling what we consider our virtues and worth. The boss may have listened apparently sympathetically and the time has come to ask him for a raise, or has it? Yet we falter. We can't seem to "close" and ask the all-important question.

The effective agent will not wait for the prospect to express a desire to purchase before giving the final impetus. Rather, he plans to bring his prospect to the desired point and then appeal deeply enough to his fundamental interests to produce favorable action. When is this point, sometimes referred to as the psychological moment, or more simply as the right time? According to some, it occurs near the end of the interview, after the prospect has heard an effective and enthusiastic presentation and after his objections, if any, have been satisfactorily answered.

Others believe that the importance of the psychological moment has been exaggerated. They agree that some moments during the interview may be more favorable to a successful conclusion than others. However, they doubt there is only one such moment during the interview or that all is lost if the agent fails to recognize the psychological moment.

If the agent closes the sale, he will no doubt feel that he moved in at the psychological moment, irrespective of whether one or more earlier efforts during the interview failed. If the agent does not close, his technique and timing were not necessarily at fault. Even the most successful agents do not close 100 percent of their interviews.

COMPLETING THE APPLICATION. If the agent succeeds in closing, he then asks the various questions in the application, making sure the applicant understands each one, and records the answers accurately on the blank. An incomplete or incorrectly completed application causes extra work in the field office and in the home office and frequently delays issuance of the policy. The applicant may even lose interest in the insurance in the meantime and change his mind about buying it.

The agent should be well trained in the proper completion

of the application. He should know about such matters as secondary beneficiary designations, and reservation of the right to change the beneficiary. Does the applicant understand the disadvantages as well as the advantages of each of the available nonforfeiture provisions? Is the applicant eligible for waiver of premium and accidental death benefits?

The new agent's elation over making the sale may sometimes be such that he does not press for some of the elements that make for persistent business. Nevertheless, he should try to obtain payment of the first premium with the application and explain to the applicant the advantages of the conditional or binding receipt. The proportion of monthly premium business is increasing, but the agent may well first suggest annual, semiannual or even quarterly payments. Further, in many cases life insurance is more likely to accomplish the purpose for which it was purchased if the contract provides for payment of proceeds under an income settlement agreement rather than in a single sum.

PLANNING OR PERSONAL WORK HABITS. The daily work of most gainfully employed persons involves planning to some extent. In the case of many clerical and factory workers, their work is planned for them. In the case of the self-employed physician, lawyer and the life insurance agent, the planning is largely up to the individual.

The discussion of what to include in a sales training program for the new agent has now covered prospecting, approach, sales presentation, answering objections, the close, and completing the application. Since each day has only 24 hours, not all of which can be devoted to the job, every working hour should be well spent.

To perform his various duties properly, the agent must plan his days and his weeks. Planning is not easy. Since the agent is so much his own boss, it takes drive and determination to self-impose a strict schedule and *stick* to it.

Most outstanding agents are good planners. The new man should be trained to plan his work at the earliest possible moment and to make such planning a habit. Good habits adhered to pay off. "Every human being in this world has habits. They may as easily be good habits as bad, and a habit once established is the greatest and strongest of all motivating forces." Many life underwriters spend part of Saturday and Sunday planning the following week's work.

The agent's daily schedule should provide for a number of different activities in the performance of his duties:

1. Prospecting
2. Making contacts and selling calls (initial calls)
3. Preparation of cases for calls
4. Selling interviews (followup calls) and closes
5. Calls to deliver new policies
6. Policyowner service
7. Office detail
8. Planning and recordkeeping
9. Study related to his career
10. Self-development reading

The first seven activities have been called direct and are almost involuntary; the last three, indirect and entirely voluntary. Nos. 1 through 6 require no further mention. No. 7 refers to the various clerical or routine matters an agent must attend to in the course of his work, such as handling necessary correspondence and arranging appointments for interviews and for medical examinations.

With respect to the eighth activity, planning has already been discussed. Properly kept records can be very valuable to an agent. At the start, naturally, his policyowner and prospect file will be quite small; however, appropriate notations will show him when he last called on whom, what changes have occurred in a man's family or business situation, when his age will change for insurance purposes, etc. Records will show an agent how many people he is actually calling on daily and weekly, his ratio of interviews obtained to calls made and of sales to interviews, the amount of his average policy and his income. Records will also enable him or his manager to determine the age, occupational and income groups with whom he is most effective.

Life insurance is a big field, and the new agent cannot learn everything about it during his initial training period. Continued study related to his career is necessary. Even after he has become an experienced salesman, the agent should remember that his business is not static. He should read and study his own company's literature as well as one or more insurance periodicals. In addition he should keep abreast of developments that may be of interest and value to his prospects and clients.

It would be difficult, if not impossible, to demonstrate definite correlation between self-development reading and increased sales. However, every agent should try to allow some time for worthwhile recreational or educational reading outside of life insurance.

THREE KINDS OF SELLING

Training programs should be designed to build the skills men need in order to sell—and then let them sell. They should not create students of life insurance selling, nor should they feed new agents more than they can digest. To these ends, basic programs are frequently limited to "package" or single-need selling, as distinguished from programing or total-needs selling, and estate planning—these can come later, when the new agent has gotten a little seasoning. In practice these distinctions are sometimes less sharp than the three terms suggest. This breakdown may be helpful in explaining them, however.

Package Selling or Single-Need Selling

What is package or single-need selling?[2] First, it is not selling a prospect a policy for as large an amount as he can be

---

[2] Sometimes a distinction is made between package selling and single-need selling. In the former, an agent bases his sales appeal on the merit of a particular package or *policy;* with respect to single-needs, he stresses a particular *need* of the prospect.

persuaded to buy irrespective of his needs. Rather, it is selling on the basis of satisfying a single need. The agent shows the prospect the specific need that a particular policy will satisfy: establishment of a clean-up fund, of a savings fund, of an emergency fund, of an educational fund; provision for readjustment income, minimum income, retirement income, redemption of a mortgage; wife insurance, juvenile insurance. (Here, as in total-needs selling and estate planning, many agents today can draw upon their companies' computer facilities to obtain pertinent data on prospects quickly and accurately.)

Programing or Total-Needs Selling

This is the lumping of a prospect's various single life insurance needs. The agent, instead of recommending one particular policy for one specific need, uses an analytical process in which he undertakes first to determine the prospect's objectives for himself and his dependents. Then the agent figures out to what extent the prospect's present insurance will attain these objectives. Almost invariably, analysis shows that the prospect's objectives exceed his present means of attaining them. Hence the agent recommends additional life insurance to narrow the gap.

Package selling deals with a single need of a prospect; programing deals with his total needs. If only one need is administered to, we have a single-need package. If all a prospect's needs are investigated, analyzed and solved, the resulting sale makes a total-needs package. Programing gives the prospect a better understanding of what life insurance can do for him. Further, adequate programing facilitates the solution of his financial problems insofar as these can be solved by life insurance.

Opinions vary as to the relative emphasis desirable on single-need and total-needs selling in a training program, especially in a program for new salesmen. Those who favor major or exclusive stress on package selling maintain that: most people cannot afford to buy all the life insurance they need; few people buy all their protection at one time; many buyers just aren't in the market for amounts large enough to warrant programing; and programing consumes too much of the new agent's time. In their opinion every agent should develop an organized sales presentation for a single need, and the simpler it is the better.

Others feel that even a basic program for a new man should include some training in programing. They argue that: programing is merely the lumping of individual needs; anyone who can be trained for single-need selling can be trained just as easily for total-needs selling; the new agent will be able to produce a larger volume of business early in his career; therefore, since most prospects cannot afford to buy at one time all the additional protection they need on the basis of the program analysis, the door is open to the agent for repeat business, usually the most persistent kind. The effective agent will try to get it.

Estate Planning

Broadly, nearly all life insurance selling to individuals involves estate planning to some extent. More restrictedly, estate planning involves consideration of the possession, management and transfer of substantial assets in addition to life insurance, such as real estate and securities. Persons whose estates warrant such planning possess substantial assets.

In package selling the agent seeks a life insurance solution for a single need of his prospect. In estate planning the agent seeks a life insurance solution for problems involved in the ownership, management, and transfer of a prospect's property. Usually the purchase and proper allocation by beneficiary designation of additional life insurance will contribute significantly to the solution of such problems. Such analysis will consider the effects of the estate tax, gift tax, income tax, and the statutes and decisions relating to inheritance and insurance.

The increased rate of taxation during recent years has increased the frequency of situations in which the transfer of estate assets from other forms of property to life insurance can be urged as a means of conservation. Business insurance is a common and important aspect of estate planning.

In an estate of substantial size, several persons in addition to the life insurance salesman are likely to be involved: the testator himself, his attorney, his accountant and the bank's trust officer. (In at least one state, Oregon, a decision by the highest court has severely restricted participation by life insurance representatives and other nonlawyers in estate planning activities.)

Effective estate planning requires great skill and professional competence on the part of the life underwriter. It is life insurance selling at its technical best; it is a type of selling for the experts. Even for many competent agents, training in estate planning would hardly be warranted. Such a program would be disproportionately costly in time spent to potential benefits to be realized, because they would have few if any clients possessing the means and the property to warrant such a technical approach.

The Two-Interview Method

With the increasing emphasis on selling life insurance according to the needs of the prospect, the agent should know what a particular prospect's needs are before trying to prescribe for them. Many agents find that proper preparation enables them to close a substantial percentage of their cases on their first interview. One face-to-face meeting may suffice if the prospect obviously can provide for only one or two of his most vital needs, has little or no other insurance and very few other assets.

On the other hand, many successful agents use what is known as the two-interview method, which consists of a preliminary interview and a closing interview. Assume an agent has an appointment with a prospect. Even though he has gathered as much information as he can in advance, the first or preliminary interview is largely factfinding. The agent decides what his best approach will be, supplements and confirms information he has already obtained, and ascertains the prospect's needs. In particular, he will ascertain which need the prospect considers most important and list the others in descending order of importance. Then the agent sets a date for the second interview. He may not even try to close on his first visit, although he may try to get a commitment from the prospect as to how much he can spend on premiums for additional life insurance.

In the interval between the two interviews, the agent himself or someone in the agency office (frequently with the help of the computer) analyzes the prospect's situation in detail and prepares a plan to propose to him, as to amount of insurance, type of contract, premium and the like. If more than a single need is involved, the agent may prepare some form of visual presentation, such as a graph or diagram, to facilitate his explanation to the prospect.

During the second interview, the agent makes his presentation, answers any objections that may arise and then endeavors to close. Occasionally, one or more additional interviews may be necessary. However, it has been estimated that 85 percent of all life insurance sales are made on the first or second interview. The two-interview method is useful when the prospect already has considerable life insurance, is not one who decides quickly, has already had his insurance programed by another agent, may be chart- or figure-minded, may be able to provide for full *minimum* requirements himself, and may not be able to spare the time at the first interview for the calculations necessary for a logical recommendation. The two-interview method is suitable for package or single-need selling, and for programing or total-needs selling. Cases involving estate planning frequently necessitate more than two interviews.

Legal Aspects of Training

Important legal implications are involved in the business relationship between the life insurance salesman, the *agent,* and his company, the *principal.* Legally, the life insurance

salesman is the agent of the insurer rather than of the applicant or policyowner. Under the legal rules of agency, therefore, the principal is responsible for the acts of his agent acting
within the scope of his authority, and information known to
the agent is presumed to be known to the company, even if
the agent does not transmit it.

In his dealings with applicants, insureds and other persons,
the agent is trained to operate at all times within the limits of
his authority—as expressed in his agent's contract, the application form and the policy—and to communicate to his company any information that may affect the insurability of an
applicant. This responsibility is particularly significant in the
case of nonmedical insurance, where the agent is a vital factor
in the selection or rejection of the risk. The agent completing
and signing an application participates in an important legal
transaction. Some day circumstances may arise that will require him to testify in court to his participation.

In this chapter we have described new-agent training as
conducted in the agencies. Some companies train their new
men in their home offices. Overall content of basic programs is
about the same, whether conducted in the home office or in
the field.

SUMMARY

After men have been recruited and selected, they have to be
trained for a sales career. Some have greater aptitude for sales
than others. Nevertheless, many men can be trained to sell
successfully.

Experience has shown that the trained agent does a better
job for himself, his company and his clients. While many useful activities may be considered as part of training, most programs for new agents include (1) basic knowledge of life
insurance, (2) the company's contracts and practices, and
(3) sale of life insurance. The last of these involves prospecting, approach, presentation, answering objections, close, completing the application, planning or personal work habits.

Training programs may be classified as package or single-need selling, programing or total-needs, and estate planning. The last is the most advanced; it is life insurance selling at its technical best. Even many competent agents do not become involved in estate planning to any extent.

Many agents find that proper preparation on their part enables them to close a substantial percentage of their cases on their first interview. For other cases, usually those that are more complicated or are for larger amounts, the two-interview method may be advisable or even necessary. In essence, this method consists of a preliminary or factfinding interview and a closing interview.

QUESTIONS FOR REVIEW

1. Explain why results achieved by untrained or poorly trained agents are unsatisfactory to (a) themselves, (b) their agency and their company, (c) the insuring public and (d) the entire business.

2. Formulate a fully descriptive definition of quality business.

3. Present in outline form the material to be included in a training program for new agents. Discuss the significance of each heading.

4. What is a prospect, as the term is used in life insurance? List the major sources of prospects for (a) established agents and (b) new agents.

5. Discuss the importance of planning in the work of the agent. What regular activities should he provide for?

6. Define or explain three kinds of selling based on need, so that their differences are apparent.

10 | Training the Right Manpower: Agents (continued)

N_o training program, no matter how well conceived or developed, is really effective unless it gets across to those being trained. It must result in imparting the necessary knowledge, motivating proper attitude and building the needed skills. Training of agents is usually the responsibility of the manager, irrespective of whether he does the job himself or entrusts it to an assistant. (Occasionally, as stated in the preceding chapter, new men are brought into the home office for training.) Whoever does the training must possess the qualities of a good teacher of adults: He must know his subject, have patience and be able to inspire by making men *want* to do their best.

Getting the Program Across

How does the trainer seek to put his company's training program across to new men? Regardless of the specific method used to train new men, the so-called PESOS formula is involved. PESOS is a coined word taken from the first letters of prepare, explain, show, observe, and supervise. While these steps probably are self-explanatory, a brief enlargement may be in order:

1. Prepare—The trainer must prepare the trainee to learn by showing the new man *why* he should do a particular thing.
2. Explain—The trainer must explain carefully to the trainee each step of the process to be learned.
3. Show—In this step the trainer translates the words of explanation into an actual performance of how something can be accomplished.
4. Observe—In this step the trainee begins to practice the new technique under the observation of the trainer, who corrects each mistake as he notices it.
5. Supervise—Herein the trainee continues the step until he has learned the new technique perfectly.

Most agents' training programs incorporate, directly or indirectly, these five steps. Various designations have been devised to identify training methods. Among them are:

1. *Role Playing*—A weakness of much sales training is that it is largely the passive acquisition of knowledge. Role playing strives to bridge the gap between theory and practice. As the term implies, role playing is a dramatization of the action that the trainee will need to perform in an actual selling situation. Both the trainer and the trainee participate in the office in a lifelike training session under simulated "combat conditions" (no prospect is present). By setting up a situation and using careful guidance and adroit questioning, the trainer seeks to help the trainee solve a selling problem that he cannot seem to solve alone. Frequently trainer and trainee reverse roles, the trainer taking the part of the new agent and the trainee taking the part of the prospect. There are variations of this method. If several men are being trained at the same time, the remainder of the group may or may not participate actively

in a role-playing session, depending upon the judgment of the trainer.

2. *Coaching on the Job*—This term may be less self-explanatory than it sounds. Coaching on the job involves two phases: demonstration and observation. In each phase the trainer and the trainee call on actual prospects together. In demonstration the trainer exemplifies the techniques that the trainee has learned and presumably mastered. The role of the trainee is that of observer.

In the second or observation phase it is the trainee who makes the sales presentation to prospects, and the trainer observes him in action. The trainer then reviews each such call with the trainee, pointing out the latter's strengths and weaknesses. This method gives the trainer an opportunity to determine whether the new man (or even an experienced man) is actually using the techniques he has been taught. *Ideally,* the trainer accompanies the new man *solely* as an observer to see what and how he is doing in his selling interviews, which are then followed by discussion and critique of what was said and done. *In practice,* the trainer sometimes pitches in to help make the sale when the new man is having rough going in his interviews.

3. *Joint Work*—Correctly performed, coaching on the job offers the manager a great opportunity to help his agent become a more effective man in the field. Incorrectly performed, however, coaching on the job may make a "leaner" out of a new man. He may come to expect someone else to do his selling for him. To minimize this danger, some trainers use joint work. In this arrangement the trainer is more than an observer. He actually works with the trainee in making sales calls and both participate in the interviews. If the trainer is someone other than the manager himself, commissions on sales resulting from joint work are sometimes divided between the trainer and trainee. In that event the trainee is actually paying for assistance, and the trainer works *with* rather than *for* the new man. Occasions for joint work may arise when the agent is in a slump or when he is unable to handle a particular prospect.

Duration of Basic Training

Periods vary in length from less than a week up to two months or even more. The period should be flexible, since some trainees learn more rapidly than others. Hence they may be ready for solo field work sooner. Most basic training programs aim to get new men into production on a limited basis as soon as they appear equipped to try *some* cases, sometimes in the first few days. Because of high financing levels, the "earn while you learn" idea is virtually a requisite of training. Additional training is always necessary and can follow or accompany such preliminary sales efforts. Many authorities believe that additional, more intensive training is more effective *after* the new agents have had a taste of selling.

Scope of a Basic Training Program

Companies vary greatly as to size, type of agency organization, territory of operation, concentration of population of territory—urban, suburban or rural—portfolio of coverages and attitude toward duration of training. So it is hardly surprising that individual companies' training programs differ as to content, order and emphasis of subject matter and duration. They aim to prepare men to perform the agents' duties, outlined in chapter 8. Various other factors may modify the content of a basic training program. One would be the existence of a program for precontract orientation. Another would be the requirement in some states that a new agent must take his examination for a license promptly after being contracted.

Purely to give some idea of content, a composite of a 10-day basic program follows:

First day
1. Statement of purposes of the training program
2. The institution of life insurance
3. "Our" company
4. Economic problems of life—typical situations or needs

    5. Problems of learning

Second day

Fundamentals of life insurance:

    1. What it is and does

    2. Elements in premium calculations

        a. Mortality

        b. Interest

        c. Loading, i.e., provision for expense

    3. Reserves, cash values, comparison of participating and nonparticipating insurance, nature and uses of policy dividends

    4. Basic forms of policies—whole life: ordinary, limited-payment, endowment, term

Third day

    1. Analysis of whole life contract (clause by clause)

    2. Observation by trainee of trainer's actual sales interviews with prospects

Fourth day

    1. Supplementary features of life insurance

        a. Disability benefits

        b. Accidental death benefits

    2. Other common plans

        a. Family income

        b. Family policy

        c. Various riders

    3. Settlement of proceeds

Fifth day

    1. Qualifications of a salesman

    2. How to start selling: prospecting, approach, sales presentation, anwering objections, close, planning and personal work habits

    3. Kinds or methods of selling—package or single-need

    4. Observation by trainee of trainer's actual sales interviews with prospects

Sixth day

    1. Ratebook

    2. Completing the application

3. "Our" underwriting rules and other rules
Seventh day
  1. Service to policyowners
  2. State or provincial insurance laws
     a. Licensing
     b. Rebating
     c. Twisting
  3. Supervised trial interviews with prospects
Eighth day
  1. Group and debit insurance[1]
  2. Health insurance
  3. Supervised trial interviews with prospects
Ninth day
  1. Introduction to business insurance
  2. Government insurance
  3. Kinds or methods of selling—programing, estate planning
  4. Supervised trial interviews
Tenth day
  1. Written test on material covered

Programed Learning

Preparing a new man properly for a life insurance selling career takes considerable time. The trainee is available full time for training, but the trainer, especially if he is the manager, has many other duties. As a result it is sometimes difficult for him to give the new man all the time necessary for *sales* training. In an effort to free more of the manager's time for this essential sales training, some companies have turned to programed learning or self-instruction for the mastery of a substantial part of the fundamentals of life insurance included in most agents' training programs.

Programed learning texts in general may be described as follows:

---

[1] Such treatment would be brief for the many companies that do not sell debit.

1. They are self-instructional; much of the learning is accomplished without the assistance of an instructor.
2. They are individual and self-pacing.
3. Every student learns the same material.
4. They present the content in a carefully planned, organized series of "steps" or "frames," which leads the learner through material in a logical sequence.
5. Each frame is pretested.
6. They inform the learner immediately of the correctness or the falseness of his answer.

Thus, programed learning summarizes the essential facts, eliminates the wrong answers, rewards the right answer immediately, standardizes the content so that the latter never varies and so that the student always gets the same facts in the same way. In the field of life insurance, special texts have been prepared to enable the agent trainee to learn by himself much that would otherwise require time of the trainer as well. Some companies use tapes to convey information such as how to understand and use the rate book.

Self-instruction techniques are useful for the presentation of facts in the training process. They are not complete in themselves, however. Most trainees also need the help of a trainer to actually learn how to sell successfully.

Advanced Training

Training is a never-ending process. There is always more to learn, and there are always better ways of doing things. After the new man has acquired some experience and some proficiency, he may be ready for further training, sometimes divided into intermediate and advanced training. For our purposes we shall consider all training beyond the basic as *advanced*. As already indicated, such training would include programing and estate planning. If these are included at all in a basic program, the treatment is light—first things first. Closely related to estate planning is business insurance, which may be defined as that form of life insurance designed primarily to protect a man's business rather than to benefit his family directly. Actually, such insurance does benefit the family in many instances, because equities in most businesses are passed on to the owner's heirs at death. By means of programing, estate planning and business insurance, the qualified agent will find many opportunities to render useful service to clients and to increase his own income.

Advanced training is provided in many ways. Some larger companies have carefully-developed programs of their own for those agents who they believe would benefit. More often, companies will go outside their own organization for advanced programs. Some of these facilities will now be described.

OTHER-THAN-COMPANY TRAINING PROGRAMS

American College of Life Underwriters

This organization was chartered in 1927 and confers the designation of CLU (Chartered Life Underwriter) upon those men and women who have attained certain standards of education and of proficiency in life underwriting.

As recently revised, the CLU diploma program consists of the following 10 courses, which are intended to provide educational background for the life insurance agent:

Course 1—Individual Life and Health Insurance
Course 2—Life Insurance Law and Company Operations
Course 3—Group Insurance and Social Insurance
Course 4—Pension Planning
Course 5—Income, Estate and Gift Taxation
Course 6—Investments and Family Financial Management
Course 7—Accounting and Finance
Course 8—Economics
Course 9—Business Insurance
Course 10—Estate Planning

The nature of a candidate's life insurance experience determines whether he will qualify for the CLU award on passing these 10 examinations, and upon satisfying certain other requirements.

CLU's are eligible for membership in the American Society of Chartered Life Underwriters, which has local chapters in more than 180 cities in the United States. The principal aims of this organization are to provide further education on a graduate level, favorable publicity and professional service for its members.

The American College also sponsors two other educational programs: The Certificate Course Program designed for those persons who are interested in specialized areas of study such as agency management, company management, estate planning, group insurance, pension planning, personal investments, health insurance and other courses to be developed; and the Continuing Education Program, jointly sponsored with the American Society of Chartered Life Underwriters, designed to further the professional education of Chartered Life Underwriters.

The Life Underwriter Training Council

Many companies provide only basic training for their agents. LUTC was established in 1947 to provide intermediate sales training to fit between individual companies' courses and the United States CLU program.

LUTC offers practical on-the-job training in the sale of life and health insurance. Classes, sponsored by local chapters of the National Association of Life Underwriters and moderated by successful life insurance men, are open to all life insurance representatives who meet the Council's enrollment requirements. The basic plan of instruction is the discussion-conference method under the guidance and leadership of the moderator. The program emphasizes the development of sales skills and the use of knowledge as contrasted with the acquisition of information alone.

The chief eligibility requirement for the First-Year Life

course and for the Health course is completion of at least one year's experience in life insurance selling or having sold a specified minimum of annualized[2] ordinary life premiums and a specified minimum number of cases sold. For Second-Year Life, the enrollment requirement is completion of First-Year Life or an alternate requirement based on annualized ordinary premiums and a minimum number of cases sold.

Another LUTC training activity is its action orientation program featuring a series of Action Projects. These are sales missions which require the agent-student to apply in the field material he has learned in class.

The life course, a two-year program, currently consists of 26 weekly sessions for each year. The health course consists of 12 weekly classes. First-Year Life concentrates on the sale of life insurance for personal needs including programing. Second-Year Life covers the sale of life insurance for business purposes including the businessman's problems of estate creation, conservation and distribution. The health course concentrates on the sale of disability income coverage and is designed for the career life man who also sells health insurance.

Life Underwriters Association of Canada

This organization of Canadian life insurance salesmen was established in 1906. In 1924 the LUAC received the right to conduct examinations and to grant qualified candidates the right to use the title of "Chartered Life Underwriter of Canada." Thus the letters "CLU" in Canada usually identify someone who has completed the Canadian life underwriting course administered by the Institute of Chartered Life Underwriters of Canada.

At present the Canadian CLU program consists of three parts with examinations in subjects as follows:

Part 1—Economics, business English, fundamentals of life insurance, life insurance law

---

[2] Annualized premiums are defined as the total first-year premiums that would be paid if all policies remained in force for the entire first policy year.

Part 2—Accounting, commercial law, group coverages, taxation

Part 3—Corporation finance, psychology, advanced life underwriting, case studies and ethics

It will be seen that the curriculum content is quite similar to that of the CLU program sponsored by the American College of Life Underwriters. The two organizations are completely separate entities, however.

In 1956 the Life Underwriters Association of Canada established the Life Underwriters Association Training Course. This program is designed to give the life insurance agent who has completed his company's first-year training course additional training in sales procedures and techniques. The LUATC was patterned after that of the LUTC in the United States. Like the United States CLU organization, the LUAC has a number of local chapters throughout Canada. In the area of continuing education, LUAC sponsors regional CLU seminars.

Life Insurance Agency Management Association

This is a cooperative organization of legal reserve life insurance companies; membership is by company rather than by individual. Its activities include research in all aspects of agency management, issuance of research reports and management aid publications, and acting as a clearinghouse for information on sales, which includes regular reports on totals of new business paid for and manpower data.

In the field of training, the LIAMA holds regional in-residence schools in agency management in the United States, Canada and elsewhere for managers (not soliciting agents), supervisors and home office agency personnel of ordinary and combination companies. One school, the Management Orientation School, is of one week's duration and is designed for the brand-new man in agency management. LIAMA also conducts an advanced school for experienced field management and a school particularly for the home office staff that works with that management. These schools are of two weeks' duration.

Campus Training Schools

At present there are two university-sponsored vocational schools or institutes in insurance marketing. One was established at Purdue University in 1945; the other, established a few years later, is at Louisiana State University.

The general plan of operation is the same in the two schools. Each offers a one-year course consisting of collegiate-type classes in life underwriting for resident, on-campus students, combined with actual fieldwork. Only agents under contract to a legal reserve life insurance company are eligible. The course includes two or three periods of classroom work on the campus of four weeks' duration each, alternating with longer periods of supervised fieldwork in the particular student salesman's own agency. Weekly reports on this fieldwork must be submitted to the school.

The courses of both institutes are composed of a basic part and an advanced part. Business insurance, taxes and advanced programing are among the subjects included in the advanced part. Those completing these one-year courses receive a certificate in insurance marketing.

National Association of Life Underwriters

The NALU, established in 1890, is an organization of life insurance managers and salesmen, with local chapters throughout the United States. Membership is by individual, not by company. The NALU offers no agents' training directly. It is mentioned here because it had a part in the establishment of two organizations that do offer such courses: The American College of Life Underwriters and the Life Underwriter Training Council.

Other Training Programs

Not all training courses are sponsored by companies or institutions. A number of commercial firms offer both basic and advanced textbooks in life insurance selling. Some companies use the facilities of these publishers in lieu of developing their own training material. Others integrate these privately sponsored courses with their own training programs. These courses are more in the nature of education than training and are sometimes administered on a correspondence basis.

SUMMARY

Training of agents is primarily the responsibility of the manager, whether he does the job himself or entrusts it to an assistant. Whoever does the training must be able to teach adults.

Most training programs involve the so-called PESOS formula: prepare, explain, show, observe, supervise. Among the specific training methods used are role playing, coaching on the job and joint work.

Basic training of new agents may last from less than a week to two months or more. Even most longer programs aim to get new men into production on a limited basis within the first few days. Content varies. Among the subjects commonly included are: some history of "our" company and its policy line; fundamentals of life insurance; analysis of major policy provisions; use of ratebook and other sales materials; service to policy-owners; and pertinent insurance laws.

Advanced training comes later. Sometimes companies provide it themselves. More often they use the training facilities of other-than-company organizations. These include the American College of Life Underwriters, Life Underwriter Training Council, Life Underwriters Association of Canada, Life Insurance Agency Management Association, campus training schools and commercial firms.

QUESTIONS FOR REVIEW

1. What is the so-called PESOS formula? Name and describe three common training methods that incorporate this formula.
2. List the subjects or activities commonly included in a basic training program for life insurance agents.
3. Describe programed learning. State briefly its potential significance in agents' training. Does your company use programed learning (a) in the home office, (b) in the field?
4. Name five of the organizations that sponsor training programs for agents of life insurance companies. Describe each program briefly.
5. Compare briefly the contents of the two programs leading to the CLU award in the United States and in Canada.

11 | *Supervision and Motivation[1] of Agents by the Manager*

W̶hen a man has been recruited and trained to be a full-time agent, both he and his manager expect that he will succeed—otherwise it would have been a waste of time and money to place him under contract, finance him and put him through a training program of the type that has been described. Nevertheless, the new man should not be neglected just because he has completed his training. Not even the best program can assure automatic followthrough by the trainee. Supervision is necessary.

Supervision by the agency manager[2] has been defined as the process of observing, evaluating and guiding an agent in the performance of his duties, including those activities designed to assist the agent in putting into practice the knowl-

---

[1] Sometimes the term "continuous training" is used to include both supervision and motivation.

[2] In larger agencies the manager may delegate such supervision to an assistant manager or to an agency supervisor.

edge and skills acquired in training. The manager analyzes the agent's knowledge of the job, his attitude toward it, his skill in performing it and the work habits[3] he has formulated— and seeks to bring about improvements in these areas. Supervision is less concerned with imparting new information to an agent than with ascertaining whether and how he is using the training already given him. The only ideas that will work for an agent are the ones he puts to work.

Sometimes supervision and motivation are considered to be a single activity of the manager. We will reserve motivation by the manager to mean inspiring the agent to want to do his best, that is, to realize his full potentiality.

Necessity for Supervision

Supervision by the manager (or by an assistant) may seem unnecessary. The new man has been trained. Presumably the trainer was competent. If for no other reason than that he is a mature individual who wants to earn a living for himself and his family, the new man should want to succeed. He knows that earnings will be in proportion to the success of his efforts, so his efforts should be good. What more does he need? And what more should or can his manager do? If the new man just gets out and sees enough people, won't he succeed?

Effort alone does not assure success in life insurance selling —the effort must be properly directed. Success depends as much on the *quality* as on the *amount* of activity. Usually one agent is more successful than his colleagues because he works more efficiently, rather than because he works harder, than they do.

Probably no practice ever makes perfect; in the case of life insurance selling, practice—unless it is the right kind—may not even make better. Some agents soon reach a modest plateau of accomplishment above which they rarely rise but from which they sometimes fall. Contrary to popular belief many

---

[3] Usually referred to as the KASH formula: knowledge, attitude, skill, habits.

agents do not improve with experience. In study after study, failing agents list lack of supervision as one of the main causes of their difficulties.

METHODS OF SUPERVISION

Like recruiting, supervision is an active, not a passive, process. Experience shows that "supervision left to chance too often is supervision left undone." To be effective, supervision must evaluate the agent's performance under actual field conditions. To prescribe intelligently from his supervision, the manager must have facts. How can the manager obtain them?

In general, there are three methods: personal observation, personal interview, and recordkeeping.

Personal Observation

The best way for a manager to find out what his agent is doing is to watch him do it. Under this method the manager does much of what he did when training the new agent. By means of role playing (page 167) with the agent, the manager can prepare the way for going into the field together for as long as a full day, if possible. He works with the agent, observes him in action, but should remain silent during the actual sales interview with a prospect. He should not take over to make the sale if the agent stumbles. A critique is held as soon after each joint call as possible.

Unquestionably this method would be the best one to evaluate the agent's performance under actual field conditions and thereby ascertain both his strengths and weaknesses. It is of course possible that the agent may pay more attention to what he has been taught if the manager is with him than if he is working alone.

However, this method usually is not practical for either agent or manager. Carried on extensively, personal observation becomes joint work, and joint work may provide for the sharing of commissions with the man who works with the agent. Further, the manager just hasn't that much time for any one agent. He has many other things to do; among them is finding time for other agents who are similarly situated and who also are entitled to supervisory assistance.

Personal Interview or Conference

Also known as the "post mortem" or "playback," this method is a substitute for personal observation. The manager does not accompany the agent into the field. By skillful questioning, he endeavors to find out what happened in a given sales interview as soon as the agent returns to the office. This method has obvious limitations. It consumes a lot of time if the manager wishes to develop the full picture. Even then, the manager may be unduly influenced by what he assumes the agent has acquired in the way of knowledge and skills. And, of course, the agent may still convey a picture reflecting more what he wishes had taken place rather than what actually did.

Recordkeeping

In view of the limitations of personal observation and personal interview as methods of supervision of agents, the most feasible method is recordkeeping. In this method the manager evaluates his agents' performance by examining their own reports of the work they have done, supplemented by some personal observation and followed by a personal conference. Recordkeeping by the agents constitutes the most practical method of providing the manager with the constant flow of facts on which to base his continuous supervisory activity. Assuming the manager knows how to use records as diagnostic instruments, advantages attributed to this method include the following:

1. The manager can save a great deal of time. Instead of spending a good many hours in the field with, or across the desk from, each agent under supervision, he need

spend only a few minutes daily or weekly evaluating performance data furnished by each such agent.

2. Records provide a valuable picture of an agent's ability. Even personal observation may be subjective to some extent. Also, records are available for periodic review.
3. The need to furnish records forces the agent to maintain them. Since a good set of records includes outlines of plans as well as of results, he must plan the use of his time.

To the extent that records are a substitute for actual work by the manager with an agent, they do have certain disadvantages:

1. Records alone, no matter how well kept, do not tell all that personal work with an agent in the field can convey. Without *some* personal observation, how can the manager know just how an agent handles himself when interviewing a prospect?
2. Many agents dislike keeping records. It is to be hoped that an agent's aversion will disappear or at least diminish when he recognizes that the use of records can improve his own performance.
3. There is at least a possibility that some agents will exaggerate reports of their activities. Naturally, any evaluation by the manager of performance based on such records is of little value.

For maximum effectiveness the manager needs some kind of checklist to guide him in evaluating the work of an agent. Some managers use a questionnaire. Among the questions commonly included are the following:

1. What was the agent's production last year?
2. What is his estimated production this year? Has he met the quotas called for by his own goals set at the beginning of the current year? If not, why not?

3. Is he getting enough business from present policy-owners (repeat business)? Can he get more?
4. Does he keep a plan book or similar record? If so, what does it show as to the policy plans of insurance he is writing? Has he written business in any of the new markets he may have planned? Can he upgrade his present market?
5. How effectively is he applying his training as to prospecting, approach, sales presentation, answering objections and closing?
6. What is his attitude toward life insurance in general and toward his job in particular?
7. How many applications is he submitting monthly? On how many lives? For how much insurance? For what average face amount? For what average premium per sale? How often does he obtain cash with the application?
8. How much business is declined by the home office? How much business is "not taken out"?
9. How well does his business persist? How does his lapse record compare to those of other men in the agency? In the company as a whole?
10. What is his ratio of interviews to calls? Of sales to interviews? Is he improving in these areas?
11. Has he any personal problems that the manager may be able to help solve?

Another form of checklist is a performance analysis sheet. Basically such a sheet will provide for examination of the following areas:

1. Personal effectiveness
   a. Ambition
   b. Getting along with people
   c. Self-confidence
   d. Enthusiasm for job
   e. Managing personal affairs

2. Work habits
   a. Daily planning
   b. Full day's work
   c. Keeping records
   d. Analysis of results
3. Prospecting
   a. Continuous prospecting
   b. Getting results
   c. Getting information
   d. Getting introductions
   e. Eliminating "suspects" (names of persons whom the agent has called on but who are not likely to apply for insurance)
4. Skill in selling
   a. Approach
   b. Sales presentation
   c. Answering objections
   d. Close
   e. Delivering the policy
5. Quality or persistent business
   a. Cash with application
   b. Use of settlement agreements
   c. Average amount of policy or premium
   d. Collection frequency
   e. Grade of prospect

On the basis of his own records the agent may be asked to rate himself under each subheading above according to one of five broad categories: high, above average, average, below average, low. The manager, on the basis of the same records and such other information as may be available (e.g., personal observation), also rates the agent. With these data as a foundation, the manager can better evaluate the agent's present performance and find his strong and weak points. Proper analysis is essential; not all agents have the same difficulties, nor do they all succeed or fail for the same reasons. Then the manager can confer with his agent—to retrain him when or where necessary; to get him to build his strengths further and overcome his weaknesses; and to help the agent do things better for both his clients and himself.

Records Kept by Agents

If the agent is to keep records useful to himself and to his manager, they need to be in convenient form. Companies furnish various forms to their agents. Among the kinds of records in use are the following:

Daily Workbook or Worksheet

This is a common type of record. In general, it provides for such information as:

1. Cases the agent expects to close during the period (often a week), showing the name and the amount of each
2. Referred and other qualified leads, showing for each the name and address, age or date of birth, approximate income, occupation, family setup and best time for interview
3. Day-to-day activities, listing the people to be seen together with their ages or dates of birth. For each person seen, the agent indicates whether it was a call or an actual interview; if the latter, whether a preliminary or closing interview. If a sale resulted, the agent will show whether he obtained payment of the first premium with the application. Frequently there are spaces to enter hours spent in the field, in the office and in life insurance study.

From a careful review of an accurately kept book or sheet, the manager can get some idea of how and what his man is doing. Not every item is equally significant, and solutions to questions may not always be apparent. But such records will tell the manager where to look. For example, it is an unfavorable sign if the agent plans to see only three or four people each day—that's probably not enough. Maybe the agent has run out of prospects, maybe he is becoming discouraged, or maybe he isn't putting full time on his job as a life insurance salesman.

Plan Book or Chart

Another useful supervisory record to be kept by the agent is the plan book or chart. Frequently agents are urged, if not actually required, to outline their sales objectives for the entire year, month by month. First the agent estimates how many dollars he will need to earn to meet his living expenses. Unlike a man on a salary, the life insurance salesman does not know just how much he is going to earn during a given month or year. Presumably he will want to aim higher than the minimum he needs in order to allow for savings, recreation and emergencies. Once he knows how much he needs to earn, the agent can estimate how many calls and interviews he must obtain and how much business he must produce to achieve his objectives in terms of income dollars. Obviously, the market in which he solicits will affect the volume of business he needs to produce. $15,000 of 20-payment life will yield a much bigger commission than $15,000 of term because of the higher premium for the 20-pay policy. And $15,000 sold to a prospect aged 40 or more will mean a larger premium and larger commission than the same amount on the same plan sold to a prospect aged 25. (It may be noted that these examples point to the desirability of keeping records in terms of premium dollars rather than of face amounts of policies.) Analysis of his past records will be a useful guide to an agent in projecting his future earnings and may make him more receptive to the manager's supervisory efforts to show him how and why he can do better.

Sales Method Index

Another of the supervisory tools in use is the Sales Method Index, introduced by LIAMA in 1948 and revised frequently since. Its purpose is to identify specific strengths and weaknesses in an agent's work habits. Properly used, the SMI enables the manager and the agent to analyze the latter's sales methods—his activity, his prospecting, his market, his presentation. Each day the agent answers a group of questions in the SMI (currently 42) about each sale he attempted that day, whether he was successful or not. "Successful" life insurance sales attempts include only those in which a signed application was obtained and forwarded to the home office. "Unsuccessful" sales attempts include those in which the agent submitted a specific proposal and tried to close but no application was signed and he did not obtain a confirmed appointment to see the prospect again within 30 days. (Sales attempts involving group, weekly premium and salary savings insurance, and pension and annuity business are excluded from the tabulation in the SMI.)

The agent continues this procedure until he has recorded 30 sales attempts in the SMI. His answers are then summarized. Such a summary will help show where the agent is getting his prospects, the types of prospects with whom he is succeeding, the effectiveness of his presentation and whether he is fitting the types and amounts of policies to his prospects' needs.

The Sales Method Index can be used in at least two ways. First, continuous completion of the SMI makes possible a comparison of the agent's present and past activity and results. Daily recording by the agent of facts concerning each sales attempt facilitates supervision. Second, the manager can use the SMI to obtain either a cross section of the prospecting and selling habits of a group of agents or a single sample of one agent's recent selling activity.

The SMI is a supplement to and not a substitute for other supervisory records and activities. Used in conjunction with them, the SMI furnishes the manager valuable facts to give his agents a critical appraisal of how they use the training they have already received and to guide their future training into the most profitable channels.

LIAMA has also developed a health insurance edition of the SMI.

Developing a Program of Improvement

Recognition of a problem is important; doing something about it is even more so. Regardless of what method of supervision he uses, the effective manager will try to come up with specific recommendations. He will try to develop a program of improvement for each agent whom he supervises in order to enable the latter to overcome his weaknesses and capitalize on his strengths.

Assume, for example, that a manager recognizes that a particular agent's prospecting technique is weak and that the reasons for this weakness lie in two or more of the following areas:

1. He does not obtain referred leads when he delivers a policy.
2. He does not use referred leads when he gets them.
3. He has few centers of influence.
4. He does not qualify or evaluate prospects before he sees them.
5. He is unable to recognize "suspects."
6. He calls on too many old friends.

Such specific prospecting weaknesses call for specific recommendations for improvement. General slogans like "see more prospects" accomplish little by themselves. If possible, the manager should tactfully obtain the agent's agreement as to what his weaknesses (and strengths) are. The manager may recommend particular literature on the subject of prospecting. He may also ask the agent to discuss prospecting with one or more of his colleagues who are skilled in this area. Further, the manager should assure himself that the agent follows through and uses the new knowledge acquired.

Detailed treatment of the development of an improvement program is beyond the scope of this text. However, the procedure suggested for improving prospecting should be repeated for other areas of the agent's activity, such as his market and his presentation. A complete and specific list of weaknesses and strengths should cover all phases of the agent's job. Since no two salesmen in an agency are likely to have exactly the same weaknesses and strengths, the programs of improvement that the manager develops are likely to vary considerably.

.   .   .   .

Much of the discussion of supervision has emphasized new agents, primarily because we have been dealing with the development of new men through recruiting and training. Established agents also need supervision. They may get into a rut and need to be brought out of it—better yet, the manager should try to keep them from losing momentum. Established agents who are doing at least a fair job can easily get the feeling that they have been forgotten, although they usually contribute most to the success of an agency. They may well think that the new men are getting all the attention. Proper supervision will minimize this danger.

The manager should be on the alert for evidence among his established men of declining enthusiasm for their work, ineffective selling skills, need to develop new markets, and decreased physical and mental vitality. The wise agency head will be available to the "old hands" when they need help. Because of the heavy turnover among new men, those who remain under contract after several years may be more valuable to him and to the company.

Motivation

Supervision and motivation are closely related. Briefly, supervision is making sure, in a constructive way, that the agent is doing what he has been trained to do. Motivation goes farther. It is creating an atmosphere in which every agent will want to do his best work. It is making an agent want to succeed in reasonable proportion to his capacity.

None of us can work at our maximum efficiency constantly, no matter how energetic we are. This is true of life underwriters. Call it motivation, inspiration, stimulation, morale-building—agents need it to do their best. Motivation is the term most commonly used in agency operations.

Earlier there was a reference to the KASH formula—an agent must have *knowledge* of the job, the right *attitude,* a sharp set of *skills* and good work *habits* to do his job effectively. Motivation directly affects only attitude. It is not a developer of knowledge, skill or habits.

Necessity for Motivation

As in the case of supervision, motivation might seem unnecessary. The agent knows what he must do to succeed. He knows what he has to do to increase his effectiveness as a salesman and counselor and thereby increase his earnings—he will have to study, drill and drive himself. But very few agents *will* do all this entirely of their own accord. They won't want to enough unless somebody "inspires" them.

In many occupations a brief slump may hardly be noticeable—and perhaps is not especially serious. In the field of selling a service like life insurance, such a slump is dangerous. Unless it is checked, the enthusiasm essential to successful selling may give way to an attitude of indifference or discouragement. When that happens, it may be difficult to rekindle the spark. And if an agent can no longer get excited about his business and his work, he probably no longer belongs in it. But motivation is not mere peptalking or trying to keep men in an emotional dither. Agents soon build up an immunity to that kind of motivation. The manager must try to find and release the spring that will create in each of his men the urge to realize his capacities.

That spring will not be the same for all men. In the case of a new man, presumably training and supervision will keep him on his toes for a while. After a time, though, he too will need motivation. And the established agent needs to feel that he continues to be a vital part of his agency. If he is neglected or thinks he is—as when new men are receiving primary attention—he may become discouraged and lose enthusiasm for the business, reduced efforts may decrease his effectiveness, and his production may decline. At worst, the agency may have a failure in a man who might have been a success. At best, it will have a medium-production career man who will never realize his potential.

Motivation is predicated on the existence of good morale among an agency's salesmen. The former will not be effective without the latter. Some agencies have good morale and are well motivated; others have poor morale and are not well motivated. Either way the situation is attributable in large measure to the leadership qualities of the manager. He should be both able and willing to work for good agency morale. Agents may think that their manager is able but not so willing. The manager may *think* he is willing, but his men may not agree.

As already stated, agents look to their managers for leadership. According to a LIAMA study, agents look to their managers for the following qualities in somewhat the following order:

1. Interest in agent's welfare
2. Approachability
3. Knowledge of life insurance
4. Sincerity
5. Helpfulness
6. Fairness
7. Friendliness
8. Cooperativeness
9. Sympathy
10. Enthusiasm
11. Generosity
12. Skill in selling

Only two of these qualities, (3) knowledge of life insurance and (12) skill in selling, pertain to technical competence. All the others are qualities of leadership. Nine of the first 10 qualities that agents expect from their managers are in the field of human relations and morale.

THE HOW OF MOTIVATION

The manager must accomplish objectives through the efforts of other people. Assuming a receptive corps of agents, how does a manager possessing the necessary leadership qualities go about motivating or inspiring them to want to do their best? Broadly, there are three ways or approaches, all aiming to develop and maintain interest and morale: personal or private conversations with individual agents; agency meetings and study groups; and sales promotion or prestige-building activities.

1. *Personal or Private Conversations*—In this approach the manager directs his efforts to the individual agent:

a. Find and create wants—and then intensify them. The more things a man wants, the harder he will work for them. Ego recognition also plays a part; the desire for approval is strong in all men. Agents are important and want to be considered important.

b. Sell him a bigger concept of himself. Even good agents often underestimate their abilities. It is part of the manager's job as motivator to instill self-confidence in his men; the most effective way is to convince the agent that he, the manager, has confidence in the agent's capacity for greater accomplishment.

c. Develop his skills. Psychologists say that men like to do those things that they do well. Applying this idea, the manager should try to motivate the agent to become so skillful in prospecting, approach and presentation, answering objections, closing, completing the application, and work habits that he will be eager to demonstrate his skill with prospects.

d. Rekindle enthusiasm. Perhaps "keep enthusiasm kindled so that rekindling will be unnecessary" would be even more accurate. It is easier to keep a fire burning than to let it go out and build a new one. The effective manager will remind his salesmen what life insurance is and does, that all life is uncertain but that as long as men wish to provide for their families there will be a need for life insurance and for other men like those in his agency to sell it.

2. *Agency Meetings*—These offer the manager an opportunity to motivate his entire sales force collectively as distinguished from individually. The main objective is to keep agents up to date on such matters as:

a. New company information
b. Rules and practices
c. Sales contests and special campaigns
d. New sales ideas or demonstrations (with help of agents) of new sales or training techniques
e. New organized sales talks

Agency meetings are not held solely for the purpose of motivation. Exchanges of agents' ideas and experiences can also be valuable. However, the competent manager recognizes that attendance at and participation in a constructive agency meeting can give each salesman a deeper sense of belonging. Wisely planned and run, such meetings have substantial morale-building potentialities.

There need be no set schedule for agency meetings. Some managers hold them at regular intervals, such as weekly. The frequency is less important than the *purpose*. If the manager hopes to motivate his men, there must be a definite reason for each meeting. A talk on an appropriate subject by a visitor from the home office might constitute a good reason.

3. *Sales Promotion or Prestige-Building Activities*—Overall sales promotion is conducted by the home office agency department. However, the manager himself has numerous opportunities for this kind of motivation:

a. Agency sales contests, as distinguished from company-wide contests—The prize usually is not of great intrinsic or monetary value; recognition itself is a valuable award. (Companies operating in New York must conform to the requirements of Section 213, which limits the intrinsic value of prizes.)

b. Agency bulletins publicizing such information as:
    1) Announcement of appointment of new agents
    2) Production achievements of agency or agents
    3) Names of qualifiers for company's national agents' convention, also for CLU, LUTC, LUATC, NQA (National Quality Award), MDRT (Million Dollar Round Table), etc. (Sometimes the manager will also mail announcements of such accomplishments to selected clients of qualifying agents.)
    4) Sales ideas, news of sales contests, local and company-wide
    5) Personal items about agents and their families
c. Newspaper advertising—Sometimes the manager will feel that some of the items in 3b warrant paid space in the local press.
d. Individual letters to his agents—What the manager says in such communications would vary according to each agent's particular situation at the time.
e. Recognition of agents' participation in worthwhile community activities—Life underwriters do more than their share as good citizens in the communities where they live; more often than not they are leaders in worthy enterprises.

Personal Problems

Most of us don't do our best when things bother us, when we think we are unappreciated, when we think others are being favored at our expense. Life insurance salesmen are affected that way too. And when they are, their effectiveness suffers. An agent may have a lot of things on his mind: At home there may be sickness, domestic trouble or financial problems; on the job there may be frustration, discouragement or a feeling of insecurity. Some agents may look to their manager to hear their problems and give them guidance. But the majority are reluctant to take the initiative in telling what is troubling them. The manager should be on the alert for signs of difficulties and make himself available and even encourage an agent to unburden himself. He may have to recharge or reinspire his man and assure him of his interest, sympathy and desire to help.

. . . .

In this and the preceding three chapters we have described the duties of the manager with respect to recruiting, training, supervision and motivation of his men. For convenience these four manpower-building activities have been presented under separate headings, but they are not sharply distinct; in fact, they are closely interrelated. Also, while it might seem that comprehensive programs for these activities would assure their success, such is not the case. For one thing, even today not all companies encourage as much attention to effective manpower building as these chapters may have suggested. For another, not all managers are equally qualified and willing to accept the responsibility for such manpower building.

At the same time we should point out that not all agents are either outstanding salesmen or failures. The business has room for and needs many salesmen of average ability who can and will earn an average income by selling enough life insurance properly to prospects of average income and average needs and by serving those persons satisfactorily. Such agents are not experts and probably will never lead their companies in sales. However, they solicit many hundreds of thousands of worthy prospects whom top producers seeking a high average policy are not likely to be interested in.

Despite the best efforts to recruit, train, supervise and motivate only men whose prospects for success are better than average, results are far short of 100 percent—just as they are in comparable programs in other industries. Some agents drop out before they have completed their training program. Others drop out soon after. Some remain under contract with indifferent success for a year or even longer and then give up. Still other agents will be terminated, not necessarily because they have not tried but because they don't have or can't acquire what it takes to make the grade as life underwriters. All such departures contribute to the turnover discussed in chapter 8.

Companies and managers are unhappy about *excessive* turnover, although the problem is by no means peculiar to life insurance. But there is also a positive side. Until a perfect means of recruiting, training, supervision and motivation is developed, there will always be agents who hindsight indicates should not have been hired. The sooner they leave the business, the better for themselves, their companies and the insuring public.

Summary

Recruiting and training of promising men do not assure their success as agents. Their sales efforts must be supervised, because practice alone does not make perfect.

Among the methods available to a manager to supervise his men are (1) personal observation, (2) personal interview and (3) recordkeeping. Because of the limitations of the first two, the most feasible method usually is recordkeeping by the agent, supplemented by some personal observation by the manager. Kinds of agents' records include (1) daily workbook or worksheet, (2) plan book or chart and (3) devices such as the Sales Method Index.

Closely related to supervision by the manager is motivation, which aims to get agents to want to do their best. Methods of motivation by the manager include (1) personal or private conversations with individual agents, (2) agency meetings and study groups and (3) sales promotion or prestige-building activities. Sometimes a manager may be able to bring about effective motivation by helping an agent with his personal problems.

Questions for Review

1. Explain fully the scope of the term "supervision" as applied to life insurance agents.

2. Describe briefly three supervisory methods that enable a manager to obtain the information necessary to supervise his men. Which of these three usually is most feasible? Explain why.

3. Outline a procedure for developing a "program of improvement" in the achievement of life insurance agents.

4. What is motivation? List the three main ways managers use to motivate agents. Describe each in some detail.

5. Discuss briefly the effectiveness of programs to recruit, train, supervise and motivate agents, indicating their effect on turnover.

12

Supervision and
Motivation by the
Home Office

*B*uilding a successful field organization takes much
time, effort and money. Once a reasonable degree of efficiency
has been attained, it becomes important to prevent backsliding
and to do a progressively better job. But maintenance and increase of effectiveness are not self-generating. This means that
responsibility for supervision and motivation of agencies must
be shared by the field manager[1] and the home office agency department.

SUPERVISION BY THE HOME OFFICE

In chapter 4 we indicated that overall responsibility for field
activities lies with the home office agency department, although
the execution is in the field. Home offices need to know just
how their policies are being carried out. Basically, supervision

---

[1] Supervision and motivation by the manager were considered in chapter 11.

of the field organization by the home office aims to help managers do their part in attaining the agency department's objectives. Such supervision supplements supervision on the local or managerial level but is more extensive. Supervision by the manager aims to make sure that individual agents are doing what they have been trained to do. Supervision by the home office aims to make sure that agencies are discharging their duties in accordance with home office objectives and rules. It is supervision of the agencies as a whole rather than of individual agents.

Supervision is handled differently by different companies. At one extreme there may be little supervision of the field so long as operations seem to be going satisfactorily. At the other extreme, supervision may be both extensive and intensive with respect to all phases of agency operations. And there is a vast middle ground in between, with variations according to company objectives, organization and size.

Major Areas

The performances of individual agents in a particular field office give an important clue as to how that agency is operating. Companies seek specific information over wide areas of agency activities, including:

1. *Manpower Development*—Prospective agents interviewed or recruited, men placed under contract, training programs in operation, men terminated and for what reasons, etc.
2. *Performance of Each Agent*—Kind of market, number of calls, ratio of calls to interviews, ratio of interviews to sales, amount of insurance sold and on what plans, proportion of cash with application, NTO (not-taken-out) ratios, total premiums on business submitted, average premium per policy and per $1,000 of insurance, frequency of premium payment, persistency of business
3. *Performance of Agency as a Whole*—Overall picture

based on aggregates for individual agents in No. 2 to obtain similar data on an agencywide basis; also, total figures for volume written and actually paid for, and increase in amount of in-force business

Sometimes reports on these activities are developed in the home office, and sometimes by the agencies themselves, frequently with the help of the computer. The home office agency department can analyze this information carefully to measure the progress of individual agencies and of the total field organization. Progress is relative and rarely in absolutes. The home office seeks to determine which way, on balance, each agency is heading. If the general trend is up, what are the weaknesses and how can they be overcome? If the trend is down, how can the decline be halted? Agencies rarely wither overnight. Superficially, an agency may seem to be thriving and the manager himself may be unaware that deterioration has set in. Prompt remedial action as a result of conscientious and vigilant supervision from the home office may reverse the downward trend before a major overhaul of the agency is necessary.

Companies can derive much pertinent information from the various reports they obtain about the field. Most companies believe, however, that there is no satisfactory substitute for personal, firsthand inspection trips to various field offices by members of the home office agency department.

Supervisory Organization

Several factors affect the form of organization of supervision from the home office: size of the company, number of agencies, geographical scope of operations, lines of business sold (ordinary, group, debit, health), and type of agency system in use. Managerial companies control all agency operations and require a commensurate home office organization to supervise their agencies. General agency companies reflect various degrees of autonomy. For purposes of this discussion, differences in supervision between general agency and managerial companies will be disregarded.

Various titles are used to identify agency department men who do this type of work. Among them are: field supervisor, superintendent of agencies, line superintendent and director of agencies. In this discussion they will be known as *home office field supervisors*. Such a designation will distinguish them clearly from men who hold supervisory positions in the agencies themselves under the manager or the general agent.

Home office field supervisors must be able to direct and guide others. Frequently they have had life insurance sales experience as agents, assistant managers or managers. Frequently, they are responsible for recruiting new general agents or branch managers. Supervision may be regional in nature, according to geographical areas commonly called zones. Each home office field supervisor is responsible for a number of states or provinces. Some reside in the zones they cover and visit the home office only occasionally. Others are headquartered in their company home office and make frequent trips to their zones. In some companies supervision is organized along functional lines, with supervisors being specialists in some particular phase of agency operations, such as recruiting of agents, training of agents or agency finance. Hence one such supervisor will take up only recruiting matters on his visits to his company's agencies; another will visit those same agencies for training, etc.

Scope of Field Visits

Supervisory visits to the field cost money. If they are to be of maximum benefit to the agency and the company, such visits must be well planned, and the manager and the home office field supervisor should be adequately prepared. Surveys indicate that managers welcome visits from the home office, want supervisors to stay long enough to accomplish useful purposes and want advance notice of the topics to be covered. Further, managers feel they should be able to add to the regular agenda such topics as they consider important.

The supervisor can prepare himself for field visits to a particular agency by analyzing various reports and other available data concerning that agency. For example, he will have production records of men in each agency he visits and can review these and related information with the manager and sometimes with the agents themselves. He should consult other departments to ascertain how well the quality of business submitted meets home office underwriting requirements, if persistency is satisfactory, if service to policyowners is satisfactory, etc. Thus the supervisor will have maximum information before his visit concerning the strengths and weaknesses of each agency on his itinerary, and he will be able to emphasize those aspects of the agency's operations that require the most attention. Commonly he will have a formal questionnaire or checklist to guide him in his interviews with the manager and other agency personnel. Specific areas include:

1. Analysis of present organizational structure
2. Recruiting of agents
3. Training of agents
4. Agency costs and profitability
5. Conservation of business
6. Elimination of unsuccessful agencies or possible establishment of new offices
7. Sales promotional activity[2]
8. Campaigns and contests[2]

A number of factors affect the *frequency* of home office supervisors' visits to agencies:

1. Company policy—This may call for annual, semiannual or quarterly visits; some companies follow no regular schedule but conduct visits as circumstances warrant.
2. Availability of supervisory personnel—As already indicated, managerial companies tend to have proportionately larger supervisory organization because of the greater measure of control exercised by the home office.
3. Distance of a company's field offices from the home office

---

[2] May be considered as part of motivation by the home office, to be discussed in the next section of this chapter.

(or from the headquarters of the resident supervisor responsible for that area)—Cost and time are involved.

4. The situation in a particular agency: its age, size, the experience and competence of the manager, its current problems—Occasionally an emergency may arise that requires immediate attention.

Length of an agency visit varies from one day to two or more. The duration depends largely on how much time circumstances in any particular office may require. The visit should be long enough for the home office field supervisor to do a good job.

Supervision by the home office usually involves an element of inspiration. For the most part, however, it is factual and specific. Such supervision requires a great deal of hard work and long hours, often under pressure. On his trips to the field the supervisor is asked to offer solutions to many kinds of problems in the agencies he visits. At the same time he is supervising and seeking information as to how effectively the agencies are operating. Considerable paperwork is also involved. The supervisor analyzes the information he develops in each agency and then submits a written report concerning his findings. Usually such a report includes specific recommendations for the consideration of the chief agency executive. In the case of a field supervisor with authority to institute changes in his agencies, the report would include the nature of those changes together with supporting reasons.

MOTIVATION BY THE HOME OFFICE

As is the case with supervision, motivation by the manager is intensive and concerns only his own agency, while motivation by the home office is extensive and concerns all the company's agencies. Aside from the motivation generated by visits of home office agency department representatives, motivation by the home office consists primarily of various activities commonly included under the heading of sales promotion. This term will be used to include all activities intended to help agents write more and better business. These activities will be considered under two groups:

1. Those intended to make it easier for men to sell
2. Those intended to recognize sales accomplishments of agents.

For convenience and brevity, the first group will be identified as *facilitating* activities; the second, as *recognition* activities.

Chapter 11 showed what the manager himself could do to motivate his men. Sales promotional activities to be considered now originate in the home office. Many companies, especially larger ones, have staffs devoting full time to this work. Others may use the services of outside organizations, such as advertising agencies or sales consultants.

Facilitating Activities

ADVERTISING. A well-trained corps of agents can sell a substantial volume of life insurance even if their company does no advertising. (Such companies benefit somewhat indirectly from the institutional advertising of organizations like the Institute of Life Insurance.) Conversely, companies that have tried to sell life insurance solely by means of advertising, i.e., without an agency force, have generally been unsuccessful.

Companies consider advertising a means of communicating with large numbers of people. Thus most life insurance advertising aims to create an awareness of the particular company, to create recognition and some understanding of the needs people have for its products and to demonstrate how the company's agents can serve the readers' or listeners' needs.

Companies use one or more of the following media in their advertising: newspapers, "popular" magazines,[3] radio, televi-

---

[3] Companies also run advertisements in insurance trade publications, but these are addressed to brokers and agents of other organizations rather than to the general public.

sion and direct mail. Advertising may be general or specific. The former type may feature such subjects as thrift, health, ecology, the value of the agent's services and the excellence of its own training program—but without an actual sales message. Only companies operating over a fairly wide area are likely to employ this type of advertising.

Specific advertising is more common. Usually it features a particular contractual benefit, a new policy and the like. Radio or television may ask the audience to write the company for further information or to consult the telephone directory for the location of the company's nearest sales office. Newspaper or magazine advertisments may include a reply coupon.

Of the five media mentioned, only direct mail can effectively introduce the name of the agent to the reader. This medium consists of folders or brochures usually prepared by the home office agency department and distributed to the field. They are commonly imprinted with the name, address and telephone number of the individual agent, and are mailed to persons he considers prospects for life insurance.

Proper selection of names is vital to the success of any direct mail campaign. The most expertly conceived and elaborately prepared campaign will fail if too many of those to whom the literature is sent are uninsurable, are unable to purchase life insurance or for other reasons are not genuine prospects. The agent must know his market as well as his product. Effective use of direct mail requires that agents list only names of persons about whom they know enough to believe that there is a good chance for a sale. And a prompt personal followup by the agent is essential to capitalize on direct mail.

Companies do not expect that their advertising will prompt many people to contact local agency offices and ask an agent to call. However, most people prefer the known and advertised product to the unknown and unadvertised one, whether the product is shoes, air conditioners or life insurance. In a well-conceived and well-executed campaign, the prospect first encounters the name of the company by means of advertising in one or more of the following: newspaper, magazine, radio, television. The name becomes more familiar when the prospect receives one or more pieces of direct mail from that company's agent in his city or neighborhood. When the agent then telephones to introduce himself and ask for an interview, the names of both agent and company have become known to the prospect. Advertising has paved the way.

No formula has been devised that would apply to all companies under all circumstances. Companies' approaches and objectives differ.

SALES LITERATURE. In addition to using regular advertising media, companies may provide a wide variety of sales literature in order to help their field representatives. Such literature includes:

1. *Sales Bulletins*—These are sent to the agencies on a variety of subjects. Among them are: changes in rules, sales statistics of various kinds, successful sales presentations, analysis of a new law, announcement of a new policy or discontinuance of an old one, liberalization of provisions in existing policies.

2. *House Organs*—Many companies use articles in such publications to feature the successful techniques and other accomplishments of their managers and agents, or sometimes an exposition of an agent's or manager's philosophy of his work. Such articles present ideas that may be helpful to other members of the field organization. They also are a form of recognition for the men whose accomplishments are published.

3. *"Reminder" Advertising*—In this category are items the home office offers to agents gratis or for a nominal charge: pads, pencils, calendars, address books, sporting events schedules, birthday and policy anniversary cards. These usually bear some identifying imprint such as the names of the company and the agent and the address of the latter.

4. *Miscellaneous Printed Materials*—These items are variously designated as booklets, folders or envelope stuffers.

Some of this material may be included with premium notices.

Recognition Activities

Chapter 11 described devices *managers* use to stimulate their field forces to greater success in their sales efforts. Most home offices encourage competition on a companywide basis. In some cases a man may compete against certain requirements; in others, against other agents. Such activities include the following:

1. *Production Clubs*—Most companies have at least one of these "clubs," frequently more. Various designations are used. For example, in one company the agent who pays for a minimum of $500,000 of new life insurance in one year qualifies for his company's Field Club. The man who pays for between $500,000 and $800,000 becomes a member of its Honor Club, whereas the one who pays for more than $800,000 qualifies for the President's Club.

   There has been a trend away from determining eligibility for membership in a production club solely upon the amount of insurance an agent sells. To an increasing extent companies are basing an agent's eligibility for club membership, for a given year, upon the total amount of the premiums for his business or the total amount of his commissions. A similar trend has appeared in the determination of winners in companies' sales contests.

   The "app-a-week club" is another common device. Here the objective is to see for how many consecutive weeks the field underwriter can submit (not necessarily place or pay for) at least one application.
2. *"Institutional" Awards*—Chief among these are the Million Dollar Round Table and the National Quality Award. These forms of recognition are conferred by organizations other than the agent's company. As designa-

tions whose qualifications are uniform throughout the business, such awards enjoy recognition beyond the company's "walls."

The Million Dollar Round Table was established in 1927 and is used in both the United States and Canada. Its major objectives are to raise the standards of sales conduct and to promote the concept of professional employment in the field of life underwriting. Membership in the MDRT is restricted to persons paying for at least $1 million of business in the immediately preceding year. Eligibility requirements reduce the credit for term insurance and place some arbitrary value on commissions for group insurance in determining credits for membership in the MDRT. The salesman who qualifies in six consecutive years becomes a life member of MDRT.

The Leading Producers Round Table (LPRT) is the health insurance counterpart of MDRT.

The National Quality Award was developed by the Quality Business Committee of the Life Insurance Agency Management Association in 1944. The National Association of Life Underwriters, representing the fieldman, was joint sponsor. Since 1945 the award has become one of the major projects of NALU. The Life Underwriters Association of Canada also uses the NQA designation and confers it for substantially the same performance.

The purpose of the National Quality Award is to improve the persistency of business written by life insurance salesmen. It is granted each year to those agents who maintain in force a satisfactory percentage of the business they wrote in the two preceding years. It is not an award for large production.

The Health Insurance Quality Award is the corresponding award for health insurance. HIQA is not conferred in Canada at this writing.

A recent addition (1965) to the group of "institutional" awards is the National Sales Achievement Award, for which both ordinary and combination agents can qualify. The National Association of Life Underwriters sponsors the NSAA. Briefly, a candidate for this award must be a member of a local life underwriters association affiliated with NALU. To qualify for a given calendar year, he must satisfy minimum requirements as to (1) his income from first-year and renewal commissions for life and health insurance sales, (2) the amount of new premiums he wrote and (3) the number of lives he insured.

3. *Quotas*—Frequently the home office sets production goals both for individual agents and for agencies. If these goals are realistic, they can be very effective in encouraging a man to attain or even exceed his quota for a given period.

4. *Contests*—The most popular and most comprehensive companywide recognition device conducted by the home office agency department is the sales contest. Most companies have at least one such contest annually.

Usually contests are conducted according to some kind of quota. Volume in one form or another is a major factor in determing winners among a company's agents. Points may be awarded on the basis of the amount of (a) written or submitted applications, (b) submitted and issued business, (c) paid-for business, (d) annualized commissions, or (e) some combination of these. Of the four, (a) is the most responsive and permits quick recognition for accomplishment. However, this basis involves the risk of giving undue credit to agents whose submitted volume is high but whose issued ratio is low.

The *issued* basis has one advantage over written—it eliminates business that cannot be placed because the applicant fails to complete all requirements or proves to be uninsurable. It does not, though, solve the problem of written business that cannot be delivered.

Paid-for business is a better measure of production than either (a) or (b) because it eliminates qualification on the basis of business that either will not be issued or will not be delivered if it is issued. The paid-for basis is simple to administer and winners are easily determined. However, this basis is subject to the objection that there may be a time lag between date of production and date of reward. Also it gives little credit for policy plan or amount of premium.

The *annualized* commission basis is perhaps the fairest of the four. Annualized commissions are the total first-year commissions that would be paid if all policies remained in force for the entire first policy year. This basis recognizes both volume and policy plan. It is, however, more difficult to administer.

Regardless of the basis used, it is difficult to construct a sales contest that will be fair to *all* participants. Hence the rules should be such that every man who works effectively will have some chance of winning something.

5.   *Conventions*—Closely related to contests as a means of recognition are company agency conventions. Usually an agent's success selling business determines whether he attends the convention. Qualification requirements vary widely but commonly involve one or more of the following:[4]

a.   During the qualifying period, which may be as short as three weeks or as long as a year or even longer, the agent must *pay* for a certain minimum of new business. Sometimes the company imposes a limit on the amount of term insurance that can be included for qualifying purposes, or it bases qualification on first-year commissions earned rather than on new-business volume.

b.   Company rules may further stipulate some minimum total of annual premiums or a minimum of lives insured.

---

[4] Companies operating in New York must conform to the expense limitations of Section 213, referred to in chapter 6. Wisconsin and Illinois also impose some restrictions.

c. The agent must show a certain minimum persistency rate on first-year or on first- and second-year business.

d. There is a prorate arrangement to cover those men who join the company after the qualifying period has begun.

Agents who qualify are guests of the company at its agency convention. Attendance builds prestige, and some companies inform an agent's policyowners of his success.

The convention itself is partly educational, partly inspirational, partly recreational. Senior company officers address the group on various subjects of interest to the sales force, such as changes in rates, additions of new benefits to existing policies and introduction or announcement of new plans of insurance. Some time will be devoted to promotion of the company's objectives. Panel sessions may be held to present new sales and other techniques, and agents have an opportunity to exchange ideas and experiences with men from other agencies.

There has been a steadily greater emphasis on the educational and business aspects of agents' conventions. One reason may be the interest of the Internal Revenue Service in the form and character of convention programs generally. Ordinarily, the expenses incurred by an agent for attending a convention are defrayed by his company. The question has arisen as to whether such expenses should be considered taxable income to the agent. In at least two court cases, the decision has been no, provided such a convention is held primarily for business rather than vacation purposes.

PROS AND CONS OF CONTESTS AND CONVENTIONS. Perhaps the chief argument against sales contests is the belief that they result in the production of business which is below the company's regular standards and that such periods of increased production are followed by slumps. There may also be a drop in production just *before* a contest begins, because agents may be tempted to hold off submission of some applications in order to have these counted in the contest. High cost, especially of conventions, is another common objection. Further, there is some feeling that contests are out of keeping with the concept of the agent as an adviser to his clients.

On the other hand, agents sometimes feel they are forgotten men. On the job they are battling competition from other companies' agents, competition from other businesses for the public's dollars, indifference on the part of many who need protection, and indifference—or so they think at least—on the part of their companies. Letters and other literature don't quite offset the lack of frequent personal contacts with the home office.

Most companies do run contests and do have conventions. They feel that well-planned contests, with effective post-contest followup, recognize the natural rivalry among men to excel and that they increase agents' total production, especially that of marginal men. Since contests are usually based on individual production quotas, the selling efficiency of individual agents will increase. At the same time they are having a little fun.

Specific benefits accruing to men attending well-run agents' conventions have been summarized as follows:

1. The prestige that comes from qualification and attendance
2. The educational value of the program
3. The opportunity to learn from informal conversations with more experienced agents, as well as with those who have similar problems
4. The better understanding that comes through personal contact between home office and fieldmen
5. The development of loyalty, esprit de corps and enthusiasm that result from group undertakings
6. The formation of new friendships and cementing of old ones

Even the detractors concede that the recognition provided by contests and conventions can "recharge" agents when their enthusiasm starts running down. In one company executive's words: "The aim of the convention is to provide an opportunity for qualifying representatives and company personnel to meet and get acquainted. Its value cannot be measured in dollars and cents." Another has said: "The convention is an opportunity for our salesmen to talk things out with management, to exchange ideas, to gain concrete, helpful information—and to renew the conviction of being a vital, necessary and responsible part of the company."

SUMMARY

Responsibility for supervision and motivation of agents is shared by the field managers and the home office agency department. Supervision from the home office aims to help managers do their part in attaining the agency department's objectives, and to assure that agencies are discharging their duties in accordance with home office objectives and rules.

Major areas of such supervision of an agency include manpower development, performance of each agent and performance of the agency as a whole. Various factors affect both the form or organization of supervision and the scope of agency visits.

Aside from the motivation generated by agency visits of home office agency department representatives, motivation from the home office consists primarily of various activities commonly included under the heading of sales promotion. Such activities embrace efforts:

1. To make it easier for men to sell, such as advertising and sales literature.
2. To recognize sales accomplishments of agents, such as production clubs, institutional awards, quotas, contests and conventions.

QUESTIONS FOR REVIEW

1. List three major areas of agency activities in which the home office agency department is vitally interested. State the scope of each area.

2. Outline the work of a home office field supervisor before, during and after a visit to his territory.

3. Enumerate and evaluate briefly the several advertising media used by life insurance companies.

4. Discuss the various life insurance printed materials broadly covered by the term "sales literature."

5. What provisions are usually included among the requirements for qualifying for attendance at an agency convention? Discuss the pros and cons of contests and conventions.

6. Does your company hold contests and conventions? If so, why? If not, why not? What does it use in their place?

13 Office Organization of the Field

The activities of a life insurance agency are twofold: sales or production, and office or clerical. Agencies are established primarily to develop new business. However, the office activities are also important.

These must be performed in every agency, whether it is a one-man operation with a single office worker or a large, departmentalized organization with assistant managers, agency supervisors, various specialists and a comparable force of a cashier or office manager, assistant cashiers, premium clerks, secretaries and typists. Larger agencies may have an office staff of 25 or more.

FIELD OFFICE FUNCTIONS

The office work in an agency may be conveniently grouped into four functions: (1) that relating to new business, (2) that relating to the collection of premiums and other moneys due

217

the company, (3) that relating to service to policyowners and beneficiaries, and (4) that relating to service to agents.

1. New business—This function includes the following:
    a. Processing of applications—Each application must be checked for errors or omissions before it is mailed to the home office. Company underwriting rules specify when an inspection report and a medical examination of the applicant will be required. If a new application necessitates inspection, the agency will order one from an independent reporting agency. If the case involves medical examination, the agency will have the applicant examined by a physician on the company's approved list. The agency will then forward these reports to the underwriting department in the home office.
    b. Preparation and maintenance of daily or weekly production reports for all applications submitted— While such reports may be developed by the agency, more often they are prepared in the home office from each application submitted. For each application such a report might show the date, the name of the agent; age, name and address of applicant; amount of insurance, plan of insurance, amount of premium and mode of payment. The report would also show whether the applicant is already a policyowner and whether payment of the first premium accompanied the application. Usually, the home office also prepares for each agency the necessary office records for all policies issued.
2. Collection of premiums (and other insurance moneys due the company)—This function includes the following:
    a. Renewal premiums—These constitute by far the greatest proportion of all amounts collected by an agency. Such collections are deposited in the agency bank account and reported to the home of-

fice regularly, usually daily. Many companies collect renewal premiums through the home office or through centralized collection agencies rather than through their sales agencies.

   b. Policy loans and policy loan interest—In some companies insureds pay these types of indebtedness to the agency, which then reports such payments to the home office.

3. Service to policyowners and beneficiaries—This function includes the following:

   a. Transactions involving contractual payments: death benefits, matured endowments, surrenders, disability benefits—Although such checks usually originate in the home office, they often are sent to the agency for transmittal.

   b. Processing of documents in connection with:
   1) Change of beneficiary designation
   2) Assignment
   3) Change of plan of insurance
   4) Change of mode of premium payment
   5) Issuance of policy loans
   6) Addition of miscellaneous riders and endorsements, e.g., "common disaster" and "spendthrift trust" clauses
   7) Change of names and addresses of interested parties
   8) Issuance of premium extension agreements
   9) Reinstatement of lapsed policies
   10) Election of optional modes of settlement

4. Service to agents—This function includes the following:

   a. Providing information requested by policyowners —Some service is rendered to policyowners and beneficiaries indirectly through agents. Frequently an agent receives a request for information from a client. If he does not have the answer immediately he may ask the cashier for assistance. Then when the agent has obtained the necessary information he transmits it to the policyowner or beneficiary.

b. Assistance with company forms—New applications should be checked promptly and carefully so that the agent can be informed of any errors, omissions or additional requirements.

c. Notification of changes in policyowner status—In the case of old business, the office should inform the agent immediately regarding such matters as an overdue premium, a change of policyowner address, change of beneficiary or a prospective surrender.

The Cashier[1]

The office functions just described are usually the direct responsibility of the agency cashier. (In some companies the cashier does not report to the agency manager but to the home office.) In addition he exercises limited discretion in interpreting home office regulations, and conducts correspondence and interviews with policyowners, field representatives and the public.

The qualifications for the job are considerable. They include: knowledge of the life insurance business and of company rules and procedures, capacity for assuming responsibility, ability to supervise a small or even a large group of workers, courtesy in dealing with the public, and good judgment, initiative and cooperativeness.

In a very small agency the cashier may be the only office employee. If there are other employees in the office department of the agency, the cashier:

1. Trains and supervises these employees. He is immediately responsible for the quality and quantity of the work they perform.

---

[1] Also known as office manager, agency controller and (in Canada) branch secretary.

2. Decides questions that are beyond the authority or ability of the other employees.
3. Has the authority, in some agencies, to hire and discharge office personnel.

Some employees reach the position of cashier by progressing through subordinate assignments. New cashiers may be brought to the home office for training, or a number in the same geographical area may be brought to some central location. To guide the cashier in the administration of his duties, companies prepare detailed manuals of procedure, variously designated as cashiers' manuals, office manuals or operating manuals, which serve as a ready and valuable reference when questions of company rules and practice arise. Managerial companies and those where the cashier reports to the home office frequently transfer or promote cashiers from one agency to another. Such transfers are less common if the cashier reports to a general agent, since he usually is an employee of the general agent rather than of the company.

Location of Agency Offices

At one time most life insurance sales offices, like most home offices, were located in the main business sections of their respective cities. Consensus was that a central location was essential to successful operations. Many companies are now domiciled in suburban areas, and many field offices formerly situated in downtown areas have followed suit.

A number of factors have contributed to this trend. The outskirts of a large city or its suburbs usually offer better parking facilities and lower rentals. There has been a continuing movement of population from urban to suburban areas. Agents themselves may live outside the city and find a suburban business address more convenient. As more and more policyowners pay their premiums by mail rather than in person, they have less occasion to call in person at the agency office. Some never visit the office where their policies are on record, so that the location of the agency office is of little importance to them.

Centralized Collection Agencies

In some of the larger cities where they have two or more sales agencies, some companies also maintain a central collection office. No agents operate out of such an office; its activities are limited to premium collections for all contracts on record with any production office in that city. Such a collection office also handles requests for policyowner service.

Several advantages are attributed to having a centralized collection office in the multiple-agency city:

1. It relieves the agency manager of many administrative details related to the collection of renewal premiums.
2. It gives the sales force more time to concentrate on new business.
3. It simplifies the establishment of new sales offices in metropolitan areas.
4. It makes possible a substantial saving in expenses of collecting renewal premiums. The cost of collecting 10,000 premiums monthly through one centralized agency is less than the cost of collecting the same number through three or four production agencies.
5. It improves and standardizes service to policyowners.
6. It saves time at the home office, which needs to deal with only one set of reports and with only one office instead of with one report for each sales office in a given city.

Possible disadvantages of such an arrangement are that:

1. The manager may feel that the removal of the collection and service functions from his agency results in some loss of prestige.
2. The agent, who does not ordinarily visit the collection office, is not in as good a position to see that his clients receive proper service and advice.

3. The decrease in contact between the producing office and the policyowner may reduce opportunities to write new business.

REGIONAL COLLECTION AGENCIES. Some companies have also established *regional* collection offices. These are similar to centralized collection agencies. However, as the term implies, the operations of a regional office are more extensive. Instead of serving the sales agencies of only one city, it serves all agencies located in a sizable geographical or population area.

DECENTRALIZATION AND "RECENTRALIZATION" OF ACTIVITIES. Some years ago there was a trend among companies to delegate to field offices authority to perform a number of transactions that had long been restricted to the home office. Such decentralization included granting of policy loans and payment of death claims and matured endowments (occasionally surrender values also) up to specific limits. A few companies even authorized their agencies, within carefully controlled ranges, to underwrite and issue new policies. The basic purpose of such delegation, of course, was to speed operations and thereby improve service to policyowners, beneficiaries and agents.

More recently, primarily because of the increasing use of electronic data processing equipment, there has been a trend to "recentralize" in the home office transactions that had been decentralized some years earlier. Among these are mailing of renewal premiums and accounting for such premiums, as well as commission calculations, programing a prospect's insurance needs, and periodic production of policy and policyowner data for use in conservation and policy review service activities.

SUMMARY

The activities of an agency office may be divided into sales or production, and office or clerical. The latter in turn may be divided into four functions: (a) that relating to new business,

(b) that relating to the collection of premiums, (c) that relating to service to policyowners and beneficiaries, and (d) that relating to service to agents. The office functions usually are the direct responsibility of the agency cashier.

Formerly most life insurance sales offices were located in the main business section of their cities. Today, however, many are located in suburban areas. A number of larger companies have established centralized and regional collection agencies, whose activities are limited to premium collection and policyowner service.

Development of computerized operations has resulted in some transfer of agency office activities to the home office.

Questions for Review

1. Into what parts may the office work in an agency be divided? Outline the activities included in each function.
2. List the qualifications and duties of an agency cashier.
3. State the advantages and disadvantages attributed to centralized collection agencies.

14 | Conservation

Life insurance is valuable whether policyowners "live, die or quit." It does the most good if they don't quit, i.e., if they don't lapse or surrender their protection until their life insurance has accomplished the purpose for which they originally purchased it.

The word "conservation"[1] suggests preservation or wise use. In life insurance it means preservation of business in force or wise use of such protection.

Closing a sale is one thing; keeping the business on the books is another. As stated in chapter 4, the increase in the amount of a company's in-force business is a more significant measure of its progress than the amount of new business written each year. "The business that stays is the business that pays."

When a policy lapses before it has fulfilled its purpose, all concerned lose. The policyowner and his family lose valuable protection; the salesman loses income from renewal commissions and perhaps a source of contacts for new sales. For the agency and the company, lapse, especially early lapse, means loss of insurance in force, expenditure of time and money

---

[1] Sometimes known as "persistency," although these terms are not exactly synonymous.

225

and, sometimes, a dissatisfied ex-customer. Conversely, all concerned benefit when business persists.

THREE PHASES OF CONSERVATION

Conservation in life insurance may be considered as embracing three phases. In order of decreasing importance and effectiveness these are:

1. Broadly, conservation at the source
2. More narrowly, prevention of lapse
3. Reinstatement after lapse

Conservation at the Source

Numerous studies confirm that, with respect to conservation of life insurance at least, "an ounce of prevention is worth a pound of cure." But prevention has a much broader meaning than just to keep a policy from lapsing. Conservation begins at the source, at the time the insurance is sold. The importance of the life insurance agent in conservation can hardly be exaggerated. The agent writing a given policy is the most important factor in its persistency—the kind of salesmanship largely determines the lapse rate.

If the agent sells a prospect the right policy for his needs and sells it skillfully, the policyowner will usually have a proper appreciation of the value and benefits of his protection. As previously stated, the first year or two are the most critical for the persistency of a policy—and it is more likely to remain in force if the agent who sold it remains under contract with the company. The agent writing a policy is the most important factor in its persistency. Well-written business persists better. Conservation work after issuance of the policy is of limited value. Consequently, companies continue to try to recruit, train, supervise and motivate men who will sell persistent business.

Some terminations are unpreventable. Policyowners die, endowments mature during the lifetime of the insured and term contracts expire while the insured is alive. Such terminations do not concern us in conservation.

Major factors affecting persistency, apart from the agent himself and his sales methods, are:

1. *Income of the Insured*—Next to the agent himself, this is perhaps the most important single factor. Policies bought by persons with higher incomes are likely to persist better.
2. *Mode or Frequency of Premium Payments*—Policies on which premiums are paid annually enjoy better persistency than those for which premiums are paid more frequently. The explanation may be that the insured need decide only once a year whether he will continue his policy in force, rather than twice, 4 times or even 12 times.
3. *Age of Applicant*—Generally speaking, persons in the 30–55 range are better off financially, have greater need for coverage, are more responsible and are more likely to maintain their insurance than those at younger ages. Juvenile business, which usually is purchased by people in that same 30–55 age range, has also been shown to persist to an above-average degree.
4. *Policies for Large Amounts (or Premiums)*—Such contracts are likely to be bought by persons with higher incomes, who can afford to keep them in force.
5. *Policies Sold to Professional Men*—Many professional men earn larger incomes; also, they are likely to appreciate the value of their protection.
6. *Previous Ownership of Life Insurance in the Same Company*—"Repeat" business suggests that the insured is satisfied with his company and with his agent and clearly recognizes the usefulness of life insurance.
7. *Cash With Application*—The man who pays his first premium when he signs the application not only is more likely to accept delivery but also is more likely to keep his contract in force.

RATING CHARTS OR DEVICES. Can an agent learn to identify at the time of the sale those prospects who are more likely to keep their insurance in force? To facilitate the agent's efforts, companies also use various devices to improve persistency. One is the Persistency Rater developed by the Life Insurance Agency Management Association from analyses of the relationship between the persistency of a group of policies, and various characteristics of the insured and the transaction. The purpose of the Rater is to provide, at time of sale, the agent and the company with the most accurate prediction possible as to whether a particular policy will remain in force and fulfill its intended purpose.

In actual use, each applicant receives a so-called basic rater score, which depends on his income and the frequency of premium payment. In the classification of "for all men except students,"[2] plus factors are added to this basic score for: previous life insurance in the company to which the man has applied; age of 45 and over; and payment of $50 or more with the application. From this total, minus factors are deducted for: no previous life insurance; age under 25; payment of less than $10 with the application; and term insurance. The remainder is that applicant's persistency rating score. The higher the score, the better the outlook for persistency.

Many companies have some of their agents, particularly inexperienced men and those with unsatisfactory persistency records, submit a completed Rater form with each application. Some companies discourage or occasionally even decline applications that threaten to show poor persistency according to the Rater. Others relate compensation of agents to persistency of business. A number of companies use their own rating charts, which are similar to or based on the LIAMA Rater. The National Quality Award (described in chapter 12) is a means for recognizing agents whose business has shown good early persistency.

"APPROPRIATE BUSINESS." Annual premium policies for large amounts sold to men in higher income brackets are not the only

---

[2] These plus and minus factors are modified for the other rater classifications: "for all women except students" and "for male and female students."

ones that will show good persistency. Many policies for moderate and small amounts with premiums payable as frequently as monthly persist well. The expression "appropriate business" is sometimes applied to policies that are well suited to the needs and financial circumstances of the buyers, even though such sales may not meet all the normal requirements of persistent business. If agents sell appropriate policies to the right buyers on a suitable premium frequency, good overall persistency should result.

Prevention of Lapse

There are situations other than financial strain that may cause a policyowner to think he wants to drop his protection. Also, numerous lapses result from oversight or procrastination. These then involve conservation in the second or narrower sense of preventing lapse. Such conservation is undertaken by the agent, the cashier (or other qualified person on the office staff of the agency) or both. Sometimes a member of the office is the first to learn of a threatened lapse. The alert cashier will promptly notify either the agent who sold the policy or the agent who is servicing the policy.

No agent or cashier can compel an insured to keep his contract in force. But thoughtful explanations can often save business headed for surrender. The most effective prevention methods can be applied only when the conservator knows the real reason why a man wants to surrender. "Can't afford it any more" is not necessarily the real reason—he may want to use the money for something less essential. Many policyowners have found ways to continue premium payments when they realized exactly what they would be losing by surrender. Depending on the circumstances in individual cases, the agent or cashier should:

1. Show that in the case of permanent plans, payment of each premium increases the cash value and thereby, the insured's equity and, in the case of participating policies, the dividends.

2. Emphasize the benefits that the contract will provide for the insured and his family at maturity.
3. Explain that this protection may be irreplaceable if the insured is ineligible for reinstatement or for new insurance.
4. Explain that a new policy, if he is still insurable, would require larger premiums because of higher age, and that cash values would have to be rebuilt.

Specific aids in the prevention of lapse include:

1. Change in mode or frequency of premium payments, as from annual to semiannual
2. Extension of time to pay a premium (premium extension agreements)
3. Use of accumulated policy dividends to pay the current premium (on participating contracts)
4. Payment of premium by policy loan or automatic premium loan
5. Conversion of contract to a lower premium-paying plan, as from 20-payment life to ordinary life
6. Reduction in amount of insurance
7. Combination of two or more of the above

Sometimes a policyowner wishes to surrender a policy, especially one against which he has borrowed, and replace it with new insurance. Such a course is rarely to his advantage. At best he will have to bear the expense of a new policy. At worst he may no longer be insurable at standard or perhaps even at substandard rates. Careful analysis will usually reveal whether replacement has any merit.

Occasionally "twisting" is a cause of lapse. The twister may represent the same or another insurer or a mutual fund organization.

Reinstatement After Lapse

Despite the proper sale of business and efforts to prevent lapse, lapses do occur (unless the policy contains values that can be used under its automatic premium loan provision). The process of putting back in force a contract that has lapsed for nonpayment of premiums and may already be running on one of the nonforfeiture options is known as *reinstatement*. This is the least effective of the three phases of conservation. Prevention is much more effective than cure. It is doubtful whether restored business is worth the cost to the company and the agent in time and effort, because the subsequent persistency of reinstated business has been found to be poor.

While practices vary, most companies are substantially more liberal in considering applications for reinstatement than required by their contracts or by statute. (Life insurance policies issued in the United States and Canada contain a clause permitting reinstatement in the event of lapse, subject to certain requirements and time limits.) Restoration efforts usually are concentrated into the 30 to 60 days immediately following the expiration of the grace period. The several aids under "Prevention of Lapse" are also applicable to reinstatement after lapse.

The majority of companies have adopted some form of *late remittance offer* to obviate the necessity for formal reinstatement. While there are many variations, basically this is an arrangement whereby the insurer will accept an overdue premium beyond the expiration of the grace period without requiring completion of a reinstatement application or evidence of insurability. The usual period for such a late-payment offer is 10 days to two weeks, sometimes longer.

Companies offer reinstatement as a service to the insuring public, even though some may doubt the value of this phase of conservation. Experience shows that some policyowners are chronic lapsers. Some companies also feel that a man who has owned life insurance for more than a year or two should have recognized the value of his protection so that he will keep it in force without urging; if he nevertheless wishes to surrender his policy, that is his privilege.

Some agents feel they are not in a position to spend much time on reinstatement or prevention-of-lapse activity. Under the traditional and formerly almost universal commission basis, an agent may see relatively little dollars-and-cents incentive to maintain business in force or to reinstate it in the event of lapse. The agent may consider his time more profitably spent in selling new insurance.

Let us consider a policy carrying a $100 annual premium with an initial or first-year commission of 55 percent or $55, and nine renewal commissions of 5 percent or $5 each. If the agent's reinstatement efforts on a policy that has lapsed are successful, he earns an immediate $5. Writing a new policy on someone else for a $100 premium would yield the agent $55 as first-year commission, perhaps for no greater expenditure of time than saving the old policy for $5. True, this attitude does not provide the best service to policyowners and overlooks the long view of clientele building, but it is a viewpoint that some agents do develop.

As indicated in chapter 5, many companies have adopted compensation schedules providing for higher second- and third-year renewals. Such arrangements encourage greater conservation efforts on the part of agents. Even under these schedules, however, an agent has no direct financial inducement to keep business in force or to reinstate it if the commission-paying period has expired, unless his contract provides for some form of persistency fee.

This discussion reemphasizes the importance of "conservation at the source." The agent who sells the right policies to the right prospects builds a good clientele and will have relatively little trouble with lapse. Ultimate persistency depends largely on the kind of sale.

OTHER ASPECTS OF CONSERVATION

Two developments have contributed substantially to the conservation of life insurance, especially since most companies discontinued the practice of sending two premium notices. These are the automatic premium loan provision and the preauthorized check plan.

Automatic Premium Loan

Some lapses result from oversights. The insured fully intends to pay his premium. However, he lays the premium notice aside and forgets it, or he is out of town until after the grace period has expired. Lapse results and reinstatement is necessary.

The automatic premium loan provision in the contract prevents such lapses. If a premium remains unpaid during the grace period and if the policy's cash value is sufficient, the company pays the premium by lending it from this cash value at the specified rate of interest. This provision can prevent many cases of unintentional lapse. The insured should repay these loans promptly, however, or the face amount of his policy will be reduced, not only by the amount of the loan but by interest thereon as well.

Preauthorized Check Plan

Each premium due date is an exposure to lapse, inasmuch as the insured has to decide whether or not to continue payments. The higher the premium frequency, the greater the hazard of lapse.

While not a contractual provision, the preauthorized check plan minimizes this hazard. In essence the policyowner authorizes his life insurance company to draw checks against his bank account for the payment of premiums (nearly always monthly). He also authorizes his bank to honor the checks so drawn. The life insurance company deposits these preauthorized checks. These checks clear through normal bank channels and are charged against the policyowner's bank account just like any other checks.

Once the insured has initiated a preauthorized check plan for the payment of his life insurance premiums, the arrangement continues automatically. The plan remains in operation until the policyowner terminates it; he need not renew these authorizations periodically. No further action is required, except, of course, maintenance of an adequate bank balance.

The preauthorized check plan for paying life insurance premiums is widely used today.

•   •   •   •   •

Some policies may be extremely difficult to keep on the books even if they were properly sold originally. When a contract has served the purpose for which it was bought, perhaps many years before, the insured may prefer one of the nonforfeiture options to the continuance of premium payments. For instance, a father may have bought a policy years ago to assure a college education for his son in the event of his own early death. The son has long since graduated, is well established and actually is considerably more prosperous than his father. In such a case the father may decide that he no longer needs this particular policy. Being at or near retirement, he may have enough other insurance to meet his requirements and thus select one of the nonforfeiture options. Discontinuance of premium payments is not always wrong.

SUMMARY

In life insurance, "conservation" means preservation of business in force or wise use of such protection. Conservation may be considered as embracing the following phases in order of decreasing importance and effectiveness:

1.   Broadly, conservation at the source
2.   More narrowly, prevention of lapse
3.   Reinstatement after lapse

Concerning the first phase, the agent writing the policy is the most important factor in its persistency. Well-written business persists better. Other factors include mode (frequency) of premium payments, income of policyowner, age at issue, plan of insurance, payment of first premium with application and previous ownership of life insurance by insured.

Prevention of lapse is less effective than conservation at the source, but frequently a policyowner can be persuaded to keep his protection in force. Reinstatement is the least effective phase, since some persons are chronic lapsers.

Among devices that companies have developed to improve persistency are the automatic premium loan policy provision and the preauthorized check plan.

QUESTIONS FOR REVIEW

1. State the three phases of conservation. Which is the most important? Why? Which is the least important? Why?
2. List the several factors that affect persistency. Explain briefly the significance of each.
3. What is the purpose of a persistency rater? Describe the use of a rater to improve persistency.
4. Outline the arguments an agent or a cashier should present to dissuade a policyowner from surrendering his life insurance. What are some of the specific aids in the prevention of lapse?
5. Define or explain: (a) automatic premium loan and (b) preauthorized check plan. What is the purpose of each?

15 | Other Forms of Insurance Sold by Life Companies

Previous chapters have dealt primarily with agency organization for *ordinary* business. Even today a few insurers write ordinary only. The great majority, however, sell one or more of the following forms as well: health, debit or industrial, and group and allied coverages. These will now be considered briefly, particularly insofar as their organization for sales administration differs from that for ordinary.

HEALTH INSURANCE

For most persons, income stops when their ability to work stops. Many accidents and sicknesses disable persons to the extent that they are unable to earn a livelihood. Even when total disability does not result, hospital, medical and related expenses mount rapidly, and frequently cause much financial hardship. Like many other services, the costs of medical and hospital care have soared in recent years. Expenses for any protracted incapacity may easily run into thousands of dollars.

236

Such outlays constitute a severe drain upon, if they do not actually exhaust, the resources of most families.

Payments for losses resulting from sickness or injury may arise from a number of sources. Aside from accident and sickness insurance and disability income provisions in life insurance policies, such sources include: workmen's compensation, liability insurance, Blue Cross and Blue Shield plans; benefits by virtue of membership in labor unions, beneficial societies and similar groups; benefits provided by federal, state (or provincial) and municipal governments; and salary continuance plans granted by many employers.

According to a recent survey[1] about nine out of ten persons, or about 175 million, in the United States had some form of health insurance coverage as of Dec. 31, 1969. During that year benefit payments made by all private insuring organizations for hospital, surgical and medical care totaled $14 billion. Insurance companies provided such protection for more than 108 million persons. Further, persons with loss-of-income insurance received about $2 billion in benefits from insurance companies.

Nature of Coverage

Health insurance is indemnity insurance; that is, it compensates the insured for loss, specifically for loss of income and cost of medical care and treatment. Generally, if the insured is disabled as defined in his health coverage, he receives benefits (usually weekly) and reimbursement for medical expenses incurred as a result of sickness or injury. This coverage is written by different types of carriers: life insurance companies, casualty companies, companies writing only health insurance, fraternal societies, beneficial societies and so-called commercial travelers' and other associations. Our discussion will be limited to health coverage issued through *individual* policies by life insurance companies. Health insurance also is written as group

---

[1] *1970 Source Book of Health Insurance Data*

coverage. Sales and administration of group health plans are usually handled by the company's group department.

Originally, health insurance was classified as a casualty line, and was sold almost exclusively by companies and organizations that were not life companies. Later, life companies entered the field. This trend has been especially pronounced since the end of World War II. In terms of annual premium income, the usual yardstick for measuring the growth of health insurance, well over 75 percent of all the business is now written by life insurance companies or by companies with life affiliates.

Some life insurance companies have entered the field primarily because their competitors have done so. Others began as health insurers and have added life as a companion line. The majority, however, believe that life and health insurance complement each other, that they are good teammates. In fact, some companies call the team "personal insurance," thus attributing equal importance to both coverages.

Alone, life insurance protects against the hazards of death and old age but only slightly against the hazard of disability. The majority of *life insurance* policies in force today have no disability income provisions. After their extremely adverse experience with the monthly disability income provision in their life policies, most insurers discontinued offering this form of protection during the early 1930's. More recently there has been some trend toward again offering an income disability clause.

Waiver of premium alone will keep policies in force but provides no income. Hence a man without disability income insurance who becomes totally incapacitated may have to borrow upon and eventually surrender much of his life insurance. Such a course will impair his life insurance program, thus lowering his family's standard of living in the event of his death and depriving his loved ones of needed protection. Health insurance can protect against the so-called economic death resulting from accident or sickness. Together, life insurance and health insurance safeguard the insured and his dependents against all three hazards—death, old age and disability. As has been said: "Health insurance in all its phases is an integral part of the life underwriter's programing and economic adviser service. Life insurance and health insurance are teammates, since the latter helps to prevent lapsation of existing life insurance contracts.

Life insurance companies use their regular sales forces to sell health insurance.[2] Although the methods used in recruiting, training, motivating and supervising agents vary slightly for health as compared to ordinary, the *principles* involved do not. A few significant differences, or at least modifications, in methods are worth noting.

Training

While health insurance contract forms are many, basically their operation is relatively simple. Hence a new agent should be able to learn the fundamentals of health insurance more easily and quickly than he can those of life insurance.

Health insurance is a useful door-opener for the sale of life insurance. The type of training a life insurance agent receives, however, is likely to depend on the company's attitude toward health insurance. Some have been active in both fields for a long time. As already indicated, some companies were well established as life insurance companies before they entered the health field. Conversely, some organizations long prominent in health insurance write relatively little life. Companies' training emphases will reflect these differences in attitude.

Persistency

Good, well-written business will persist better than poorly written business in health insurance just as it will in life insur-

---

[2] As in the case of life insurance, some companies receive a substantial number of health applications through brokers. Some of this brokerage business originates with life insurance agents whose companies do not write health insurance.

ance. In fact, right selling may be even more important in health insurance. If the owner of a life policy lapses or surrenders, he will nearly always pay higher premiums for new protection—even if he is still insurable, he will be older. The owner of a health contract is less likely to suffer from lapse, provided he remains insurable.

The laws of most states permit companies to attach a refund-of-premium rider to their health insurance policies. Companies use different forms of riders, which are designed to encourage persistency. Commonly two elements are involved in a refund-of-premium rider: a minimum in-force period and some kind of refund or cash concession. The minimum period is usually 10 years. If during such a period either no claims or no claims totaling more than a certain maximum amount are incurred, the insured is entitled to a refund of a substantial percentage (50 percent or more) of the total premiums he paid during that 10-year period. Depending upon the terms of the rider, an insured may qualify for more than one refund of premium. The premium for a policy with a refund rider is usually larger than for one providing the same benefits but without such a rider.

Compensation

Two broad schedules of agent compensation are in effect, level and nonlevel. The former is the older and is probably a carryover from the original status of health coverage as a casualty line. As the term implies, under a level scale of commissions, the agent receives the same rate for a particular policy in each subsequent year as in the first year. The nonlevel scale is similar to that for life insurance; a high first-year commission is followed by a series of lower renewals. Particularly as life insurance companies have become predominant in the health insurance field, the trend has been to the nonlevel scale. The popularity of noncancellable and guaranteed renewable health insurance, which is closer to life insurance principles than cancellable health insurance, has accelerated this trend.

Future of Health Insurance

Insurance companies have provided health coverage for many millions of persons. The business is continuing to do so and has been constantly trying to improve its services to the public. However, recent developments may have a bearing on its ability to continue to perform in the future.

One such development was the establishment of "Medicare" and "Medicaid" by the United States Congress in 1965. Briefly, Medicare consists of a compulsory basic program (Part A) and a voluntary program (Part B), both for persons 65 and over. The compulsory, hospital insurance program provides for payment of the cost of hospital care, posthospital extended care, outpatient diagnostic services and posthospital home health services. This part (A) of Medicare is government-financed by taxes upon employees and their employers. These taxes are in addition to, and collected with, regular Social Security taxes and cease when the individual attains age 65.

The voluntary, medical insurance part (B) of Medicare helps pay doctor bills and some medical and other services not covered under the hospital insurance part. The voluntary part of Medicare is financed by monthly premiums shared equally by the persons who apply for medical insurance and by the federal government. Such premiums are usually deducted from Social Security payments.

When Congress enacted Medicare in 1965 it also added a medical assistance program to the Social Security Act. Known as Medicaid, this amendment provides for financial assistance to the states in paying health care expenses for substantial segments of the population below age 65. While not an insurance program, Medicaid provides federal matching funds to states which establish programs for medical assistance to eligible needy persons. Nearly all states have established such programs.

Another development of significance to the future of the health insurance business is the prospect of some form of national health insurance. A variety of proposals, formal and informal, have been advanced—by individual insurers, insurance trade associations, legislators, labor unions. Under some of these proposals insurance would be compulsory. Some would provide for participation by the insurance industry. Informed consensus is that some federal health insurance legislation will be enacted soon, probably during the present decade.

As is true of governmental social schemes generally, the basis of solvency for a national plan would differ from that for a private organization. Federal authority involves the power to tax. Thus benefits, and the taxes necessary to pay for them, can be and frequently are increased. An insurance company, on the other hand, is required by state law to be actuarially solvent, and the law of contract applies. Also, partly for competitive reasons, it may not be feasible or even possible to increase premiums.

Despite the substantial advances achieved in the number of persons covered and in the levels of benefits paid under private health insurance, insurance companies are not in a position to provide coverage for those who are unable to pay their share of the cost. Pressure is building for establishment of a compulsory, national health insurance scheme. Nationalization of the health insurance business would not automatically solve the pressing problems in the medical care field. Nevertheless, the future role of company-sponsored health insurance in the United States is uncertain.

DEBIT INSURANCE

More than 200 companies in the United States and Canada write this form of protection, originally known as industrial insurance. They range in size from some of the very large insurers down to very small organizations. All of the larger companies and nearly all the others also write ordinary business, and the term "combination company" is commonly applied to an insurer that sells both forms.

The name "industrial" stems from the origin of this coverage in England in the 19th century. Most ordinary policies previously available were for larger amounts than the average wage earner at that time could afford. Further, premiums had to be paid not more often than quarterly. Industrial insurance was introduced as a means of helping the heads of low-income, wage-earning families obtain actuarially sound life insurance in small amounts for themselves and their dependents. Industrial began in North America in 1875.

As the business developed, especially after the 1920s, the term "industrial insurance" became something of a misnomer. In fact, this designation has been largely replaced by "debit insurance." Other common terms used are weekly premium insurance, small-policy insurance and monthly debit ordinary (MDO). Like the original designation, "industrial," none of the substitute designations are entirely satisfactory; their meanings may vary according to the company using them. In the particular case of monthly debit ordinary, this term generally embraces policies of the ordinary type for amounts up to about $3,000 and more, with monthly premiums collected at the home by the debit agent.

Nature of Coverage

Debit insurance has had certain basic characteristics. Compared to ordinary, it is life insurance for small amounts, rarely more than $1,000 (the average policy in force is about $500),[3] with weekly or monthly premiums collected at the insured's home by the agent. Debit insurance is also sold with premium units in multiples of 5 cents, the amount of protection varying by plan and age at issue. Thus 5 cents weekly at a certain age and plan will buy a policy with a face amount of $100; 10 cents will buy one for $200, etc.

Debit premiums are payable weekly, biweekly or monthly, i.e., much more frequently than ordinary. Whereas the ordinary agent *regularly* collects only the first premium—with the application or on delivery of the policy—his debit counterpart

---

[3] Up to $2,000 is issued in Canada.

regularly collects all premiums at the home of the insured; no premium notices are sent. The contracts of many companies allow a discount of 10 percent to policyowners who pay their premiums at a company district office for at least one year. This reduction is possible because the cost of the agent's collection call at the home is eliminated. The majority of debit policyowners, however, do not take advantage of this opportunity to reduce their premium outlay.

Field Organization

Combination companies organize their sales forces on the branch office or district office system rather than the general agency system. Since managers (sometimes called superintendents), assistant managers and agents as well as clerical personnel are appointed by the company, the branch office system enables the home office to achieve a higher degree of uniformity in sales operations and service to policyowners.

Each company selling debit insurance divides the territory in which it operates into a convenient number of districts. Each district is further divided into smaller collection areas known as debits. An agent is assigned to each such debit. This sales and servicing area is agent A's alone. If a policyowner moves out of A's debit, the insured's records are transferred to the agent servicing the debit into which he has moved. (In practice a debit agent usually is permitted to write *ordinary* insurance outside his territory or debit.)

A manager or superintendent is in charge of each district office. Depending on the size of his district, the manager may have several assistant managers (or assistant superintendents) under him. Each assistant supervises a group or staff of from four to eight debit agents.

Because of the frequent house-to-house premium collections, the sale of debit insurance is best adapted to urban and suburban areas with their high concentrations of population. Thus, a large city may be divided into several districts with a number of square blocks to each debit. A smaller city may consist of one or two districts. In rural areas a single district may comprise two or more towns.

Like the manager of an ordinary branch office, the manager of a combination company's district office is responsible for the efficient operation of his territory. Usually he is a man who has been promoted from the ranks of assistant managers after a good record on a debit. Assistant managers' duties are varied: They help recruit[4] and train agents; they motivate and supervise them; they help their men sell, frequently going out with them on difficult cases; they fill in for an agent absent because of illness or vacation; periodically they audit the accounts of their men. They may also sell insurance themselves.

Training and Supervision

Fundamentally, the training of a debit agent is quite similar to that of the ordinary underwriter. Such training is geared to the needs and means of the people he will call on. It usually includes such subjects as:

1. Brief history of life insurance
2. Introduction to selling according to family needs
3. Mechanics of life insurance—how it operates
4. Use of the ratebook
5. Accounting and recordkeeping procedures for his collections
6. Analysis of his company's more popular policy forms
7. Explanation of his company's general practices
8. Prospecting techniques
9. Completion of applications (both ordinary and industrial)
10. Essentials of debit underwriting
11. Mastering of basic, simple sales talks
12. Preparation for state license examination, where required

---

[4] LIAMA's Combination Inventory for prospective debit agents corresponds to the Aptitude Index Battery for prospective ordinary agents.

One meaning of "debit" has already been explained—it is the geographical area to which a particular agent is assigned. "Debit" also means the total amount of premiums an agent is to collect each week on business in force in his territory. For recordkeeping purposes, he is "debited," or charged with the amount of these premiums, and is then "credited" with the amounts he actually collects. The amount of a debit changes from week to week. New business, reinstatements and transfers from debits of other agents are added. Claims, lapses, surrenders, policies that become paid up and transfers to debits of other agents are deducted. Debits are not standardized as to amount; they may run up to between $400 and $500.

An agent must know how to manage his debit properly if he is to succeed. He must follow a regular schedule to keep his collections up to date. While he need not be an accountant, he must keep accurate records to know where he stands each week. Basically, these records are three in number.

1. *The Premium Receipt Book*—When the agent makes his first sale to a family he furnishes the wife or husband a book which then serves as the *family's* only official record of all premium payments on that policy. The same receipt book is used to record payments on any other policies the agent may later sell to members of that family. The family retains possession of this book.

2. *The Agent's Debit Book*—This book serves as the *agent's* record of all premiums he collects. He uses a separate page for the policies in force on each family. Each time the agent receives money for a premium he records the payment not only in the premium receipt book but also in his own debit book.

3. *The Agent's Collection Report*—This is the report the agent completes regularly (usually weekly or monthly) and submits to his district office for transmittal to the home office. It shows the total amount he has collected on his debit for the period.

Aside from selling and collecting, service to his debit is an important duty of the combination agent. As a result of his regular collection calls, he is much more frequently in touch with his customers than the average ordinary agent is likely to be with his clients. The debit man will come in contact with many family situations and should be well trained to furnish the various services expected of him. Specifically, he should be able to:

1. Keep a maximum amount of his business in force. Persistency often is a greater problem in debit insurance than in ordinary.
2. Handle changes of beneficiary designation and changes of plan.
3. Process claims, maturities and surrenders.
4. Handle reinstatements
5. Handle transfers into and out of his debit.
6. Answer numerous inquiries on a variety of life insurance subjects.
7. In addition, take care of the needs of his ordinary business (which may be larger than his debit in some cases).

The nature of the combination agent's duties is such that adequate supervision is essential to assure that he is using the ideas and methods he has learned. Such supervision is the primary responsibility of his assistant manager, and is considerably more intensive than in the case of ordinary agents.

Compensation of Agents

Any suitable method for compensating the debit agent must recognize a number of factors affecting a proper evaluation of his work. First, debit insurance policyowners, on the average, are more prone to lapse their insurance than are ordinary policyowners. Second, the agent may have to call at a policyowner's home as often as 52 times a year to collect premiums, and there may be many requests for various kinds of other service. Third, the debit agent is expected to write new insurance.

For many years the "increase method" (also known as the "times" method) seemed to constitute a satisfactory reward system for the debit man's work. It endeavored to induce the agent to conserve and service the in-force business on his debit and to stimulate the writing of new business. Briefly, the increase method consisted of a commission for the amount of premiums collected on his debit, and a commission based on the net increase in the amount of his debit. Companies defined net increase as the amount of premium written and restored, minus the amount of premium terminated for reasons other than death and maturity. The effect on the commission for net increase in debit was such that conservation, or persistency, was emphasized to the extent that an agent suffered substantial penalty for "preventable" lapses.

The increase method worked satisfactorily until the depression of the 1930s. During that period many agents found it difficult, if not impossible, either to increase the amount of their debit or to prevent lapses resulting from widespread unemployment. As a result many debit companies, including the three selling the largest amounts of debit insurance at that time, adopted a new method of compensation. While there are variations as to details, this method computes the compensation for the agent separately for each of his three major activities:

1. *First-Year or New-Business Commission*—This compensation encourages the writing of persistent business because the agent usually receives this commission only if the insured pays premiums on the policy for at least one full year. Further, sometimes the commission is not payable on a policy written within three months before or after the lapse of another policy in the same company on the same life, or in the same family.

2. *Collection Commission*—This compensation is usually a fixed percentage, e.g., 12 percent of weekly premiums,

of the amount of *premiums collected*—not of the amount of the debit. If the debit is small, as may be the case in some rural areas, it is commonly provided that the agent will receive some minimum amount weekly for collecting and servicing his debit. Collection commission frequently is the largest single factor in the agent's remuneration.

3. *Conservation Commission*—This compensation is in terms of dollars rather than of a percentage. It provides the agent a financial incentive to conserve existing business. The amount of this commission currently ranges from $3 to about $12 weekly and depends on a particular agent's lapse rate, as compared with that of his entire company or with some other standard.

· · · ·

In addition to the foregoing, combination agents receive commissions for other business they sell, such as regular ordinary and monthly debit ordinary. They are eligible for life insurance and retirement benefits, and for vacation with pay. Some companies grant annual bonuses based on length of service.

It is interesting to compare the earnings of combination agents to those of agents who sell no debit business. Leading ordinary salesmen earn substantially more than leading combination agents, and there are relatively few of the latter in organizations like the Million Dollar Round Table. However, while the combination agent is not likely to find many prospects for large amounts on his debit, companywide income averages for combination men compare very favorably with those for ordinary agents. Many salesmen are now deriving a substantial part of their compensation from ordinary policies. Further, the combination agent enjoys a certain regularity of weekly income that the ordinary salesman cannot count on. Even the best ordinary producers hit spells when weeks may go by without a sale and therefore without any income from first-year commissions.

Compensation of Managers and Assistant Managers

The basis of remuneration for the manager of a district office is similar to that of a branch manager of an ordinary agency. As an employee of his company he receives a salary. The amount of this salary depends largely on the success of his district in both debit and ordinary. Company practice varies as to whether the manager is encouraged, permitted or forbidden to write business himself. The assistant manager's salary depends largely on the results achieved by his own staff of agents. Assistant managers quite generally are personal producers as well, although they are expected not to compete with their men.

Many combination companies are conducting schools to improve the effectiveness of their assistant managers. Most of these schools are conducted at the home office and are of one week's duration or less. Emphasis is on management activities, coverage of the agent's job and the duties of various home office departments, in that order. A few companies conduct schools for their combination managers, as does also the Life Insurance Agency Management Association.

Future of Debit Insurance

In the United States the annual in-force amount classified as *debit* reached a peak of about $40 billion for 1957. Since then there has been a slow decline, the in-force amount standing at about $38.6 billion at the end of 1970. In Canada the amount in force dropped from a high of about $1.7 billion for 1955 to less than $700 million at the end of 1969. For many years the three largest United States' combination companies dominated the debit field. By the end of 1967 all three had discontinued the sale of weekly premium life insurance.

Debit insurance has been gradually declining as a percentage of total life insurance in force in the United States and Canada. In 1940 it was about 18 percent of the total; today it is about 3 percent. Debit insurance has also been declining as a percentage of total insurance sold. It should be pointed out that statistics comparing ordinary with debit include monthly debit ordinary under ordinary rather than under debit, although premiums are usually collected by debit agents.

There are several reasons for the changing status of debit insurance:

1. Development of the family policy—This is a plan whereby the entire family is protected under one life insurance policy. Permanent insurance covers the husband-father, a smaller amount (usually term) covers the wife-mother, and term covers the children. Children born or legally adopted after issuance of the contract are insured without the necessity for application, home office underwriting or change in premium payable. Many families now buying family policies were formerly prime prospects for several debit policies.

2. Growth of monthly debit ordinary—Many prospects not only are able to pay a larger premium but can pay monthly or less often.

3. Financial ability of more wage earners to buy ordinary —The economic status of many former prospects for debit has improved to such an extent that they are now prospects for several thousands of regular ordinary.

4. Continuing extension of group insurance—So many wage earners are now covered by several thousand dollars of group (the average coverage per employee in employer-employee groups was more than $6,000 at the end of 1969) that a small amount of debit insurance seems unimportant. Further, many group plans also provide insurance on the lives of wage earners' dependents.

5. Availability of ordinary insurance on the lives of infant children as early as age zero—Up to the mid-1930s, a debit policy was often the only form of protection that companies offered for young children.

6. Increasing coverage provided by government Social Security.

To some extent debit insurance has worked itself out of a job. It has been the steppingstone to broader life insurance coverage for millions of families. Since combination companies write ordinary (and many of them write group also), their agents, using the debit system of distribution, are in a strong position to take care of the needs of many persons who formerly would have bought debit insurance. However, a considerable but narrowing market will remain for the foreseeable future.

GROUP INSURANCE

Nature of Coverage

Group life insurance is protection issued without medical examination on a group of persons, most often employees of a common employer, under a single contract or master policy. It is a means of furnishing low-cost life insurance on a mass basis.

Group insurance may be written either on the one-year renewable-term plan or on the level premium permanent plan. The latter is much less prevalent in its pure form. In recent years, group carriers have developed "group ordinary," under which an individual can change his protection from one-year renewable term to a level premium plan by paying a specified premium. Unless otherwise specified, "group insurance" or "group life insurance" in this discussion will be assumed to be on the term plan.

In group insurance the group of persons rather than a single individual is the unit or basis of selection. The insurance company knows that some members may be substandard or even uninsurable as individuals. However, the assumption is that satisfactory mortality will be experienced if the group is sufficiently large and if the individual covered is not permitted to determine the amount of his insurance. This restriction is necessary to prevent selection against the insurer.

Group insurance has had a remarkable growth since it was

"born" in 1911 or 1912—especially since World War II—in terms of numbers of persons covered, number of master contracts and amount of coverage. Many companies have entered the field since 1946. From 1960 through 1970, group life insurance in force in the United States more than tripled to reach $545,000 million, while ordinary life increased about 115 percent to $731,000 million in force.

About three-fourths of the *civilian* workers in the United States are now covered by group life insurance. More than 800 companies write this form of protection. The largest single group is the Federal Employees' Group Life Insurance (FEGLI), established in 1954. More than 350 life insurers participate in this plan, which provides coverage for more than three million employees of the United States Government.

Since September 1965 all persons in the *armed forces* have been eligible for Servicemen's Group Life Insurance (SEGLI or SGLI). This is term insurance underwritten in part by about 500 commercial life insurance companies, one of which administers the plan. Within 120 days after separation from the armed forces the serviceman may, without evidence of insurability, convert his term insurance into permanent insurance in one of the 500-odd companies participating in SEGLI.

For many years the standard definition of group insurance specified that each group consist of at least 50 persons. Today some states still require as many as 10, but a considerable number permit group to be written on as few as five lives (sometimes called "baby group"). Still other states and Canada prescribe no minimum number. A group of 5, 25, 50 or even 100 is not large enough of itself to assure a predictable level of mortality. But if enough such groups are soundly underwritten, the average mortality for the sum of these many small groups can be forecast.

Originally, group insurance was limited to the employees of a common employer. Today it is available to other categories including labor union groups, groups of borrowers, various associations (such as automobile dealers and restaurant owners) and so-called multiple-employer groups. Since employees of a common employer continue to constitute the largest segment of the business, this discussion will apply particularly to such groups.

Field Organization

As indicated in chapter 3, group insurance is distributed through agents. For most companies, however, this agency system differs considerably from that for ordinary, debit or health. Companies actively soliciting group usually consolidate most group operations in a single department, with its own sales and administration divisions.[5] The top group sales executive is not likely to report to the agency vice president for ordinary, and frequently the group field offices are completely separate from the ordinary agencies and have their own managers. In the home office there are usually separate group divisions for underwriting, for accounting and for claims.

The marketing of group differs substantially from that of ordinary. The prospect is the *employer,* rather than the employees whose lives may be insured. The prospect employer for group is likely to be well informed as to what this form of coverage can accomplish and is in a position to compare critically the plans of various group carriers. While the typical premium per $1,000 for group term is only a few dollars, a group contract for even a small number of persons can easily involve a substantial total premium for a large face amount of insurance.

The sale and servicing of group insurance require specialized training. Companies draw heavily on recent college graduates to build up their forces of group salesmen, often called group representatives or group specialists. Many companies bring these college trainees into the home office for an intensive indoctrination lasting several months. Here they undergo training in various phases of home office group operations,

---

[5] Some companies are only nominally in the group field. They write only an occasional case, such as on their own employees or on a few local enterprises.

such as underwriting, claim handling, office procedures, accounting and statistics.

Trainees selected for field work are transferred to regional group sales offices. Depending on circumstances, they may be first assigned to inside administrative duties for which their home office training has prepared them. These may involve correspondence with policyowners (the holders of the master contracts representing the agreement between employer and insurer), processing premium reports and the like. The new man also makes field calls with the group manager or other experienced group representative. This preliminary work constitutes useful preparation for the time when the trainee goes out into the field on his own.

The group sales representative performs many duties. While he usually does not originate sales, he works closely with the ordinary or combination agent of record in prospecting. In order to present a suitable group proposal or plan to an employer, a preliminary or factfinding interview is usually necessary, as in ordinary insurance. During such an interview the agent of record, sometimes accompanied by the group representative, obtains such background information as:

1. Whether the prospect employer has any group insurance
2. If so, the nature of such coverage
3. The person or persons with authority to decide whether or not to purchase a group plan
4. The number of full-time employees on the payroll
5. "Census" data concerning these employees: sex, age, occupation, salary, marital status, etc.

After such preliminary information has been obtained, the group representative is usually the one who develops a plan that will provide appropriate coverage for that group in keeping with the amount of money available. The cost quotation can be divided into four parts: cost per individual covered, total cost, the employer's contribution, the employee's contribution (if any). If the plan is acceptable to the employer, the group representative puts it into effect, i.e., "installs" it, after which he usually services the case completely.

Group is highly competitive, considerably more so than ordinary or debit. Profit margins are small. Many consultations with the prospect may be necessary before a sale results. In some large cases, group executives come from the home office to participate in the sales process.

Compensation

The agent of record who originates a group insurance contract is compensated by a commission for the sale and for such services as he renders after a group plan has been installed. An important collateral benefit of group to the agent of record is the opportunity to sell individual policies to persons covered under a group plan. Group representatives are usually compensated either by salary only or by a base salary plus additional remuneration, which depends on the amount of new group business they write. They do not write ordinary or debit insurance.

A substantial amount of group business originates with brokers. In many instances the agent of record or the broker is less active in selling and servicing a group contract than in the case of ordinary and debit. Agents' and brokers' commission rates for group are substantially lower than they are for ordinary and debit. How much lower may be evident from the following representative schedule of commissions payable to soliciting agents and brokers for placing group insurance:

Typical Schedule of Commission Rates for Group Insurance for Soliciting Agents and Brokers

Amounts of annual premium	First-year commissions	Yearly renewal commissions
On the first $1,000 of premium	20%	5% for 9 years
On that part of the premium in excess of $1,000 but not exceeding $5,000	20	3 for 9 years
On that part of the premium in excess of $5,000 but not exceeding $10,000	15	1½ for 9 years
On that part of the premium in excess of $10,000 but not exceeding $20,000	12½	1½ for 9 years
On that part of the premium in excess of $20,000 but not exceeding $30,000	10	1½ for 9 years
On that part of the premium in excess of $30,000 but not exceeding $50,000	5	1½ for 9 years
On that part of the premium in excess of $50,000 but not exceeding $100,000	2½	1 for 9 years
On that part of the premium in excess of $100,000 but not exceeding $150,000	1	½ for 9 years

Administration of a Group Plan

Once such a plan has been adopted, a certain amount of administrative detail must be carried out to keep operations functioning smoothly and the client satisfied. Various changes occur that require adjustment of records. First, a plan must be kept up to date to show new employees entering the plan and old ones terminating. Second, changes in an employee's status may change the amount of his insurance. Third, changes in beneficiary designations are constantly occurring and must be recorded. Occasionally, also, there may be assignments or changes of names of persons insured or of their beneficiaries.

Group plans are usually administered in either of two ways. Under one, the policyowner employer handles various changes almost entirely by himself. Under the other, employer and insurer handle these changes together.

SMALL GROUPS. It will be evident that the type of preparation, presentation and administration just described would apply only to large groups. In small cases, such as "baby group," the agent of record himself does the work as to fact-finding, installing, servicing, etc., because the amount of premium involved does not warrant the participation of a group representative.

Allied Coverages

In the debit section of this chapter it was stated that today many group life plans provide for protection on the lives of the dependents of wage earners.

Life insurance companies also offer a number of other coverages on a group basis. Group permanent and group ordinary have already been mentioned. Other related coverages include group annuities, group creditor, group hospitalization, group surgical and group major medical expense insurance. Since the methods of sales and administration are quite similar to those for group term, they will not be treated further.

Effect of Group on Other Lines

Group insurance was originally intended to provide low-cost coverage for thousands of employees who would otherwise have no life insurance protection, either because of uninsurability or because of inability or unwillingness to pay premiums for ordinary or debit.

The development of group has, as we have seen, substantially reduced the market for debit insurance. There is considerable feeling, primarily among soliciting agents and agents' organizations, that group, as it has evolved, is also reducing the market for ordinary. These men feel that group has departed from its original purpose. Their argument is that the increasingly higher maximum group limits (sometimes known as jumbo group) on a single life now cover many men, particularly executives, who do not need group in such large amounts and who would otherwise purchase more ordinary. The major points at issue are whether such large amounts of coverage on a single life:

1. Obscure the need and reduce the demand for *permanent* insurance.
2. Tend to undermine the agency system and thus deprive the purchasers of the advice and assistance they need and should have in establishing the best personal life insurance program.

Many agents and agents' organizations are also disturbed by the growth of so-called association group insurance. This is life (or health) insurance offered to groups of persons with some type of common relationship (but not that of a common employer) in which the coverage is paid for entirely by the persons insured and in which the insurability of the individuals is determined on the basis of group underwriting. Agents believe that such groups are artificial or contrived, particularly if they are formed primarily to obtain life insurance at group rates.

Company managements themselves differ as to the effect of the expansion of group insurance upon the life insurance business in general and upon ordinary agents in particular. The following viewpoints—harmful, helpful and in-between—expressed by the chief executives of three major companies reflect these differences:

"The horizontal extension of group insurance to members of associations not previously thought of as being eligible for this type of insurance has deprived the ordinary agent of many prospects. As we expand this type of insurance further and further away from the usual employer-employee type of case, we materially reduce the effectiveness of the backbone of our business—the ordinary agent."

"I predict that our home office, both directly and through their general agents and managers, will give the agent increasing assistance in pinpointing markets and other phases of prospecting. In doing this our access to mass markets through group, association coverages and the like will not be a weapon to destroy markets for the agent but a useful tool to assist him. These coverages, in short, will be turned into door openers rather than door closers."

"The continuing growth of group lines of insurance has been a storm center of controversy within the life insurance industry. About the closest we can come to consensus on the issue is that group insurance has been neither the unmitigated disaster nor the unalloyed blessing for our industry that the 'extremists' on both sides would have us believe. Our company has long since accepted group insurance and has for many years accentuated the positive benefits accruing to the agent that are inherent in group insurance."

Such questions as maximum amounts of group on one life and the merits of association group continue to be the subjects of talks, debates and discussions, involving individual agents, agents' organizations, company managements and representatives of insurance departments. As the foregoing paragraphs indicate, consensus has not been reached.

SUMMARY

Today relatively few life insurance companies limit themselves to the sale of ordinary business only. The great majority sell one or more of the following forms in addition: (1) health insurance, (2) debit or industrial and (3) group and allied coverages.

Various forms of health insurance provide protection against losses resulting from injury or disease. The greater part of this coverage has been sold by insurance companies.

Sales training methods for ordinary insurance and for health insurance are similar. Persistency is more of a problem in health insurance than in life insurance, because the policyowner is less likely to suffer financially from lapse. Today the nonlevel scale of commissions is considerably more common.

Debit insurance originated in England and was introduced in North America in 1875. A major distinguishing feature continues to be the collection of weekly or monthly premiums at the insured's home. Combination companies organize their sales forces on the branch office or district office system. Training of the debit agent is geared to the needs and means of the people he will call on. Compensation recognizes the agent's efforts for new business, collections for old business and conservation.

For a variety of reasons, debit insurance has been declining as a percentage of total life insurance in force in the United States and Canada. The dollar amount in force of insurance classified as debit reached its peak about 1955 and has been declining very slowly since that time.

Group life insurance has enjoyed an astonishing growth since it was introduced in 1911 or 1912. About three-fourths of the civilian workers in the United States are covered by group insurance.

Companies actively in group sales usually consolidate most of their group operations in a single department, with its own sales and administration divisions. Marketing of group differs considerably from that of other forms, partly because the prospect is the employer, rather than the employees whose lives would be insured. Consequently, the training of group salesmen likewise is different.

The development of group insurance has substantially reduced the market for debit insurance. There is some feeling, especially among some agents, that group is also reducing the market for ordinary.

QUESTIONS FOR REVIEW

1. Describe briefly each of the three forms of insurance, in addition to ordinary, sold by many life companies.
2. State the major respects in which sales organization for health insurance differs from that for ordinary.
3. Describe the typical field organization for the sale of debit insurance.
4. Explain the twofold meaning of the term "debit." How does the agent use the basic records on his debit?
5. Compare the traditional and the more recent methods of compensating debit agents. Compare the earnings of combination agents with those of agents who sell no debit insurance.

6. Account for the changing status of debit insurance, as compared to ordinary and group.

7. Why is the marketing of group insurance different from that of ordinary? What is a group representative? Describe his duties.

8. How are the writing agent and the group representative compensated for the sale of group insurance?

9. Describe two aspects of group insurance that have given agents' associations, company managements and representatives of insurance departments some concern.

16 | *Recent Developments*

In chapters 1 through 15 the home office and field organization of a life insurance company was treated in what
might be called its basic or "pure" form. Such a company's
"product line" is relatively simple. Through its field force, the
insurer markets conventional life insurance and conventional
annuities with one or more of health, debit and group. Changes
in product line are evolutionary: a new policy is introduced,
perhaps another is dropped, new benefits are added, existing
policy benefits are liberalized, restrictions in existing policies
are either modified or eliminated.

And the corporate structure usually is simple also. As mentioned in chapter 8, there have been *some* multiple-line organizations for many years. However, in the great majority of
cases the company has been an independent entity, operated
by its own officers and directors and responsible to its own
shareholders in a stock company and to its policyowners in a
mutual company.

Probably a substantial majority of life companies still operate along these lines. Since the early 1960s, however, developments have been extensive and more rapid. For convenience,
these will be treated under three headings: (1) other products

sold by life insurance companies, (2) changes in marketing methods, and (3) changes in corporate structure. There will also be a brief discussion of "consumerism," which is likely to have increasing influence upon life insurance companies' sales operations.

OTHER PRODUCTS SOLD BY LIFE INSURANCE COMPANIES

These are essentially equity or equity-based products: mutual funds, variable annuities, variable life insurance. The underlying assets for these products are invested substantially in equities (rather than in bonds and mortgages), primarily in common stocks. (Sometimes the terms "Total Financial Services" or "Complete Product Line" are used to embrace (a) conventional or traditional life insurance and annuities (b) the aforementioned equity products, (c) insurance sales other than life, such as property-liability.)

Proceeds of conventional or traditional life insurance policies and annuities are payable in fixed or guaranteed dollars. Under mutual funds, variable annuities and variable life insurance policies, the benefits are not fixed at time of purchase; they may vary or fluctuate. The purchaser of any one of these products needs to recognize that a fixed-dollar benefit is not guaranteed.

Equity products will be considered here primarily in terms of their possible effect upon the sales activities of life insurance companies—home office and field. The discussion will not be concerned with the mechanics of adding one or more of these three to the insurer's product line. It will be assumed that the mechanics used conform with insurance department regulations and pertinent statutes. No position will be taken as to the merits of equity products in life insurance operations or as to whether the sale of such products by life insurers benefits policyowners and their beneficiaries. The fact is that many life insurance companies sell equity products. Widespread participation by insurers is still too recent for drawing conclusions.

Insofar as the life insurance business is concerned, most companies continue to stress income replacement when income ceases, as in the event of early death, disabling illness, retirement. Equity products need to be marketed carefully. In an economy of rising standards, equity-based contracts provide the opportunity for public participation in economic growth. The sale by life insurance companies of equity products is sometimes advocated as a hedge against inflation or as a replacement for the guarantees of life insurance. Such advocacy is at least open to question.

Mutual Funds

This term was treated briefly on page 155. The mutual fund concept has been traced back to about 1860. Practically, it came into being in the mid-1920s, through corporations known as investment companies. Mutual funds are sold to individuals as well as to institutional investors at a public offering price.

By 1970, close to 250 United States life insurers had either begun, or signified their intention, to sell mutual funds and variable annuities. More than 60 companies, including some of the largest, had organized 71 mutual funds, and 34 had acquired funds.

A life insurer planning to go into the sale of mutual funds needs to decide whether it will establish a separate organization for such sales or use its own managers or general agents for recruiting, training and supervising company agents for selling mutual fund shares. The majority of such companies now engaged in the distribution of mutual funds have elected the latter course. Accordingly, this discussion contemplates that the same sales force handles funds and insurance.

Exactly how many mutual funds there are at this time is uncertain, but the number is well over 500. Obviously they have been accepted as a means of investment. Nevertheless opinion as to whether *life companies* should sell mutual funds is divided. Various reasons have been advanced pro and con; most of them relate directly or indirectly to agency operations.

Among the reasons advanced in favor of the selling of mutual fund shares by life insurers are the following:

1. Offering a wider range of financial services increases the opportunity for the public's participation in economic growth. The large, widespread life insurance sales forces will facilitate such participation. Thereby the individual company can expect to increase its own market for life insurance.

2. Sale of equity products will provide an additional source of income to the agent. To some prospects he will sell equity products; to some, life insurance; to some, both. Just as representatives of some investment firms are seeking to help their clients obtain life insurance protection, agents should make securities investments available to their clients.

3. Availability of mutual funds as part of total financial services should facilitate the recruitment and the retention of agents by providing additional client contacts.

4. Mutual funds help the purchaser offset inflationary pressures. The seller offers a product that reflects changing dollar values and counters the weakness of guaranteed dollars in an inflated economy. The decline in the purchasing power of the dollar is likely to continue.

5. Both the public and the field force "demand" mutual funds. If a prospect can't obtain them from his agent, he may buy them elsewhere. An agent who can't furnish what his prospect or client wants, may seek another company affiliation.

6. Profits from the sale of mutual funds will benefit policy-owners and stockholders, because of the more effective use of existing resources and the increased dollar flow.

Among the reasons advanced against the selling of mutual fund shares are the following:

1. Most companies are devoting increasing attention to manpower development. Yet few would claim that there

is no room for improvement. Salesmen have been trained to emphasize the advantages of the guaranteed or fixed-dollar concept, the important assurance that the face amount of the policy previously agreed upon will definitely be paid to the designated beneficiary. For mutual funds the agent will need to learn a new viewpoint and new techniques. Specifically, he will be selling a product whose dollar value at maturity is not guaranteed. The purchaser hopes the dollar value at maturity will be greater than the amounts paid—but it may be less.

2. It has not been demonstrated that the insuring public and the agents actually "demand" mutual fund shares. Many prospects are not interested in buying them, whether from an agent or from anyone else; many agents are not interested in selling them. Further, at least some companies entered mutual funds for reasons other than public "demand."

3. Purchase of needed life insurance may be neglected in favor of mutual funds. The average prospect is under-insured but lacks the dollars for both adequate life insurance and investments such as mutual funds. He needs guaranteed dollars before he needs variable dollars.

4. The Securities and Exchange Commission exercises substantial control over the sale of stocks and other securities. Hence the insurer is exposed to close regulation. Mutual fund regulations are markedly restrictive as to what the agent may convey to a prospect in a sales presentation.

5. The agent's additional income from fund sales may be too small to be worthwhile. Compensation may not be enough to make up for the commissions the agent, particularly the established agent, may have lost by spending his time selling mutual funds.

6. The long-term trend of most stocks has been upward. However, as experience has shown, values can and do go down as well as up. The image of life insurance and

of the agent who sold funds before a decline began may suffer temporarily.

7.   Many persons buy funds not because they are against fixed-dollar guarantees or because they seek a balanced financial program, but because they hope to make a profit. Life insurance companies are chartered to furnish protection to those who become their policyowners. Even if companies and their agents profit financially from the sale of mutual funds, it has not been established that their policyowners benefit from such activity unless of course they wish to buy funds themselves.

Whether mutual funds will do for the life insurance business all their proponents have claimed remains to be seen. So far not enough companies have sold enough of them long enough. A clearer picture of the optimum relationship between mutual funds and life insurance should evolve in the next few years.

Variable Annuities

Life insurance companies for many years have been offering annuities to provide retirement income of predetermined amounts or pensions, usually for the life of the annuitant. Since the dollar amount of the periodic income is determined at the time of issuance, such contracts are sometimes known as fixed-dollar annuities. They are available on both an individual and a group basis, the amount issued through group annuities being the greater of the two. As in the case of conventional life insurance, reserve funds have been invested primarily in bonds and mortgages.

A recent development is the variable annuity. Like the fixed-dollar annuity, it is a retirement contract; like the fixed-dollar annuity, it is available on both an individual and a group basis. In contrast to the fixed-dollar annuity, however, the reserve funds are invested primarily in common stocks; hence the variable annuity is an equity product. The amount of the periodic income payment is not fixed but, depending on the value of the underlying assets, may fluctuate up or down, and the investment risk is taken by the annuitant.[1]

The arguments in favor of selling the variable annuity may also be considered the advantages claimed: to relate the purchaser's income, at least to some extent, to variations in the cost of living, and to provide him an opportunity to share in the expected growth of living standards. One argument that has been raised against the variable annuity is that the cost of living of any one individual will not necessarily fluctuate directly with the cost of living in general. The Consumer Price Index is based on averages, while the cost of living of any particular individual is based on his personal expenses; these will not necessarily conform. Another objection is fear that there may be an adverse reaction against the entire institution of life insurance if the dollar benefits provided by variable annuity contracts fall short of those the annuitants were led to expect. Further, some have expressed doubt that continuing inflation is inevitable and, even if it is, that common stock investments will provide an adequate hedge against rising prices.

Of significance to life insurance companies is the fact that courts in the United States, including the Supreme Court, have held the variable annuity to be a security. Hence, the cases decided seem to establish that the Securities and Exchange Commission has been given jurisdiction to regulate the registration and prospectuses of insurers issuing variable annuities as well as companies' separate accounts funding such annuities. Accordingly, companies offering variable annuity contracts are subject to the regulations of both the Securities and Exchange Commission and the insurance departments of the states in which these contracts are sold. Among other powers, the SEC has control over companies' selling activities, sales literature, and sales load. Agents who wish to sell variable contracts must meet qualification standards imposed on them at both the federal and state levels by passing a written examination. One part

---

[1] Under some variable annuities payments may be related to some other variable factor such as the cost-of-living index.

deals with securities generally; the other, with variable contracts.

Variable Life Insurance

The term "variable life insurance" generally refers to policies in which the amount of the death benefit varies to reflect the experience of a fund invested primarily in common stocks. At this writing, variable life insurance policies have been sold to some extent in Canada, England and Holland. Before such contracts can be offered in the United States, numerous state and federal legal requirements must be satisfied. Up to the end of 1970, only six states had amended their laws to permit the writing of this coverage, though others are likely to follow. As in the case of the variable annuity, the investment element in variable life insurance will bring this product under the regulations of the Securities and Exchange Commission.

Since variable life insurance policies will probably be available in the United States in the not-too-distant future, this product deserves consideration here. Development of the variable life insurance policy is analogous to that of the variable annuity; a major purpose is to offset the declining value of a death benefit (or of a matured endowment) payable in fixed dollars.

Within the concept of variable life insurance, there is a potentially wide range of policies. As understood in the United States and Canada, variable life insurance includes the following elements:

1. Premiums are usually fixed at issue and remain level.
2. Reserve funds are invested by the insurance company in a separate account, nearly always made up of common stocks. That is, this account is not part of the assets for the traditional policies the company sells.
3. Policy benefits vary according to the investment results of the separate account. The company guarantees a minimum face amount, but the benefits may be higher if investment results so warrant.

At such time as variable life insurance becomes generally available, a life insurance company will be able to offer the public a product which has a guaranteed minimum death benefit and a potential for a larger death benefit and which will not necessarily require spending of additional premium dollars. The agent will be able to offer prospects a choice between the fixed-dollar policy and the variable dollar policy. The characteristics of the former are well known. The prospect may be willing to give up the guarantee of specific cash values and the elements of the fixed-dollar contract that depend on such guaranteed cash values, such as the traditional policy loan clause. His variable-dollar policy cash values and nonforfeiture benefits may be larger or smaller than those in a comparable fixed-dollar policy. The prospect who is primarily interested in protection against death and in the possibility of increasing the amount of his death benefit may decide to take his chances as to the level of cash values in his variable-dollar contract. Thus he may enjoy the rewards, as well as assume the risks, of the investment experience of the life insurer's separate account.

If variable life insurance is to be sold, life insurance companies are the logical organizations to do so. Companies and/or their agents will need to consider such questions as:

1. How well does the variable feature meet the public's life insurance needs?
2. How will the company determine the cost of the benefits which are guaranteed?
3. Who—the policyowner or the company or both—will bear the investment risk?
4. How difficult will this product be for the agent and his prospects to understand?
5. What will be the financial impact upon the company if it offers or does not offer variable life insurance?
6. Can the insurer cope satisfactorily with the state and federal regulations involved?
7. How will agents be compensated for the sales of variable life insurance? The basis of remuneration will have to be

one that will encourage life insurance salesmen to stress this form of protection.

In the words of one company executive: "The successful marketing of variable life insurance may well depend upon whether agents are compensated for variable-benefit policies upon the same basis as for selling fixed-benefit contracts. If they are compensated on the same basis for both products, they can be expected to sell both with equal vigor and with equal career opportunity. Differences in compensation could create a conflict of interests; the agent could profit more from the selling of the product which may not be most suitable to the needs and desires of the proposed insured."

Changes in Marketing Methods

The agency system has been the traditional means used by life insurance companies for the distribution of their products. Probably the majority of companies continue to operate under this system, using general agents or branch managers to head their field sales offices.

Since the end of World War II, however, we hear more and more about mass marketing (also known as mass merchandising). The term "marketing" was considered in chapter 4. What, then, is "mass marketing"? Perhaps oversimply, mass marketing is a means of product distribution. Like some other expressions, it has become a "positive" term and is used loosely. Partly because it means different things to different people, mass marketing is a difficult term to define precisely or even to describe.

With particular reference to insurance, the term derives from the nonlife lines. During the 1960s a number of the larger property-liability insurers began to experiment with some form of group or mass coverage to supply the automobile and home-owners' insurance needs of employees of larger corporations, which were clients of these insurers.

A life insurer engaged in mass marketing makes a broad-scale sales appeal simultaneously to a large number of prospects for insurance. Group insurance (including association group) is one example; mail order or direct mail insurance is another. The mass market may be reached through a commercial or industrial organization which has contacts with its customers through a regular billing cycle or through frequent personal contact. Thus, an insurer may offer a plan for holders of credit cards and charge accounts. Or term insurance may be available to a bank's savings account customers, with part of their quarterly interest applied to premiums. Salary savings and payroll deduction insurance are also offered by life companies.

From the foregoing it will be seen that most life companies have participated in mass marketing to some extent for some time. Specifically, group insurance, salary savings, direct mail, association group are not new.

The major purpose of mass marketing is reduction of distribution cost and the passing of such savings along to the persons insured. Participation by the individual agent may vary from little or none to substantial. There are so many variations in mass marketing that it is virtually impossible to be specific. Some of its proponents hail mass marketing as *the* life insurance sales system of the future. Others maintain that mass marketing will reach many prospective purchasers of relatively small amounts, purchasers whom debit agents formerly solicited quite generally but whom some strictly ordinary agents may not be able to reach. The impact of mass marketing on life insurance sales organizations remains to be seen.

CHANGES IN CORPORATE STRUCTURE

A holding company is a corporate arrangement in which one corporation controls one or more other corporations by owning a substantial amount of their common stock; it is a means of harnessing diverse activities. While the holding company concept is not new, significant participation by life insurance companies in holding companies is a relatively recent development. It has been estimated that in 1970 more than 200 life insurance companies were affiliated in some way with a holding company.

Insurance-related holding companies have various patterns of holdings. Sometimes the holding company may own only insurance and insurance-related organizations. In other cases, it may own a variety of enterprises, one or more of which is an insurer. A holding company of the latter type (involving companies in a variety of fields) is called a "conglomerate."

Generally speaking, the term "downstream holding company" is used if the top or parent organization is the life insurance company. The term "upstream" is used if the life insurance company is one of the subsidiaries. An illustrative chart of the downstream type appears in Figure 3.

FIGURE 3
Organization Chart of an Insurance-Related Downstream Holding Company

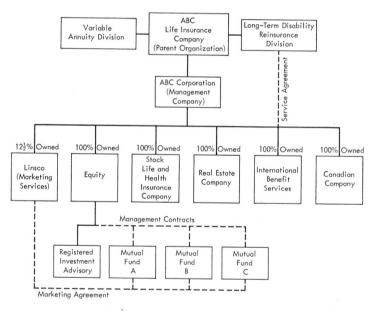

To cite one insurance-related example, a large insurer reported that during 1970 it had increased its "services to meet the growing insurance and related financial needs by (1) sponsoring a mutual fund, (2) sponsoring a real estate investment trust, (3) organizing a premium-financing subsidiary, (4) participating in the formation of a computer software corporation to serve the life insurance business." These services, which were in addition to its life insurance business, were offered through the subsidiary corporations.

Some holding companies are considerably less insurance-oriented, and include such activities as telephone utilities, publishing and manufacturing, along with insurance.

Various reasons have been advanced in favor of holding companies in the life insurance business. It is said that the use of the holding company form of structure makes possible a greater diversification of financial services. These might include, for example, the sale of equity products, investment counseling, consumer and sales finance. Agents able to offer "total financial services" would stay abreast of the emerging trends in markets and the company itself would have greater flexibility in its operations. The holding company structure allows for greater ease in the establishment or acquisition of related businesses. It is also said that there can be more profitable use of corporate funds through the holding company device and that the expectation of profit stimulates progress.

Those who have doubts about holding company affiliation by life insurance companies point out that the nature of government regulation of life company investments, which may result from having an insurer controlled as a subsidiary by another corporation, may not be of benefit to the policyowners. Concentration on corporate profits is not necessarily in the interest of the insuring public. Those objecting also fear that an insurer owned by another corporation may lose control of its own agency and other operations.

While the majority of life insurance companies operate under independent corporate structures at this time, the trend toward corporate combinations is one that may be expected to continue and one that may affect life company field and home office organization.

CONSUMERISM

In our treatment of new products, marketing methods and company organizational structure, we have been primarily concerned with the possible effect of these developments upon agency operations of life insurance companies and upon the insuring public. Accordingly, it may be appropriate to close with a reference to another recent, general development, known as consumerism. This development is likely to affect many facets of our society, including life insurance.

Words like consumption, consumer, etc., have been with us for a long time. In the economic sense, a consumer is one who utilizes economic goods. But the word "consumerism" itself (also known as the "consumer movement") is of recent origin —so recent, in fact, that only the latest editions of our dictionaries list it. As generally understood, consumerism is an expression of the desire for increased value for one's money. Though on an individual basis this objective is hardly new, it is now being expressed by organized groups.

Consumerism involves the idea of consumer protection. It involves the concept of "buyer's rights." From a position formerly called "caveat emptor" ("Let the buyer beware"), we are evolving to a position of "caveat vendor" ("Let the seller beware"). Thus consumerism is concerned with such aspects as the following:

1. The buyer's right to make an intelligent choice among products and services
2. The buyer's right to accurate information on which to make his choice
3. The buyer's right, when his interests are badly served, to register his dissatisfaction and to have his complaint heard and acted upon.

Business is said to have the responsibility to:

1. Seek out the informed views of consumers and other groups to help assure customer satisfaction from the earliest stages of product planning

2. Eliminate frauds and deceptions from the marketplace, setting as its goal not only legality but honesty in all transactions
3. Ensure that its sales personnel are familiar with product capabilities and limitations and that they fully respond to customer needs for such information
4. Facilitate sound value comparisons across the widest possible range and choice of products
5. Provide effective channels for receiving and acting on consumer complaints and suggestions, utilizing the resources of associations, chambers of commerce, better business bureaus, recognized consumer groups, individual companies, and other appropriate bodies[2]

For the most part, the foregoing statements suggest tangible, manufactured products. In life insurance, the "product" is a service, a promise to pay evidenced by a document called a contract; therefore, some of these statements need interpretation.

With particular reference to life and health insurance, companies and their sales representatives are likely to be held accountable to a greater degree in the future as to pre-sale and post-sale statements concerning policy provisions, benefits, net cost of protection, etc. True, a principal generally is responsible for the acts of his agent. True, also, companies do not cancel or contest policies except under strictly limited circumstances, and most agents give valuable services to their policyowners, beneficiaries and other interested parties. Nevertheless, although companies and agents in the overall have been serving the public well, they will be expected to improve upon present levels of performance. This is still another reason for insurers to continue to improve the training both of their agents, who

---

[2] From the Business-Consumer Relations Code adopted by the Chamber of Commerce of the United States, February 26, 1970. The complete statement also includes references to quality of the environment, maintenance and repairs of products, etc. These, however, have relatively little significance for life insurance.

are the company to the public, and of their office personnel in the home office and in the field.

There is considerable doubt that consumerism "demands". that life insurance companies offer mutual funds, variable annuities, variable life insurance, mass marketing and changes in corporate structure. Consumer *acceptance* is what will determine the success of these products and developments, even the success of conventional policies and annuities. Most people recognize the value of life insurance. It does not necessarily follow that they accept the proposition that distribution through the agency system is the best means of obtaining life insurance protection.

Predictions as to the future of the consumer movement are risky. However, consumerism is not likely to go away any time soon. Federal as well as state and provincial regulatory authorities are likely to be increasingly concerned with consumerism. The life insurance business and its agency operations will not be excepted from this concern.

SUMMARY

Many, probably a substantial majority of, companies operate as explained in the preceding chapters. However, since the end of World War II, there have been interesting developments in the product lines of some companies as well as in the means of distribution and corporate structure. Because of the recentness of these developments, it is too early to predict their long-range effect upon insurers in general and upon companies' agency operations in particular. Insurers are likely to be more involved in consumerism in the future.

QUESTIONS FOR REVIEW

1. What are equity products? State the underlying reason why some life insurance companies have begun to sell them.
2. With respect to mutual funds, outline the usual arguments advanced for and against their sale by life companies.

3. Define or explain the term "mass marketing." Comment on the statement that most life companies have been somewhat involved in mass marketing for some time.

4. From the life insurance standpoint, outline the various reasons that have been advanced for and against the holding company device.

5. Is your company involved in a holding company relationship? If so, is it of the downstream or the upstream type?

6. What is meant by consumerism? Why is it of significance to life insurance companies?

Bibliography

Canadian Life Insurance Association, *Canadian Life Insurance Facts*. Toronto, 1970.

EILERS, ROBERT D. and CROWE, ROBERT M. (eds.), *Group Insurance Handbook*. Richard D. Irwin, Inc., Homewood, Ill., 1965.

GREGG, DAVIS W. (ed.), *Life and Health Insurance Handbook*, 2nd edition. Richard D. Irwin, Inc., Homewood, Ill., 1964.

GREIDER, JANICE E. and BEADLES, WILLIAM T., *Law and the Life Insurance Contract*. Richard D. Irwin, Inc., Homewood, Ill., 1968.

HUEBNER, SOLOMON S. and BLACK, KENNETH, JR., *Life Insurance*. Appleton-Century-Crofts, New York, 1969.

Health Insurance Institute, *Source Book of Health Insurance Data*. New York, 1970.

Institute of Life Insurance, *Life Insurance Fact Book*. New York, 1971.

Life Insurance Agency Management Association, *Managing an Agency*. Hartford, Conn., 1969.

McGILL, DAN M., *Life Insurance*. Richard D. Irwin, Inc., Homewood, Ill., 1967.

MEHR, ROBERT I., *Life Insurance: Theory and Practice*. Business Publications, Inc., 1970.

MELONE, JOSEPH J. and ALLEN, EVERETT T., *Pension Planning*. 2nd edition. Dow-Jones, Irwin, Homewood, Ill., 1971.

PEDOE, ARTHUR, *Life Insurance, Annuities and Pensions*. University of Toronto Press, Toronto, 1970.

Readings for Agency Management, 1967.

STALNAKER, ARMAND C., *Life Insurance Agency Financial Management*, 2nd edition. Richard D. Irwin, Inc., Homewood, Ill., 1965.

WATSON, GEORGE N., *The Elements of Group Insurance*, 2nd edition.

Institute of Chartered Life Underwriters of Canada, Don Mills, Ontario, 1965.

The author also drew on a great deal of company material and on the proceedings and reports of several life insurance associations, especially those of the Life Insurance Agency Management Association.

INDEX

This book has been set in 11 and 10 point Caledonia, leaded 2 points. Chapter numbers are in 36 point Perpetua and chapter titles are in 30 point Perpetua. The size of the type page is 25 × 42½ picas.